CALL ME LARRY

CALL ME LARRY

A Creole Man's Triumph over
Racism and Homophobia

LARRY BAGNERIS

with Ryan Gomez

THE HISTORIC NEW ORLEANS COLLECTION

2025

The Historic New Orleans Collection is a museum, research center, and publisher dedicated to the study and preservation of the history and culture of New Orleans, the lower Mississippi valley, and the Gulf South region. The HNOC is operated by the Kemper and Leila Williams Foundation, a Louisiana nonprofit corporation.

533 Royal Street
New Orleans, Louisiana 70130
www.hnoc.org

Project editor: Cathe Mizell-Nelson
Director of publications: Jessica Dorman
President and CEO: Daniel Hammer
Design: Alison Cody

First edition. 2,000 copies.

Printed in Michigan by Sheridan
Distributed by the University of Virginia Press

29 28 27 26 25 1 2 3 4 5

ISBN: 978-0-917860-93-5

Front cover image by Jerry Click from the *Houston Chronicle*, © 1980 Hearst Newspapers, all rights reserved, used under license. Back cover images courtesy of the author.

Library of Congress Cataloging-in-Publication Data

Names: Bagneris, Larry, 1946– author. | Gomez, Ryan, 1987– author.
Title: Call me Larry : a Creole man's triumph over racism and homophobia / Larry Bagneris with Ryan Gomez.
Description: First edition. | New Orleans, Louisiana : The Historic New Orleans Collection, 2025. | Includes index. | Summary: "Larry Bagneris was raised in a large, loving Creole family during the 1950s and early 1960s. In his memoir, Bagneris recalls his activist career, starting in New Orleans as a student leader in the struggle against racial injustice, later as founder of Houston's Pride Parade, and then, following a return to his hometown, as a political organizer and mainstay of the local gay community. Bagneris also relates his observations as he travels, builds community, and finds family in queer spaces around the world—from San Francisco to New York, Tel Aviv to Bangkok"— Provided by publisher.
Identifiers: LCCN 2024043511 | ISBN 9780917860935 (hardcover)
Subjects: LCSH: Bagneris, Larry, 1946– | Sexual minority activists—Biography. | Gay activists—Biography. | Gay men—Louisiana—Biography. | Creoles—Louisiana—Biography. | Minority gay men—Louisiana—Biography.
Classification: LCC HQ75.8.B34 A3 2025 | DDC 306.76/6092 [B]—dc23/eng/20241004
LC record available at https://lccn.loc.gov/2024043511

This book is dedicated to my parents, Lawrence and Gloria, who taught me long before they left this good earth how to deal with racism and homophobia.

COURTESY OF THE AUTHOR

Larry speaking at Dallas Pride celebration [1982]
LARRY BAGNERIS PAPERS, AMISTAD RESEARCH CENTER, NEW ORLEANS, LA

CONTENTS

CHAPTER ONE / *Childhood*

First Communion [1954]
COURTESY OF THE AUTHOR

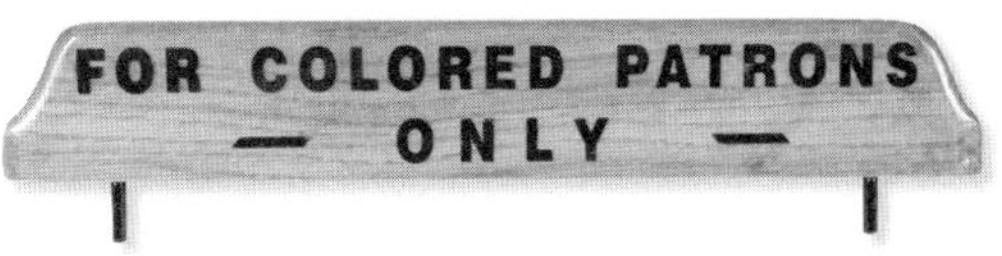

1

LIFE BACK IN THE OLD SEVENTH WARD WAS SIMPLE—YOU HAD TO BE Catholic. Not only that, if you were a Bagneris kid, you attended St. Peter Claver, a well-to-do Creole Catholic school run by the Sisters of the Blessed Sacrament: nuns of all shapes and sizes. I attended school with my younger brother, Vernel, and my older sister, Joanne. (My baby sister, Gina, was to come later.) Every day, until high school, I would walk the marble corridors, every surface sparkling clean. Every morning we would attend Mass, with full Communion to cleanse me of the day's sin. I even became an altar boy, after studying Latin for months.

I knew I was gay when I was four years old. Now, how did I know that? While other boys were into girls, even at that age I thought the other boys were hot! I was attracted to boys and remember a world full of crushes. I knew I was different from everyone else and had no idea why, but I knew for certain that boys gave me thrills.

One day I was running around the schoolyard. We were playing basketball, and I was minding my own business when a tough, stern sister called me out. She was the principal of the entire school, in charge of discipline. She hollered, for the whole yard to hear, "Boys don't run like that!" I had been flailing my hands a bit more than she liked. To model correct, masculine behavior, she put her hands closer to her body, like a boxer. "Boys run like this." Looking back, I realize how difficult society was and how heavily policed "masculine" and "feminine" behavior was, even in the sanctuary of my church and family neighborhood.

Every morning of every school day my mother, Gloria, would get up before dawn and iron khaki shirts and pants for me and my brother. With so much starch in them, she had to iron them while they were wet. Our mom would polish our shoes and meticulously plait my sister's hair with ribbons and barrettes. Vernel and I would put on our green ties, and Joanne would don a pleated skirt and white blouse. Our Creole family would never be caught with shiny cheeks, so we started each day with a spot of powder to dim the nose. My mother was the best in terms of taking care of the house and keeping everything, and everyone, clean. Watching my mother's devotion helped me understand the value of work. Work is only valuable if you do it for others, so if I was going to follow her example, I would want to help as many people as I could.

I still see her as a beautiful young girl, and I always see her as that young mother with the clear, Spanish skin and full hair that never grayed. She was short and stocky like I am, but her form was toned from all the work of running the house and watching the children. I actually think we kept her young. To ensure that we were presentable for the world, she paid close attention to the latest hairstyles and dress codes. As my brother likes to say, "she quietly outclassed most people."

The bill for Catholic school was paid by my father, Lawrence, who worked three jobs so the whole family could attend. He instilled in me a sense of equality, a sense that New Orleans was mine, as I was neither Black nor white. My Creole community can spot if I'm pretending to be something I'm not. We were taught to ignore anyone who passed for white to access perceived advantages. Why give up your identity in exchange for a paltry amount of power or expend all that energy to keep up appearances? It simply leaves you at the mercy of others to determine the outcome of your life. As Creoles, our mixed heritage allows us to empathize with and celebrate different cultures. Learning to be myself was a wonderful way to grow up. By the time I came out, I could tap this strength, knowing that hiding my identity was not the way to be free. My father didn't want me to be something I'm not. He wanted me to be happy—and gay is who I am.

Although neither of them could remember exactly when they first met, Mom and Dad had been a presence in each other's lives since they were very young. They both attended Joseph A. Craig grammar school in the Sixth Ward, and it was clear from the start that they were probably headed for marriage when they were old enough. They were wed in 1942, and over the years, Mom and Dad would create a strong team. My older sister, Joanne, would go on to teach in the New Orleans public school system for over forty years after marrying into the LaFonta family. My brother, Vernel, grew up to be a successful actor, singer, dancer, and playwright with a Broadway hit, *One Mo' Time*. My younger sister, Gina, became a doctor.

While we were growing up, Mom and Dad were very much in control. They didn't even drink! Instead, Daddy smoked cigarettes, and Mom loved church bingo and playing horses at the Fair Grounds. Both knew they had to be steady forces when it came to raising their kids. In the prevailing hostile racial environment, they wanted us to be careful how we conducted ourselves in public. It was all to support their general wish that we move up in the world. In their way, Mom was eager to craft fantasy experiences while Dad was good at being frank, grounding us with realities.

One day, Vernel asked Dad if we were white or colored. "Why do you ask?" my father replied with a touch of bemusement. Well, Genie and

Vincent were a couple of Italian boys we had always played with. Both were eager to watch the latest Western at the movie theater and invited us to come. We all knew the movie theater was more for their kind than ours, but our friends convinced us we could be white just for the day to attend the movies with them.

Dad's reply was that you couldn't switch color in a day. In fact, he convinced us that it was better to be colored. We could go to our own Carver movie theater where—for the same price as you'd pay for one movie at the white theater—we could watch two movies, with a cartoon and a side of popcorn, ice cream, and cherry coke. Compared to the Tivoli, the Carver was integrated, if mostly Creole, and brand new, with air conditioning. White people didn't dare go, but after our report, Genie and Vince now begged us to let them join our outings to the Carver.

Mom and Dad expected nothing but A's and B's from my brother and sister. Yet when it was my turn to share my report card, my B's and C's were met with sympathetic smiles. Something felt strange about this special treatment, but if that meant less work, that was fine by me. This went on until the third or fourth grade, when two of my favorite instructors—Sister Regina Pacis, who had taken a liking to me, and Ms. Heath, an African American lay teacher—both noticed that I wasn't doing well in spelling at all. Despite the B's and C's I earned in my other classes, my spelling earned only F's.

Everyone was concerned: I was a good kid, so there had to be some explanation for those F's. My instructors finally urged my family to have me examined by a doctor they recommended at the Eye, Ear, Nose, and Throat Hospital, near the library on Elk Place. After a few "beep beeps" and a few "boop boops," the prognosis was in. There was nothing they could do—I could only hear in one ear! Years later, doctors would determine that since birth, one of my ears had lacked a structure that transmits vibrations from the eardrum to the inner ear. In the 1950s, there wasn't any technology to improve my hearing, so I was technically deaf.

And since spelling back then was taught through sounds—"say 'ka' for 'K'"— I couldn't spell it because I couldn't hear it! In time I grew to master reading lips. My mother made sure my disability didn't affect my attitude. "He can hear whatever the heck he wants to hear," she pronounced, insisting that my hearing was not an impediment, and that I would not be missing out on any of the world around me. Her positive approach saved me.

My mother, Gloria, came from a refined Spanish background whose origins lay in Central America. Her family owned the Diaz Trucking Company—pronounced "DYE-azz"—which did business hauling heavy loads in and out of the city. Her father, Herman, and his brothers were mainly concerned with racehorses, leisure, and money. I always found them self-centered and quite reserved, compared to my father's family. They would probably agree, proud that their behavior matched their pedigree. Sunday dinners at the Diaz home with my great-grandmother, Camille Jamet Diaz, born 1877, were a tradition for the entire family. Two dozen extended family members were often found at these dinners. Crystal and china, not paper and plastic, were the standard. On weeknights, Camille served her dinner on the kitchen table, but on Sundays, lace tablecloths, floral centerpieces, candles, and wine were called for. Disciplined and stern, my great-grandmother insisted on formal dining manners, and a whole array of different spoons and forks. As soon as I was old enough, I did everything I could to avoid these uptight dinners.

But there was more to my mother's side of the family. Every Catholic clan has the example of a matriarch who keeps things together, and ours was no exception. Armantine Lumas—my Mami, a title we emphasized on the second syllable—was the second youngest of a New Orleans Creole family of three brothers and four sisters. The girls of the family were very pretty and worked together at El Trellis cigar factory off Canal Street, where they cut and rolled cigars all day. At age fourteen Armantine was working downtown and spending her evenings off with her beloved sisters—playing cards, attending vaudeville and burlesque shows, and often visiting the various jazz clubs around the city. At fifteen she was married to another teenager: a troubled relationship. Herman laid down strict rules for his wife, demanding she stop wearing makeup and silk stockings, and spend less time cavorting with her sisters and friends. He even locked her in the bathroom one night to keep her from going out, but she escaped through the bathroom window, never to return to his house.

As both were devout Catholics, divorce was not an option, so they separated. Although just a teenager, Armantine was left to raise their child—my mother—on her own. Her parents and siblings helped out—and attractive, young Armantine soon found a man she could love while still protecting her freedom. She and Fred Calloway would stay together for the rest of their lives, finally marrying in middle age.

Herman was still in the picture, a stern and imposing figure, when I was little. But when I was five or six he severed his ties with the Diaz Trucking Company and moved to Los Angeles to further his fortune. My mother looked forward to his occasional visits home, even though I didn't. I didn't know or care whether he chose to deny his heritage and pass for white in California—a common practice for many Creoles who moved to the West Coast to start anew.

But if Herman was a mystery I didn't want to solve, Fred was a role model. Seeing my fair-skinned grandma fall in love with a Black man—in spite of segregation—taught me to ignore society's petty ways of measuring a man. A steamship cook, Fred showered us with gifts from Europe, Africa, and the Middle East, including an accordion that my siblings and I would use to drive Mom up the wall. My step-grandpa always brought home thick steaks and cooked us lavish dinners with ingredients from all around the world.

Mami lived on St. Peter Street during my youth, and on our visits we would sit on the back steps of her house, looking past the fig trees in the yard toward the nearby Baptist church. When the sounds of the choir wafted our way, everyone praising the Lord with shouts and song loud enough for the entire neighborhood to hear, we would start to giggle and make fun of them for their loud, rollicking services. But whenever Mami caught us cutting up, she always reminded us in a stern voice, "You must *not* make fun of them, or anyone, for their religion!"

Mami was known for her kind heart, easy laughter, listening ear, and solid advice. She and her sisters maintained their closeness, leaning on each other for support and understanding through marriages, children, and grandchildren. I was particularly close to my Great Aunt Mamie and her husband, my Uncle Frank, whom I admired for taking care of my mom and my siblings while my father was at work. I remember spending hours of joy playing with my cousins or, slightly less enjoyably, riding with my uncle on his buggy as he sold produce in the neighborhoods. "Fruits and vegetables!" he would call. "I got watermelon, ladies, red to the rind. If you don't believe me, lady, peep through your blinds." This was my first exposure to hard work, and I didn't like it. The sun was too hot, and I didn't enjoy hustling people.

Mami always had an open mind and was never judgmental, and we realized later that she was more than accepting of gay people. She would never ridicule so-called "queers" and even defended those in the Black community who were assigned male at birth but came to live as women. She considered them beautiful. She had a tremendous love for me, and we always had a special connection. Sorry to say, but I really was her favorite. I didn't realize then what I do now, which was that one of her brothers was gay—but that was never talked about openly. My life was filled with nothing but love from and for my family.

Don't get me wrong. As lovely as it was growing up in New Orleans, it has always been a racist place. Even though my siblings and I could pass for white, my mom and dad taught us to be proud of ourselves and would kick our asses if we ever tried to lie about who we were. In 1950s New Orleans, the Creoles were but one of many different ethnicities and shades that lived quite close together, in equal parts peace and hostility. With such fluid definitions and high stakes, one could be tempted to try to pretend to be white, and many did. The choice to do so was a fork in the road between an easier but fragile future or an honest but more difficult life. My parents chose honesty for themselves, and for me and my siblings—and they felt responsible for helping us celebrate the fruits while protecting us from the consequences of that decision.

Our family's first home had been in the Lafitte projects, at 710 North Rocheblave, where my father had settled after the war. The apartment featured a balcony and hardwood floors—but by 1952, with three young kids, my mom insisted on higher standards. And so we moved a few blocks over and settled into one half of a shotgun double at 2738 St. Ann Street, around the corner from the Zulu Social Aid and Pleasure Club's headquarters on Broad.

It took about a mile for our squad to walk up St. Ann Street to get to St. Peter Claver. In one direction, two blocks over, we had white people that didn't want niggers in their neighborhood. But two blocks in the other direction, we had Black people with their own dictionary of insults. We were light-skinned, or "high yellow." Some of the neighborhood kids were quite mean, so I had to learn to fight at a very young age. I was the oldest boy in the family, and as Lawrence Bagneris Junior, I was taught young that if something ever happened to my father, the family's fate would be in my hands.

Even as a small child, as we walked to school, there was nowhere to hide in our crowded and mixed city. As the older brother, I had to make sure my siblings could feel safe walking to school. Some blocks had warped chain-link fences. Some blocks had barking dogs and crowing roosters. Many sidewalks turned to gravel or grass as we walked. Porches and stoops sometimes interrupted our path. Mother insisted that we hold hands, particularly when crossing the street.

Each day, I knew it would come, and I had to prepare Vernel and Joanne. A large white family, a mother with about nine kids, waited for us.

It seemed like she had one dress that she turned inside out each morning, instead of washing or changing. And from the mouths of missing teeth, we heard "Nigger!"

"Nigger! Nigger, nigger, nigger!"

And so, each day, I had to remind my brother and sister how silly it was that we were so well groomed and well dressed and still had to be taunted. If my race was enough to trigger them, can you imagine what they would do if they knew I was gay?

Halfway on the walk to St. Peter Claver, at Galvez and St. Ann, was my other grandma's house—my father's mother, Louise Imbert. She had immigrated from France with a few relatives when she was young, a white European with fair skin looking for fame and fortune. She married Nemour Bagneris, of Haitian heritage but born in Louisiana, with whom she shared the French language. From family photos, I could see he was a Creole, with fair skin, white hair, and green eyes. He could have passed for white. Nemour was much older than Louise and died the year I was born. Growing up, we took the Creole pronunciation of the family name: Bon-ya-RIS.

Although I was still only an altar boy when my grandmother Louise died, I have plentiful memories from growing up in and around her house. I remember her as a very sweet and loving Frenchwoman—an impression that I still struggle to reconcile with family stories about her early years in New Orleans, when she was known to run numbers games! Family members sometimes called her a "casket girl," a New Orleans term that hearkens to the days when single Frenchwomen ventured out to the colonies to get married with a *casquette*, or trunk, in tow. She had entered into an early marriage in Louisiana, with a white man, and had three children with him. But she separated from her first husband relatively young and got the chance to spend a long life with my grandfather Nemour.

Together, Louise and Nemour kept a neat, impeccable house, down to the monogrammed towels. The French and Spanish sides of my family share a taste for lace and lettering to feel classy. Though kind, I always thought of my paternal grandmother as reserved—and it was hard, despite hearing those tales from my aunts, to picture the days when Louise and my uncles would collect and distribute lottery payouts. The entire bunch occupied a thirteen-room house on the corner of St. Ann and Galvez, full of people of different ethnicities who spoke French, Spanish, Louisiana Creole, and English. Thus, from a very young age, I was exposed to a range of colors, year in and year out, particularly around Christmas and New Year's. Each holiday brought a new reason to celebrate. My grandmother's home was the default venue for first Communions, graduations, confirmations, and preparation for family picnics as well as civil and religious holidays. As a whole, the family was secure and confident in themselves and their middle-class station. My aunt Jeanne Dowden, my father's sister, became one of the first teachers in the family, working at the segregated Valena C. Jones Elementary School.

Despite the persistence of some social taboos, the entire neighborhood was quite integrated. People from across the city—or outside, like my mother's family, who were from Honduras and Guatemala—fell in love and settled down in the Seventh Ward. Roaming, resident chickens could be found in many backyards, as is sometimes the case even today. Filling out the large house where my father had been raised were two of his sisters' families: Aunt Inez had a kid with a Black husband, while Aunt Carmen Rita lived on the other side with her six children, who helped take care of my Grandma Louise.

With so many comings and goings, my father's family was always celebrating life to its fullest. Between the two families, I preferred the Bagneris side because they were more inclusive. Their attitude was markedly unusual for the time, as neighbors of different colors often lived side by side but went to different schools and sat on different ends of the bus. Growing up in the Bagneris household, with over twenty-four members whose heritage drew from different cultures, was a gift in the middle of a hostile, segregated society.

My father, Lawrence Sr., was a fun-loving, happy-go-lucky man who worked hard to provide for his children and to replicate the family gatherings he'd enjoyed growing up within his large family. He and his seven brothers and sisters had no contact with their three half-siblings, who lived across town. Those kids were raised by their white dad and couldn't risk admitting that they were related to Creoles. When Louise died, in June of 1960, those children were careful not to cross the parish line from Arabi to attend a Black family's funeral.

My father had come back from his World War II service in France with a bigger view of the world. He was playful, supportive, and creative, which is remarkable given that, even with his Army service, it had been difficult to get the job he held in the post office. He was grounded by his family history: free people of color who first immigrated to New Orleans in 1850 and never strayed far from the Seventh Ward. Just like my mom, he was on the short side, but thinner, as he was a lifelong smoker. Every day I'm thankful that he was not only my biggest cheerleader but also a friend who always had time to share his wisdom.

Dad had experienced the world and was interested in other nationalities, and he passed this spirit of curiosity on to us. In that day and age, and despite little disposable income, we could still expand our horizons: we would take a ride on what we called the Belt, taking the Broad Street bus to the Canal streetcar and then the Dumaine Street bus back home, passing through all kinds of neighborhoods along the way. Downtown, on Canal Street, the department stores were lit up for every holiday with elaborate decorations, drawing in shoppers. When the buses went down Dumaine we saw row after row of large homes very different than the shotguns in our neighborhood. Down Broad Street, we would see the smaller mom-and-pop shops and storefronts.

No one worked harder than my dad. When the northern oil and gas men of the Petroleum Club needed a clean table for an elegant dining experience, it was my father's job to serve them from 10 a.m. to 2:30 p.m. Because he out-cultured most of them and was well mannered, he made

Neighborhood party at the Bagneris house on Tonti Street [1960s]
COURTESY OF THE AUTHOR

good tips and picked up even better gossip. After a nap, he would work at the post office from 6 p.m. to 2 a.m., sorting mail. Mardi Gras season was extra busy: he served as valet to the pages, kings, and captains of the krewes of Babylon, Hermes, and Momus. His presence was needed late into the night and into the next morning when he served the drunk, tuxedoed blue bloods at elaborate breakfasts. This was his hustle to keep us in private schools. My dad always had a smile and warm greeting for everyone he met.

Beyond feeding the family, Dad's hard work extended to ensuring that he set a good example for his boys—especially me, as I was the oldest son. One day, walking home from school, my brother Vernel suffered a sneak attack from older boys who found him an easy target. I ran four blocks to our house yelling "Daddy! Daddy! They're beating Vernel up!" In bed, tired from work and resting for the next shift, he calmly explained that "if you don't go whip their ass, I'm gonna whip . . . *your* ass!" With no choice left, I ran back and found those two boys on top of Vernel. I grabbed them both, threw one on the ground, and dragged Vernel away. After that I was confident that I could protect my family. Again, as the oldest boy in a Black-Creole family, this was my dad preparing me, should he ever depart, to be next in line to take the reins.

Just the next week, a cocky, blond Creole kid from the neighborhood thought it would be good fun to provoke me. I had just swept my porch. It was spick-and-span when he appeared from the bushes to surprise me with a large, ice-cold 7 Up, which he splashed all over me and the porch. So I beat his ass. Immediately, with his stern voice, Dad called me inside. "You will not be beating anyone up! You are to protect yourself and your siblings, but you are not to be aggressive." I then knew the difference, the necessity of balance, not to walk this world as a weapon—but still, I had never felt more confident that I could protect myself and my siblings.

Just like all New Orleanians, my family and childhood friends would enjoy the hot summers at the breezy Pontchartrain lakefront, making sure to stay east of Franklin Avenue with no exception. No signs were needed, no markers were worth erecting. If we didn't want to be harassed, we left the white folk alone, west of Franklin, and sometimes even that wasn't enough to protect us.

My loving father, of course, tried to spare his children from the sting of racial discrimination. He just wanted us to enjoy a day out at Lincoln Beach, the beach where we belonged. It took two buses to get there, including the Hayne Boulevard bus, which typically only Black people rode. New Orleans buses had a movable wooden sign that could be attached to the back of a row of seats. "For colored patrons only" was stenciled on the wood. The sign was called a "race screen," and Black people had to sit or stand behind it, helping the driver make sure that at least the first-row seats were always open for white riders.

One day, on the Hayne bus, my dad and I had to stand because Black people filled all the seats except that front row. I asked him, "Why can't we sit there?"

His reply was simple: "With the wheel under the seat, you don't want to sit there. That seat would be too hot. It's better to stand and feel the breeze come in."

Perhaps I wasn't so innocent as I remember, for I had my suspicions. As much as my father loved me, I concluded that he wasn't telling me the real truth. The front seat was left empty for miles while plenty of Black people came and went, standing. It was clear that it didn't take too much for people of color, African Americans in particular, to stay intimidated into avoiding those front seats. My dad always had a marvelous way of putting a positive spin on things. He'd always find good in a negative situation, to protect us from what otherwise would have been painful.

I still don't know where he got that attitude, but I remember seeing it often. To this day, I think he's amazing.

The first time I felt called to leadership outside my family circle happened in the halls of St. Peter Claver, where we had patrol boys: fifth-grade crossing guards who helped younger students across Ursulines Avenue and St. Philip Street. We all wore white patrol belts and shiny metal badges. We took our duties seriously. Together with our tasks and spiffy uniforms, we had a deep sense of schoolyard loyalty, often in the face of pervasive racism. On one occasion, we felt like one of our own was bullied—by a nun! This one sister, white like all the Sisters of the Blessed Sacrament, would tell us in class that everyone was created equal, but we had a sure feeling that she wasn't comfortable with just how dark this one boy was. Even though she wasn't head of the patrol program, she didn't quite like his "look" in the patrol group photos and wanted to kick him out. So, confronted with this challenge, I had just the solution—revolt! On my word, each patrol boy found the muddiest patch of curb in sight and shoveled dirt on their belts with their badges. Then, one by one, they each thumped their cold pieces of tin on the desk of the principal, Sister Stephanie. Now, Sister Regina Pacis, head of the patrol program, had seen this protest coming and knew I was behind it. With a bemused look, she invited me and the other patrol boys into the principal's office, and after a brief chat, our friend was reinstated on the patrol.

I remained a patrol boy for the next few grades, years that brought greater confidence in public—and greater uncertainty in private. When I was in eighth grade, I went to the downtown library and quietly looked up "homosexuality" in the card catalog. "Gay" wasn't a term people used to describe themselves back then, and homosexuality was a word that turned stomachs. Following the call number on the card, I went up to the second floor. Like a spy in the movies, I was convinced I was being followed. I checked, double-checked, and triple-checked behind and ahead to make sure the coast was clear, and with my heart beating as loud as a drum, I found the book that matched the card. I was a teenage child, scared to death, and trying to find what I needed to keep me from being attracted to boys. Just as I suspected, I learned that day that I had a mental illness!

Even decades later, the pain still feels all too real. There was only one conclusion: I needed to make a plan. First, I could tell no one. Then, I thought ahead to high school. In the fall, I would attend St. Augustine, the premier Catholic boys' school in our community. If my mind was broken, a correction would be needed to allow me to fit in. Being a ho-mo-*sex*-u-al meant dying and burning in hell. I may not have been too worldly yet, but I knew there were people eager to damn those sinners to keep them from infecting anyone else. Like *The Scarlet Letter* or *The Crucible*, being outed meant losing friends, expulsion from school, and ejection from society. Whole lives were rightly destroyed as payment for perversion.

The church was the center of my life and my family's life, interwoven into our upbringing and education. I had been an altar boy for five of the eight years I was in elementary school. Since entering high school as a *homosexual* was unacceptable, I had no choice but to pray really, really hard as I prepared for confirmation—a coming-of-age ceremony for young Catholic boys akin to becoming a man through a bar mitzvah. In preparation for the event—which the archbishop himself would attend—I did the Stations of the Cross over and over again, and at each of the fourteen stations of Jesus's passion, I begged the Lord with a personal, impassioned plea to cleanse me of my attraction to boys.

I had actually looked forward to confirmation, for I knew that when I approached the altar, the Holy Spirit himself would appear to wash away all my sins. My dreams of holding men close in my arms would be replaced with a different, a better kind of love. And so the moment arrived. With Archbishop Rummel present, I was anointed with the oil and received a holy tap on the face. And that was it. That was it. Nothing had changed. Trembling, I returned to my pew in the church, crying because those feelings remained, and if the Holy Spirit couldn't intervene, my problem was mine alone to fix.

Sexual exploration of any kind, with boys, with girls, was still no doubt sinful and wrong. That meant I was sinful. That meant I was wrong. I was wasting the gift of life and needed to torture my guilt away. If I was gay, I was going to hell. If my deformation was so strong that a tap from the Archbishop couldn't change me, I thought, maybe a physician could.

Desperate to see a psychiatrist, I worked for two summers to save money. The priests at St. Augustine had me paint windows, clean bathrooms, run the bookstore, and hawk Purple Knight backpacks, calendars, and key chains. By my sophomore year, I had saved enough money to see a psychiatrist on St. Charles Avenue, the grandest street in the city. There I was, aged sixteen, handing over the price of a month's mortgage. The doctor carefully counted out the $238, and once the money was in the cash box he had just the answer: shock therapy.

The Holy Spirit was certainly in no hurry, but now it was right on time. It arrived inside of me as a well of anger and came out with a yelp: "You can stick that shock treatment up your ass!" I'm still surprised I really said that. The Spirit was there that day to make sure I wasn't going to allow anyone to destroy my brain, and that same Spirit walks with me every day, to this day. Through the Holy Spirit, I know the difference between right and wrong.

Perhaps a change really did occur upon my confirmation. During that ceremony I took the name Lawrence George Joseph Bagneris Jr. to acknowledge my selection of St. Joseph as my patron saint. Joseph was already featured in my father's name. I've always looked up to the Josephite order, given their devotion to St. Augustine High School, and St. Joseph's Day and Night are important celebrations in New Orleans. Perhaps it was St. Joseph's spirit that entered me that day and continued to protect me as I grew. To this day, I give him homage by attending Mass on his feast day, March 19, as well as on my birthday. It was St. Joseph again who must have set up the next coincidence.

With a much lighter wallet, I got back on the streetcar to ride downtown from the doctor's office. At the end of the route, on Canal Street, I noticed a picket line protesting in front of the Maison Blanche department store for discriminating against Black people. That was the day of my awakening, my first participation in a public demonstration. I tapped a protester on the shoulder and asked, "Want to take a break?" I was happy to carry the sign myself and proceeded to picket up and down Canal Street.

We certainly caught the attention of the shopping crowds. A Black woman whispered a warning, admonishing me to "take care of things with your Mama" rather than rock the boat and put Black jobs in jeopardy: "Nothing! You ain't nothing, troublemaker!" At least she respected the picket line! Many white families ignored us and continued to shop like normal. A much older white woman hocked a wad of spit on me. She let me know I was "poor white trash!" With my light skin, she didn't even bother to insult me correctly!

Happening upon the protest for Black rights sparked the idea that maybe one day there could be a liberation movement for gay people also. In my child's mind, I thought the barriers to freedom for Black and gay people were as simple to knock down as bowling pins. Surely, the faster we could achieve equality for people of color, the faster we could move on to gay equality. It was my first glimmer that homosexual and gay acceptance was a possibility. With the wisdom of a sixteen-year-old, I knew the race problem would be an easy fix, so I joined the protest. Piece of cake, right?

Even if the Declaration of Independence and its preamble are just words written by flawed men, I've always loved those words and still somehow believe in equality, justice, and all the principles that America is supposed to uphold. The work is never over, but I look back fondly at that first naive day as a great introduction to the task of making a better world.

Interior of a New Orleans bus [1949]
CHARLES L. FRANCK STUDIO COLLECTION AT HNOC, 1979.325.6234

NO SMOKING
FOR COLORED PATRO
ONLY

CHAPTER TWO / *High School*

St. Augustine High School [1978]
PHOTOGRAPH © OWEN MURPHY
HNOC, GIFT OF THE ARTS COUNCIL OF NEW ORLEANS, 1996.93.70

2

FOR CREOLE BOYS, THE WORLD BEGAN BOTH IN THE GARDEN OF EDEN AND AT the corner of London Avenue (today's A. P. Tureaud Avenue) and Hope Street. St. Augustine High School has been a historically Creole and African American Catholic all-boys institution since 1951. It has long served as the center of our community, and the experience I gained through the school will last with me forever. For our families, entrance into St. Aug was an aspirational dream, and I knew I wanted to go from the time I was eight. Can you imagine being so little, encountering something as large, loud, and inspiring as the school's famous marching band? Nothing better explains St. Aug's commitment to prestige, academics, and culture than the straight, disciplined lines of the Marching 100. As a child, all I ever wanted to be was a proud Purple Knight, where I knew I could grow to be my very best.

By the age of fourteen, I began to realize the amount of sacrifice my parents were making to raise their children. I was learning what it took to keep children in Catholic school and what it took to keep them fed. And so I made a conscious decision: if life required sacrifice, I was going to devote my energies to my community.

When it came time for incoming students to register for St. Augustine High School, we were all slotted into A, B, C, or D ranks based on academics. Those in the A classes were presented with more challenging material, while those in the D classes needed extra help.

Filled with ambition, I was assigned to the B class. I couldn't wait to tell my mother. Brimming with excitement, I exclaimed that I had got into B class! Her reaction wasn't quite what I expected. I thought she would be proud—but when she said "Oh my god!" with concern on her face, I realized she was worried that the pace of work would be too much for me. By then, we had known for years that my hearing wasn't the best. And even if I knew that I wasn't quite college scholarship material, I still wanted to bring home an award—even if it wasn't an academic award—when I crossed that graduation stage. So I prepared to win something. After four years of high school, I was one of only two students who had not missed a single day of class. So, on graduation night, I was able to receive a perfect attendance award in front of everybody, including my mom. My experience at St. Aug made me the man I am today: independent, with total self-respect.

Some inner turmoil notwithstanding, my high school years were incredible! I was part of a tight-knit cohort of great people. We hung out together, partied together, celebrated homecoming games and danced at proms and parties. My mother jumped at the chance to host house parties, having grown up as an only child. With my baby sister Gina born in 1963, and four children in total, celebrations had to be big! Everyone was invited. Just imagine our house on Tonti Street in the '60s, on a large lot with a wide yard, a basketball hoop and a garden transformed into a Hawaiian luau, Viennese ballroom, or Mexican fiesta.

Upon Mother's orders, I would always pass out invitations far and wide. But one day, my friend Earl Barns gave me quite the dare. Since he was Black, he just knew that I wouldn't invite him to my Creole party.

"Of course I'd invite you, why wouldn't I?" I asked him.

"All you high yellows," he replied, "you just don't do that." Well, I wanted him at the party, and I wanted to prove him wrong, so I invited him. Inevitably, one of my Creole neighbors muttered to my Dad, just as Earl was pulling up: "Now, who is that dark guy coming in?" Thank goodness for Dad, who exhorted our neighbor to "just sit down and let the kids enjoy themselves. If he's a friend of Lawrence's, he is welcome in our home." Earl ended up having a great time, and I was happy he was there, along with all kinds of kids, a group much wider than our "high yellow" community. Despite society's hang-ups on color, which pained me deeply, I loved hosting a good gathering, and I wanted everyone there.

I learned to keep house from my mom, who maintained a home so gleaming that we could eat off the floor. Dad adopted the same sense of neatness and order in his car. It still boggles my mind that Dad was able to work three jobs and Mom was able to keep everything timed perfectly, providing him—and all of us—with clean clothes and dinner. As Mom and Dad had met when they were children, all they had known was being part of a team. From that base, they proceeded to perfect the way they presented themselves to the world, a valuable survival tactic and a commonplace for all Creoles. We had to make sure, in the way we spoke, dressed, kept ourselves, and practiced manners, that we were better than everyone else. This was our required attitude in order to survive such a hostile racial environment.

Now, I don't know if you would call me a skeptic, but I was never one to believe in Santa Claus. He seemed invented by the very department stores I was told to avoid. But Mom and Dad wanted my childhood Christmases to be warm and magical, and kept inviting Santa into our home. Even when I had reached the ripe old age of sixteen, my parents wanted to see me wait at the chimney, so they said, "Son, you've been a good boy. I think Santa wants to stop by. What would you like him to bring?" Being the smart-ass I've always been, I wanted to call their bluff. So I told them that

Santa had to bring me a movie camera. See, we out here in the 'hood never saw anyone our shade with a movie camera. That was the height of technology, and it needed film and lenses and reels.

I nearly fell over when I opened a box marked "Lawrence" on Christmas morning. "Damn! There just has to be a Santa Claus. Only he could afford this!"

I hate to spoil the surprise, but it wasn't Santa who brought me the camera. Brand new, the movie camera had come not from the North Pole but from a pawnshop on Airline Highway. It came not by sleigh but in the arms of my mother, who took the long trek back by bus. She told me all this many years later. To this day, I'm still guided and astonished by the sacrifices my parents made so that my brother, sisters, and I would feel supported—and I owe them for that example alone. Dad worked three jobs, Mom cooked and ironed every day, and I'm forever grateful that my family taught me just how to step up to the plate.

Whether it was December or April, my parents made every holiday magnificent. On Easter Sunday morning, I'd wake up surrounded by baskets on every surface, full of foil-covered candy. In preparation, Mom would collect money from Dad and go wild with Easter baskets, cellophane, and blow-up bunnies. Despite her stiffer upbringing, Mom was happy to let loose like Dad's family did. Not one step later, after the baskets, you'd find the whole dining room table smothered in vases of lilies. Easter Sunday was a fashion show for the whole neighborhood. All my neighbors were dressed in the finest suits, and my pals and I were no exception. One year, green suits were in, so I couldn't wait to step out in my tailored outfit. The knot on my skinny tie was undoubtedly perfect, and my pocket square was starched and straight as a razor. You can be absolutely sure they matched. But as soon as I sauntered down the street out of church, who did I find? Eight of my teenage pals, wearing the exact same green shade!

My friends and I would take the lap from Corpus Christi Church on St. Bernard Avenue down to Dixiana Bakery off Broad Street every Sunday after church. I can still taste the bakery's impeccable glazed donuts. Sunday was made even more special because it was a chance to catch up with the sisters, young ladies who went to all-girls Xavier Prep while we went to St. Aug. I realize how lucky I am to have many of the same friends today.

Such was the natural ebb and flow of the year. Through the winter, leading up to Mardi Gras, Mom would make costumes and start our cycle of king cake parties. Starting on Twelfth Night, January 6, friends and family would gather to share a king cake, with a hidden plastic baby inside. The person who received the baby in their slice would be the king or queen of the party and would save their allowance to buy the next cake and host the next week's party, all the way through the Carnival season. When Fat Tuesday finally arrived, Claiborne Avenue was a beautiful stage for a succession of Skeletons, Mardi Gras Indians, and Zulu floats.

After Mardi Gras we would celebrate St. Patrick's Day, as the nuns at our school were Irish. St. Joseph's Day arrived two days later. St. Joseph is my patron saint, and it so happened that the priests at my high school belonged to the Josephite order. We would celebrate Joanne's birthday later in March. Gina's birthday would follow in June, Vernel's in July, and my own in September.

Our neighborhood was at the center of everything we did. Virtually all our friends and family lived within the same small collection of blocks, within our church parish. Survival depended on staying within this safe space, with festivals at church and family gatherings at home. Running rampant through the city was unthinkable, as no white folk would tolerate any such incursion. Doesn't that sound familiar? Doesn't it feel just like today, where Black and brown kids are getting shot for crossing the wrong lines?

It's much easier for me to remember the wonder in those not-quite-innocent days. To help pay for my tuition, Father Grant, our principal, offered to let me run the school bookstore. I enjoyed the responsibility. And my freshman year, I was finally in a position to realize my childhood dream

The St. Aug Marching 100, with Larry on clarinet (second row, second from left), from *The Knight* [1960]
COURTESY OF THE AUTHOR

of being in the famous St. Augustine Marching 100 band. I didn't play an instrument yet, so I was given a choice when I joined. Thanks to seeing Pete Fountain on television, I picked the clarinet. To this day, I can't keep a tune. But even if I only really heard half the notes, my rhythm was impeccable. The butch discipline of the march was my favorite aspect of band, and I can always keep a tight line.

Freshmen in the band made great target practice for the seniors. The first away football game of the season was hours away, in Bogalusa, and we were made to sit in the back of the bus with plenty of shoving, pushing, and pinching. A mosh pit was guaranteed. This gauntlet, however, failed to puncture the good cheer of the road, and the bus was filled with all manner of singing and games. It was so loud that no one noticed that I had taken a seat up front. My big sister, who was a popular cheerleader, introduced me to all the seniors on the bus—and their suitcase of wine hidden under the seat.

Bogalusa's football team was barely ready for us, and I certainly wasn't ready for Bogalusa. The good wine spirits took quite the hold on me, in a way I'll never forget. The Marching 100 took to the field, with their famous discipline. *Halt! About face!* Except, tipsy and skinny, I didn't hear the last part. I kept on walking and walking and found the goalpost before I caught the rest of the band, at the opposite side of the field. Sick to my stomach, I made a show in front of both teams by hurling into the end zone! My band director turned bright red; I had never seen him so angry. I knew I was due for a paddling, if I didn't cause him a heart attack first.

Try to imagine band bus trips from my perspective, with all the young, fit, and glowing young men. We Creoles know full well the abundance of beautiful features our people have collected from every continent. "Behave yourself!" was my constant reminder. To make sure, I would often take girls out on dates. It was easy to have a good time. Once we turned eighteen, the House of Joy—a neighborhood bar, long and skinny like a line—was always our last stop. And we all took turns hosting house parties. Our dens and our yards kept us in quite a sheltered world, where it was easy to develop deep friendships. News spread easily in a community where everyone shared aunts and uncles, and nobody wanted to be known for their bad manners, so each guest made sure to pitch in at the end of the night to clean up. Unwelcome in the Black community as well as the white, we excelled at making our little world warm.

However, no pillow fort could truly keep the rest of the world out. Many priests and leaders in our church had taught us that we had the ability and obligation to change things for the better. And so, my freshman year, I found a political cause. Back in those old days, the parade held on Mardi Gras morning by the Zulu Social Aid and Pleasure Club was a mess! It was a far cry from the well-organized and beloved operation of today. I saw their parade as sloppy and undignified, almost embarrassing, and the NAACP agreed.

Despite my relative youth, I was possessed with the urge to circulate a petition written by the NAACP, calling for a boycott of the Zulu parade until they cleaned up their act. I made speeches at my old grammar school to teach the young kids about getting involved with reform. Even our priests encouraged our activism, and the whole affair was great practice in hustling signatures. Our campaign called for Zulu to acquire a regular parade route from the city and to stop getting blackout wasted, all in the name of the Black community. The city had never given Zulu an official route before, but uproar in the Black community forced their hand. The way I saw it, both the city and the Zulu organization needed to set a better example of cooperation, decorum, and fun, for everyone's benefit. My brother snitched to my parents about my speeches and rabble-rousing, but all he could conclude was that I was a damn good speaker.

Years later, the chance to ride in Zulu would be the honor of a lifetime. Zulu reformed itself into a strong community organization, and for Mardi Gras 1991, Lena Stewart—a great friend and a staffer for New Orleans city councilman Johnny Jackson Jr.—invited me to ride with the subkrewe of Diamond Cutters. Lena and Johnny had accompanied us in the March 1987 and April 1993 marches on Washington for gay and lesbian rights, and I was so grateful to join them in Zulu for several years in the 1990s and 2000s.

It must sound surprising today, but the priests at St. Aug really exposed me to and encouraged my interest in activism. Can you imagine them taking me to the White Citizens' Council meeting at the Municipal Auditorium? Squeezed between the white priests, it was easy to sneak in. Imagine the roar of the crowd when a white son and a white daughter ran around with black faces and hair frayed like yarn. As they ran up and down the aisles, the booming question—and simple answer—echoed over the rafters: "Now, how could you ever want your kids to go to school with these mongrels?" I was safe, but deep behind enemy lines, hiding in plain sight as the crowd took joy at calling the kids the worst kind of names.

In the street, the same White Citizens' Council would chant, "Two, four, six, eight, we don't want to integrate!" and it was easier in those public protests for us to reply with a hearty, "Three, six, nine, twelve, kiss my ass and go to hell!"

My activism was sharpened through my work at the Negro Betterment Council, a club that had formed at St. Augustine and had grown to include civil rights leaders of all shades. Picketing the downtown department stores was our first priority.

Up and down Canal Street, it was clear the stores wanted nothing from us but our money. The city made the rules, and any color was welcome to shop—but we were to come, buy, and leave. At Maison Blanche, for instance, Black people could forget about trying anything on before purchasing—and for us, all sales were certainly final. Not a single worker from president to mailroom was anything but white. One gross bathroom in the basement was reserved just for us. If we were hungry, we were welcome to have lunch anywhere else. Segregation was so clear that everyone in the city was strictly programmed not to imagine otherwise.

The Maison Blanche picket line became my regular habit from 1960 to 1964. Inevitably, one day we were all arrested and taken to the juvenile detention center at Dorgenois and St. Philip. The center wasn't far from my home—and it was a spot I knew well, as I had often visited the police precinct building to collect my bike if it was lost and found. Nothing frightened me about such a familiar place. Compared to the specter of jail, juvie was a relief. After thirty minutes, my dad arrived to pick me up on his way home from work, sighing to me, "Boy, I'm thirty-two years old. I've never been arrested in my life."

"Maybe if you had gotten arrested instead, I wouldn't have to for the both of us!" I shot back. I was always the smart-ass.

Inside, however, I feared his disappointment. He was just trying to protect me. "We're going to leave your mother out of this and get you home," he said, thoughtful as always. I would be arrested for protesting multiple times in my life. But it was only later on, when I was living in Houston, that I realized I wouldn't be here at all if my father had done what I was doing. He saw the injustices in the South when he returned home after serving his country in WWII. Yet in his time, the authorities would've taken no prisoner. Any yelp, and he would've been hanged.

Even the Most Reverend John Patrick Cody, Archbishop of New Orleans, wasn't exempt from my protest. Our priests had taken some of us to the National Catholic Conference for Interracial Justice in Memphis in 1965. We gave ourselves away when we asked the New Orleans delegation directly: If the Catholic Church was willing to go so far as to hold this conference, why were our high schools still segregated? The official spokesman blew smoke left, right, and in all the familiar corners. He equivocated about all aspects of integration, trying to argue that separating all of us and catering to our "special needs" was a more effective approach to education. Of course, the root of the matter was always financial. Even as a child I knew that if all the white people pulled their kids out of the parochial schools, the church would be stuck with the bill. I wanted him to admit that. But the delegation wanted us to trust them that it was more orderly to keep our schools segregated. One of my beloved white instructors at St. Aug, Father Richard Wagner, supported my inquiry. Can you imagine: a priest standing up to his fellow priests, to the archdiocese itself, to exclaim that this segregation thing was all so wrong!

So I kept demonstrating, marching with my peers from Woolworth's to Maison Blanche and Frostop, a local chain of burger joints. The Baptist minister Avery Alexander was a pillar in those days, our very own Martin Luther King. He stood together with the Reverend A. L. Davis, another Baptist who led marches and demonstrations. Each of them came from big churches uptown and were almost in competition with each other to see who could move the largest crowds. Davis eventually became a city councilperson, and Reverend Alexander became a legend in 1963, when police dragged him by the heels up a staircase for protesting City Hall's segregated lunchroom. I'll never forget the lesson Reverend Alexander offered me as a young protester: always keep your hands visible while picketing. You never knew what illegal things the authorities could invent in your pocket as a reason to harass you. Imagine my complicated feelings in the 1990s, when I ran against the reverend for state representative.

Whatever the police may have thought, my smart mouth wasn't about to slow down. I was "hardened" after so many civil rights arrests, knowing the juvenile detention center would be the ultimate stop. So I got a little cocky one day in 1963. The police kept their sirens quiet in white neighborhoods but enjoyed blaring them in other neighborhoods. Yet on this day, as they carted me off to juvie, they didn't bother to turn on their sirens, and I didn't miss the opportunity to remind them. In the back of the unit, I told an officer, "You're still discriminating against us—you think our class isn't worthy of your siren!" I challenged the cop to let everyone in the neighborhood know that a car full of demonstrators was coming. "Let's hear some noise!"

Despite their disdainful looks, I knew the cops were only taking me back to the usual destination. I knew Dad would always fetch me, and I'd be okay.

My service on St. Aug's Negro Betterment Council—where, my senior year, I made president—was an invaluable introduction to the art of politics. Father Robert Barnes, a white Josephite priest, was always generous with his attention to Council matters, as were other white activists on our side of the struggle. And in 1964, with Lyndon B. Johnson running for US president, I made my first real foray into national political advocacy. Thanks to the venerable Clarence "Chink" Henry, an officer of the International Longshoremen's Association—a strong union of mostly Black workers—the cavernous ILA union hall on Claiborne near Washington Avenue was made available for a Council fundraiser to benefit the LBJ for USA campaign. As a budding emcee, I was often at the mic, to the regret of many. The day of the fundraiser, brimming with attitude, I announced to the packed hall that I was refusing to work in any more segregated presidential campaigns. Immediately, Chink pulled me toward stage right with his longshoreman's grip.

"What's wrong with you, boy?" he demanded. Chink explained the complicated reality that even though the Democratic National Committee segregated its campaign efforts, the Black community benefited because our organizations were assigned separate line items in the DNC's budget. This was how money was allocated to pay its Black campaign workers. If funding for both Black and white groups had been combined, all that money would likely skip our local coffers, and DNC support for working Black operatives would evaporate.

As my high school graduation drew closer, I had to decide whether I could afford to go on getting arrested. I chose to continue, keeping my mother worried to tears. She even showed up at City Hall one evening, after I had snuck out of the house. My parents used to lock the windows, so I wouldn't go to nighttime protests and get hurt. When I heard Mom cry "Lawrence!" in front of the whole team, I was so embarrassed. Fortunately, before she pulled me away by the ear, a choir struck up—and I'll never forget singing "We Shall Overcome" with my mother.

By then I was looking to go to college, a goal that would remain out of reach without credit for a foreign language. After two years of Spanish class, I still hadn't passed, probably because I couldn't hear half of what was being said in either language. So for two summers in a row, I went to Booker T. Washington High School, on Earhart Boulevard, to make up those credits. Man, was Booker T. tough. Even the principal knew about the tradition of the Last Day Melee, at the end of summer school, when the darker kids would beat up all the light-skinned kids as payback for all kinds of petty beefs. To tamp this down, the principal gave us our grades a day early and instructed us not to come back. At least back then, the bullies were just fighting with fists, not shooting with guns.

The dark students always accused us light-skinned kids from across town of trying to pass for white. They weren't altogether wrong. I knew many friends with family members who had escaped New Orleans for California to pass for white, cutting ties with their old community. However, I had been raised to know that I was not to pass for any damn thing. "You are who you are, and accept that!"—I'd heard those words every day since I was young.

Just weeks before graduating, I was selected as the master of ceremonies for the biggest event in our high school community, the St. Augustine Symphonic Band fundraising gala. For this special day, the school would fill the city's Municipal Auditorium to hear the band perform classical music. To soothe my stage jitters, I memorized the whole thirty-eight-page program to introduce such classic pieces as "Rhapsody in Blue." As much as I now enjoy making a speech, public speaking then would force me to the bathroom often. This job needed to be perfect. For weeks I worked on memorizing each line and word in the script to polish away any mistakes. My selection was an honor, and I had to rise to the occasion.

To my relief, the night went well, though not without its own funny moments. For instance, my Uncle Frank, though large hearted, was a drinker. My Aunt Mamie had to keep him tied to the chair, as he couldn't keep from hollering, over and over, "That's my nephew! You're doing great!" I could hear him all the way from the stage and could only regain my focus when Dad took him for a walk. Though embarrassed at the time, today I can appreciate the pride he felt in me. Again and again, my family and community put in place a structure that inspired excellence: doing one's best, whatever one's capabilities were.

That night in the auditorium, I certainly felt I had the knack of it. The bright lights and warm crowd had me feeling so cocky, I started to add my own quips and jokes. Soon, I had gone completely off script, not realizing the stage crew was supposed to take their cues from the written program—and my freestyling was wreaking havoc for them. After another of my grand monologues, the curtains opened and Mr. Freeman, an older teacher, was caught running across the stage to move a prop. The audience was amused, but in my nervous state I misinterpreted their laughter and assumed they were laughing at me! Devastated, at home that night, I found my pillow and bawled. What an awful performance! Of course, no one noticed; if anything, they likely had enjoyed the imperfections. A weekend of rest left me feeling much better.

CHAPTER THREE / *College*

Xavier University campus [1965]
XAVIER UNIVERSITY OF LOUISIANA, *XAVIERITE*, STUDENTS ON CAMPUS, PRINT, ARCHIVES & SPECIAL COLLECTIONS

3

AS THE SUPREMES WERE CHARTING THEIR FIRST HITS AND THE BEATLES WERE leading the British Invasion, I graduated with St. Aug's class of 1964. The Creole world that raised me was so tight knit and protected that Xavier University of Louisiana across town seemed like a different world. Xavier was founded by St. Katharine Drexel in 1915 as a high school; it became a college in 1925 and is today the only historically Black and Catholic university in America. Back in those days, we didn't think of it as "historically Black" because any institution I could attend was plainly segregated. All my friends who had a future in higher education attended Xavier, as it was the clear option for St. Augustine and Xavier Prep grads. The commute from home required back-of-the-bus rides through a minefield of colored and white neighborhoods of varying hostility.

College hadn't been a clear choice for me. Since I had been born with poor hearing, I didn't think I would do well in school, and I thought the

Army was the only other option. The military was unacceptable to my father, but he preferred expressing himself through example rather than lecture. At Mardi Gras balls, the white upper crust likes to show off in black tie—and as was their habit, they always needed a little help. So my father brought my brother and me along on one of his gigs to affix bow ties, snap together cuff links, and load our "betters" into strange, big-headed costumes.

As you can already tell, it's not quite my thing to bend my knees to anyone, nor did I really want to spend any time in the king's and captains' rooms to assist any old rich man with his shoes. One officer of the krewe couldn't make up his mind. I'd tie his shoes, and suddenly he'd sneer, "Too tight." After trying again, his shoes were "too loose," then "too tight" again. Fed up, I shot back, "Tie your own damn shoe!" My dad almost had a heart attack over my insubordination. But he knew I got the message of why he'd had me join him at work. His lesson was clear: the servitude I had just experienced was my future if I avoided earning a college education.

Thankfully, in those days, we had our version of allies. An executive of King Cotton, the wiener company, was also a member of the krewe and noticed the whole shoe exchange. He called me over and had me work with his kids, who were about my age and needed assistance with their elaborate Carnival page costumes. At the end of the evening, he gave me a hundred dollar bill and said, "Keep that attitude. It will serve you well in life."

At eighteen, I was finally of legal age, and there was a bigger world to experience—I could start going to bars in the French Quarter. At the time, I was still dating girls. In fact, I almost married a girl to avoid being outed at the beginning of college. Meanwhile, I had a few boyfriends at Xavier, and we had to be quite careful to keep our Xavier and French Quarter activities separate. I could never quite know who would discover or spread my secret. Throughout these years, I was fortunate that my bedroom was in the front of the house, offering me the privacy to escape my family's gaze. They never put any pressure on me to settle down quickly, but I still didn't want them knowing what time I was coming in and out. I had a curfew of 1 a.m., but New Orleans was a twenty-four-hour city.

Then, as now, the French Quarter was a lot of fun. Gay life centered around the corner of Bourbon and St. Ann. Two large clubs faced each other on the downriver side of the corner. The Caverns, on the lake side, was a piano bar that attracted an older crowd; Pete's Place, on the river side, was named after clarinetist Pete Fountain, who had once kept the joint as his performing space. Worn-out plush lounges looked upon a stage and dance floor at Pete's. One block away was Lafitte's in Exile—still running to this day—held together with burlap and plywood, available for the quick hookup. Beneath a veneer of propriety, the Quarter in the 1960s was every bit as queer as it is today.

Perhaps it was even more so, with an additional cluster of gay bars in the Upper Quarter, near Canal Street. Near the epicenter of Iberville and Royal there was Wanda's, a showroom for rent boys and nightly fun. Above Wanda's was the Safari Lounge. And at 604 Iberville—upstairs, of course—was the Up Stairs Lounge, with a truly mixed clientele that differentiated it from other hangouts. It welcomed Black and white patrons of every genderbending expression and was popular with drag queens, theater types, and a prehistoric trans community. On Sundays, it served as the home of pioneering gay friendly services performed by the Metropolitan Community Church.

The Up Stairs Lounge is infamous today for the 1973 fire that killed thirty-two gay people. Today, the fire is commemorated as a tragedy. But at the time, polite society preferred to look the other way—and the victims went largely unmourned by the city. My mother's reaction to the Up Stairs Lounge fire was very touching. She wondered aloud, "Why were those people treated that way, they're human beings!"

These upper blocks of the Quarter were a natural home for Wanda's and the Up Stairs because, at a time when New Orleans's waterfront was rougher, they also featured a series of Greek sailor bars. Some of my friends lucked out and found overnight berths on board ships as guests of

Cafe Lafitte in Exile, 901 Bourbon Street [1962]

PHOTOGRAPH BY DAN S. LEYRER
COLLINS C. DIBOLL VIEUX CARRÉ DIGITAL SURVEY AT HNOC, N-396D

tan sailors, well built from working on the ocean. Personally, I stayed right on dry land. I could just imagine waking up offshore, on a ship that had launched, headed straight across the Atlantic!

To me, the French Quarter was paradise. Adrian Bousqueto, from my Creole neighborhood, was a few years older than I was and knew the French Quarter's queer world well. He was like a big brother, bouncer, and nurse during a time I wasn't quite so sure of or comfortable with loving guys. He knew I'd already had three girlfriends—and that those young women were lovely, but none gave me any special spark. He suggested that I needed to separate the new gay friends I was meeting from my old straight friends. So I started introducing myself as Larry when I was out in the Quarter rather than Lawrence, the name I had used with family, at school, everywhere. This way, if any friend, guy or girl, called for Larry on the home phone, I would know immediately that I had met them in a gay rather than straight environment.

Adrian understood me and gave me the space to ask questions in a fun, safe environment. Even so, the gay world was still rather daunting. I was afraid to even use the bathroom! They were kept quite dark, and I had heard stories of all the rowdy men. Every time I needed to go, Adrian would drive me all the way back to my house. Finally, after the fifteenth time or so, he got fed up and marched me straight to the nearest hotel instead.

Life was still dangerous for homosexuals, who lived on the fringes of society. One night, Lafitte's kicked out a rich kid whose father was a special consul from far away. Enraged at being cut off, the drunk took his truck and drove it right into the bar—an episode that some old-timers in the neighborhood still remember as "the Mendoza Incident." The jukebox by the front door was sent right to the back of the bar, but otherwise no one was hurt. However, in the commotion, I was outed in a small way. My brother, a few years younger, came to check on friends that he knew were regulars at Lafitte's and found me! And only us gays hung out there! So it was that night my brother found out I was gay, and vice versa.

One day during my freshman year of college, I got a call from Kathy Vick, a top aide for Hale Boggs, whom my family admired greatly. Hale represented Louisiana's Second Congressional District in DC. Despite an upscale upbringing, Congressman Boggs was very much a man of the people, just as comfortable with Black crowds as he was with white ones. We still celebrate him today for having the courage to be a full integrationist. A successful politician, he rose to the rank of House majority leader. After Hale's untimely death in a 1972 plane crash, his wife Lindy—a real Southern lady who had wit and will to rival her husband—was elected to his former seat. She served eighteen years in Congress and another three years as ambassador to the Vatican.

Kathy was calling to ask me to join the Young Democrats of New Orleans. My first reaction was to ask her, "But isn't it white?" At some level, I was always inquisitive about why people would want to invite me to anything! But Kathy replied that the Boggses were looking to get people of color into the Democratic Party—and she added that I had been recommended by Dutch Morial. Dutch was a pioneering jurist and was soon to become the first Black member of the Louisiana House of Representatives since Reconstruction. He would go on to even greater fame as the first Black mayor of New Orleans.

I attended the meeting and soon ran to become the first African American vice president of the Young Democrats of New Orleans. I would remain active politically throughout my college years, continuing to march and demonstrate for civil rights. I applied my leadership skills to lighter pursuits, as well, helping to organize Xavier's first homecoming parade.

But at some level, I was still a kid. With all the parties at college, it was easy to lose track of eighteen credit hours, and I flunked nine. My name was added to the wrong kind of dean's list—and not too long after, I was called to the office of an old nun with a familiar face. She was Sister Stephanie, who had known me since her days as principal at St. Peter Claver, when I led the revolt of the patrol boys. With classic parochial directness, she led me to fear God in precisely the right ways. She had known all my business since grammar school, and now, as dean, she knew exactly what was necessary to get me to graduate from Xavier.

At the time, I was majoring in elementary education. This was not due to a love of toddlers but because the program featured no foreign language requirements. I really wanted to be a political science major. Knowing full well my strengths and weaknesses, Sister Stephanie was willing to approve a change of major, provided I take four separate level-one classes in French, Spanish, Russian, and German—a workaround that would allow me to complete my degree. Sister Stephanie let me in on a secret: academia is a bit of a game, and while you need to play by the rules, formal requirements aren't the key to a true education. Before dispatching me from her office, she demanded that I take a job with my father at the post office.

From the very beginning, my parents had made sacrifices to raise their family and put their four kids through Catholic school. By now, those kids were growing into young adults: my sister Joanne and I were in college, and my brother was preparing to enter a college theater program. In this environment, it was only natural that I had to give something back.

My dad had so many jobs that there was plenty of work to share. Remember, he was a breakfast and lunch waiter until two o'clock, took a siesta in the afternoon, and then started his second job at the post office. In my new routine, I joined him from six in the evening until two thirty in the morning, every day, Monday through Friday. Evening hours were prized, and it was unusual for a new employee to start with such a choice assignment. It had taken my father fifteen years to gain a shift that would allow him to work a second job. Thus, there were grumblings from the white staff at the privilege I had been granted—but our friend Hale Boggs had put in a call to the local postmaster, whose office was an appointed one, and he approved my schedule.

I thoroughly enjoyed commuting with my father each day. And while I made sure to contribute to the family budget, I soon had saved enough for a white Ford Fairlane, with money left over to have it equipped with the latest eight-track technology. Etta James's seminal album *At Last!* had been a favorite in our home and now accompanied our daily commute. Soon, Dad and I knew every word, from the soaring strings of "Anything to Say You're Mine" to the rough moans of "Tough Mary."

I learned so much from the way my dad carried himself in the workplace. He was loved by everyone in the post office, where he played the role of mediator, helping people communicate and joke around. He was always blunt and funny. At the Petroleum Club—before it left New Orleans for Houston—he earned the respect of the ruddy-faced local oil barons. But these were complicated relationships, and one experience is instructive. One Carnival season, he was assigned to assist the captain of the organization in putting together the annual ball. More than any annual king or queen, the captain bears responsibility for the ritual, logistical, financial, personal, and bureaucratic aspects of an organization's ball and parade. One evening, as the captain's head swam with these responsibilities, he grew hungry. Without a thought, he called on Dad to fetch him a roast beef po-boy; my father was happy to oblige, as part of doing a good job. Downstairs, at the building's cafe, Dad placed the order, only to have a redneck behind the counter tell this "boy" there was none for him there. When the captain learned his liege and representative had been so insulted, his own sense of power and propriety was affronted. Taking time away from his duties, the captain fired the racist cashier on the spot.

While my dad was honored, he knew that the story wasn't a simple one. This was an easy anecdote to prove to me why I needed an education. His own finishing school had been the Army. He taught me that I needed to finish college to avoid being anyone's pawn.

I could tell my father anything, and I'm blessed today by his wisdom. We grew to be friends very quickly as I grew up, particularly once I began contributing to the household's general fund and had a say in how we spent it.

Times were changing in America, and the fight for civil rights sometimes hit close to home. The economy was strong, and around 1964 my mom selected her dream home, in the Gentilly Terrace neighborhood. It had ample bedrooms, a living room bar, and a large yard—everything she wanted, except for Black neighbors. But despite my dad's steady work at the post office, our combined family income didn't qualify for a mortgage until my older sister became a schoolteacher. Now, Gentilly Terrace was a white neighborhood, but because Mom did all the house shopping, it was easy for her to get approved to purchase 4611 Touro. They thought she was Hispanic! As soon as my dad and sister arrived for the signing, the realtor found out what he was in for—the first Black family in his territory. Soon, there were new rules and red tape pushing the closing off further and further. But Mom wanted what she wanted, and that was that. It didn't matter to Mom that she was breaking the block. She was the lawful owner, she had secured a mortgage, and she was ready to move in.

And so we moved to Gentilly Terrace with my mother's strong spirit intact, whether the neighbors liked it or not. In preparation for our first Christmas, I was installing holiday lights one day when a "friendly" white neighbor came over to greet my mom with the news that she would soon be leaving the block—"but not due to your family," of course. "Our house was just a bit too small, and we're looking for something bigger." Normally quite demure, my mom surprised me that day by replying bluntly, to the neighbor's face, how strange it was that "everyone's house in the neighborhood was suddenly too small," and that the cascade of "For Sale" signs had only begun when our family moved in. "Go on, Mama!" I climbed down from my ladder to proclaim. "You're Martin Luther *Queen*!"

Thankfully not everyone left. I still remember the white man who posted a sign announcing, "This is my neighborhood! I'm not leaving. Why don't you stay?"

Our home was the natural place for everyone's birthday and holiday celebrations, and New Year's Eve 1965 was no different. As our house began to fill with the usual cast of characters, I began to drink and drink and drink. I thought it would be no problem to drink bourbon, rum, and vodka, all mixed together. (For years to come, I could still summon the smell of the cruel concoction.) My friend Rudy was coming back home, and I was terrified.

Rudy and I had grown up together in the same neighborhood and shared a friend group. Alone among all my friends, he had joined the Army. And his sendoff party at the House of Joy, after high school graduation, had been one of the lowest nights of my life. We drank and drank and, feeling safe with Rudy, I drunkenly came out to him. He was immediately appalled. His face and body dripped with disdain. I had come out to the wrong person.

Now it was New Year's Eve, and I wanted to show off our new house—on our newly integrated block—to all my friends. Trying to forget about what had happened in the past, I invited Rudy, who was home for the holidays after finishing basic training. My friend Adrian had been a godsend the previous spring, comforting me after the debacle at the House of Joy and reassuring me that he'd persuade Rudy to keep quiet. And he'd kept his word: months had passed, and our circle of friends showed no signs of knowing my secret. But now, as the New Year's party got underway, I grew terrified. Rudy had the power to out me in front of everybody. So I drank.

Approaching midnight, Rudy's car turned the corner, and the sight of him was enough to trigger my nerves into hurling. I threw up all over myself, and my dear father had to take me to the shower, clean me up, and keep me from passing out.

New Orleans gay bars were thick with the same racism that permeated the rest of the city. But since the clientele assumed I was Puerto Rican or Mexican, they had always invited me in. I appreciated everyone's friendliness and didn't waste much time worrying about it.

Easter Sunday was then and is still a popular springtime holiday in New Orleans—a time to dress up and celebrate the season. The spring of

New Orleans march in support of Selma civil rights activists, with Larry at lower right [1965]

XAVIER UNIVERSITY OF LOUISIANA, *XAVIERITE*, STUDENTS ON CAMPUS, PRINT, ARCHIVES & SPECIAL COLLECTIONS

1968, once church services and egg hunts had concluded and my family headed home for a nap, it was time for me to slip out in my favorite white double-breasted suit and see my friends in the Quarter. After hitting the bars, a bunch of us gathered at my good friend Walter's apartment, in an Esplanade mansion. But man, was I in for a shock that day!

Now, before I tell you what happened, I should say a few more words about Lindy and Hale Boggs. I was really blessed to have these special people in my life. They had even invited me to attend the Jesuit Giant, Georgetown University, with their support. Because I was sensitive about being gay, Black, and deaf, I thought it better to stay close to home for school. Throughout my Xavier years, however, they continued to encourage my activism. Congressman Boggs was up for reelection in 1968—and he asked college kids who had worked with him in the Black community to appear in a television ad. I was more than happy to assist, without quite thinking it through completely.

So there my gay friends and I were at Walter's apartment when the Boggs commercial came on, and there was my face, with the words "Xavier University" written underneath! Walter leaped in front of the TV in an effort—he thought—to protect me. To the extent that I'd thought about it, I had assumed that my gay friends knew that I had attended St. Augustine—and, presumably, knew about my Creole heritage and had no issue with my race. But Walter knew the gay community was more racist than I realized. Overnight, after that commercial, people at the bars and in the Quarter suddenly kept me at arm's length. It was a sobering lesson.

Still, if there's one constant in my life, it's that I've never gotten truly hurt or angry at other people's reactions to my race or my sexuality. Instead, I've always gotten even. After the Boggs commercial aired, I ended up making cards and handing them out to tricks, just to roast them: "You got fucked by a nigger!" embossed in script.

At Xavier, I had been lucky to find a mentor in James Schaffer, a white professor who ran the drama department. He was the sponsor for our local fraternity, which organized many wonderful trips, and for our drama-themed Mardi Gras organization, "The Greeks."

Tall, handsome, and bald, Professor Schaffer was popular among students and faculty alike, despite being out of the closet. Everyone was comfortable with him, and that alone helped me glimpse a life where being gay might be natural and accepted. I felt safe around him from the start. Up to then, my gay experiences had been confined to playing around in the messy and promiscuous French Quarter, which I had found to be dehumanizing. But at our fraternity's first fall retreat at the Creole Center in Slidell, I was moved to come out. There among the picnic tables and shade trees, a pressure built within me, and I started to cry. I was in the swimming pool, and so was Professor Schaffer, and while we were alone I exclaimed, "I'm gay, and I don't want to be."

It was so simple and must sound banal today, but for gay people, it sometimes takes a long time to feel validated. Professor Schaffer was the first to teach me that being gay is something to embrace because there's nothing wrong with you. Having someone in your corner is the truest feeling of liberation. So it was natural for me to turn to him again, for comfort, after that New Year's Eve party. He responded with words that have stuck with me to this day. "Look," he said, patting my back. "You should never let anyone upset you to the point that you destroy your life. To hell with Rudy. If he says anything, if he holds it against you, I'll take care of it personally."

Professor Schaffer was there for me every semester at Xavier, watching me grow from a freshman to a senior. What a time to be coming of age! My internal struggles were mirrored by external convulsions: year by year, the political temperature was rising. Somehow, we gays knew that eventually our moment would come. That moment would arrive in 1969—our year, the year of liberation, the Year of the Queen.

Earlier in college, at one of my darker moments, Professor Schaffer had promised to take me to New York. He wanted to give me a sense of perspective, to show me a world of romantic possibility broader than what I was finding in New Orleans. And so, true to his word, he and I met up at

LaGuardia Airport in the spring of my senior year. The spirit of '69 was in full bloom, and I felt like I was swimming in a mysterious soup, awash in political stirrings and artistic happenings. It was thrilling.

Gays were still being hunted down, of course, but Greenwich Village was soon to contain the critical mass of queers necessary to foment revolution. Our first stop was Julius' bar, where in 1966 gay activists had successfully challenged a law that prohibited two men from having a drink together as a date. In an era when information was passed by pamphlets and word of mouth rather than instant texts, the only place to meet other gays was at the speakeasies. There were more gay bars at that time than exist today! And in New York, as in New Orleans, they catered to all tastes and classes.

Professor Schaffer and I shared a meal of hamburgers and drinks before he announced that he had his own, ahem, "appointments" to attend to. I was twenty-two and he was in his fifties, and he knew that there was a whole world of young people I should be exploring. He directed me to the Stonewall Inn—and we agreed to catch up later at the Hotel Edison in Times Square, where we were staying.

It was May in New York, and so many young queers and lesbians were in the street, flirting, playing games, catching up. While all the gay bars had their cliques, the Stonewall Inn—under the purview of the Mafia, its windows covered by plywood—had a reputation for inclusivity. I had never seen such a mixed crowd of queers. There were trans people and Puerto Ricans, drag queens and African Americans, hippies and Asians and country boys.

Before it got famous, the Stonewall Inn kept a loud tribal beat playing each night. The sight of lovemaking—that is, glances and looks, caresses and embraces on the dance floor between two men or two women—was a sight I had never seen before. Straights had had their bars, parks, and lovers' lanes for as long as I could remember, but the scene at the Stonewall Inn filled me with hope. It didn't help that I had seen *West Side Story* just recently. On this night, I was a full-blown romantic.

Professor James Schaffer [undated]

XAVIER UNIVERSITY PHOTOGRAPHS COLLECTION, XUPC011.05.A.58.1.003, XAVIER UNIVERSITY OF LOUISIANA ARCHIVES & SPECIAL COLLECTIONS

Larry at a photo studio near the Stonewall Inn, New York City [1969]
COURTESY OF THE AUTHOR

Then boom! The lights were on! The police came in with their billy clubs, bashing anyone who looked at them wrong. They started to line people up one by one to demand their IDs. Back in this era, thanks to "decency" laws pushed by overzealous politicians, gay bars operated under constant threat of police raids. Sometimes, especially when a bar was run by the mob, the raids happened during less-busy daylight hours, after some quiet negotiations between police and ownership. Sometimes the raids happened when the police were simply bored, or needed to look good for their supervisors and the press. Newspapers were eager to publish mugshots for bosses and mothers to see. Rap sheets of indecency were enough to follow you throughout your whole life, jeopardizing career, family, and housing.

Police raided Stonewall all the time, and fortunately for me, I was surrounded by veterans. My night had begun like many of my first nights at gay bars, by finding a boy with whom to make cutesy-eyes. This time, it was an Italian kid from Brooklyn. When the lights came on, before I knew it, I felt a large thud and I was swept off my feet, into the bathroom. "Follow me! Follow me!" my new comrade prodded. With my heart pumping and my head spinning with tales of illicit love, *West Side Story* had come to life, a little more than I expected. My Italian friend led me by the hand and showed me how to climb out the bathroom window, onto the street—and in the back of my mind, "There's a Place for Us" played. I moved to the fire escape and began to cry. He asked, "What's wrong?" I responded that this was romantic, just like *West Side Story.* He responded, "Great, but move your ass, or we're gonna be arrested!" Had that come to pass, my life would have been completely ruined. Back in New Orleans, outside of confidantes like Adrian and Professor Schaffer, no one knew I was gay. No one at Xavier University, the post office, or anywhere had any inkling. The police raid jeopardized the sense of security and community that I had been lucky enough to enjoy my entire life.

Professor Schaffer understood how I felt after the raid, and he made a point of calmly continuing to tour me around New York. But I kept breaking down and crying. Within me, passion, frustration, and glimpses of glory needed release. It hadn't been too long since I had held a picket sign on Canal Street, fighting for civil rights. I now recognized my naivete in thinking it would be easy "to solve the colored thing." It wasn't easy. None of it was easy. I had rejected electroshock therapy, but I was still struggling as a man who loved men—torn between feelings of love and rejection, and sensing at last that there needed to be a civil rights movement for gay people. I cried at the responsibility ahead of me, the inevitability of the hard work ahead for my spirit, advocating for rights while fighting lie after lie. Just as I had to fight against the assumed inferiority of Blacks and women, I needed to fight against the assumptions that gay people were dangerous and that we abused children. Society never questioned these and many more lies—and I cried at the thought of the mountain ahead, a mountain that had to be climbed and could not be avoided.

With my college career drawing to a close, and my horizons expanded by travel, I prepared for the biggest move of my young life. I had been lucky enough to score a pair of job interviews. The first, with Foley's department store, in Houston, went well. The second, with Johnson & Johnson, in Chicago, took place in late August 1968. I arrived dressed in a sharp suit and answered all manner of questions the best I could. As I retired to my hotel bedroom that evening, the tensions of the day—my anxieties about my career choice—were compounded by tensions brewing on the streets below. Watching the increasingly agitated crowds protesting outside the Democratic National Convention, I decided, "I'm good. I am not getting my face kicked in today!" By the time Mayor Daley unleashed his forces to "pacify" the demonstrators, I was home in New Orleans, watching on television.

The thought of working for Johnson & Johnson was tempting. But Dad, in his wisdom, knew that Chicago would be too cold—and the better money would disappear with the higher expenses. Plus, the interstate was still brand new, and travel between Chicago and New Orleans could be quite a hassle. And so the spirit drew me to make my new life in Houston as an executive in the stationery division of Foley's. I already had quite a few friends in Houston and knew the lay of the land. It turned out that my Creole flavor was better suited for Houston, with its boots and pickup trucks, than Chicago, with its suits and its class-conscious, surburban attitudes often enforced with violence. And Foley's was a very different, more relaxed place to work than Johnson & Johnson.

During my visit to interview for Foley's, I happened upon "Splash Day" at the beaches in Galveston, a short hop away from Houston. One day a year, on the hush, gays from far and wide would arrive in Galveston. There were no rainbow flags back then, but everyone knew, from word of mouth, exactly which section of beach to mob in order to flirt and frolic. The authorities looked the other way, as Galveston's businesses had come to rely on our late-summer escapades for an economic boost, after the family crowds had dissipated with the start of the school year. It was a wonderful experience to mingle with all of these gay people and realize I wasn't the only one. That, together with the quality of the gay bars on Westheimer Road, cemented my decision to move to Houston to start my career.

After wrapping up one last semester at Xavier to finish my degree in political science, and with my last paychecks from the post office saved up, it was time to say goodbye to the nest. This is a tough moment for every mother, particularly mine. The morning I left home in August 1969, my mom got up and fried chicken and made sandwiches—knowing there weren't many restaurants along the way that would welcome a Black man. That's how we had to travel back then. I could have been indignant. But I was excited for my move to Houston and eager to start my gay life all over again in the big city.

CHAPTER FOUR / *Houston Beginnings*

Larry (center, rear) at Easter party in Houston [1970s]
COURTESY OF THE AUTHOR

4

HOUSTON'S MONTROSE NEIGHBORHOOD WAS FIRST DEVELOPED IN THE early twentieth century as a streetcar suburb, and today it features single-family homes as well as a gritty drag with colorful bars and galleries. Then and now, it's the place to be. Flanked by a pair of universities—Rice and the University of Houston—it attracted well-heeled professors to its pre-war bungalows, which in time were occupied by hippies of all shapes and sizes. Where the counterculture led, the gays were sure to follow. Open around the clock, Art Wren's Silver Dollar cafe, on Westheimer, was a draw for many. The eponymous owner, Art, always wore suspenders, and his wife had bright red hair and welcomed all of us so well that we became regulars.

I moved into the first floor of a complex on West Main Street a few blocks from the large intersection of Alabama and Shepherd, near the Alabama

Theater. The apartment was a little bitty thing, but I bet it will come as no surprise that it took no longer than a month or two for the pad to be the top spot. In October, I threw a Halloween party with my dear friend from New Orleans, Al Freitas. It was supposed to be a small affair, but coming from Louisiana, I did things correctly—catered with good food and a keg for all to enjoy. Soon enough, word of mouth spread, and what was supposed to be an intimate affair turned into a legendary rager. Nearly a hundred fifty people came and started filling out the patio, spilling into the parking lot! And when I say that everyone came, I mean that anyone came! People, old and young, spilled in from both the hippie and the gay worlds, with colors that spanned all shades and just as much Spanish spoken as English. What a blast! This was the first time I saw that a diverse gay community was possible—that my friends could form a constituency.

Thus, from the start, Houston was a great experience. I got to know all these exciting and wonderful people and I was comfortable in a culture that seemed so much like the one in New Orleans. Houston's community was queer, friendly, laid-back, and multiracial. However, Houston was a newer, bigger city, which allowed it to be more accepting. There was the added advantage of not having to run into relatives or friends from my past. I could start my great adventure in building my identity with a clean slate.

Spending time with our chosen family is so important for the gay community. This meant spending as much time as we could in our living rooms, our bars, and our clubs. Certainly, my friends and I enjoyed the bars. We did, however, live lives beyond the watering holes. We got to know one another intimately by gathering in people's homes and apartments. Hosting and hanging out at parties was how the gay community developed.

I found the bar and club scene in Houston preferable to the one in New Orleans. Back home, the Quarter bars functioned more like meat markets, whereas the bars in Houston were better suited for gossip, friendship, and socializing. In those days, gay bars were concentrated in Montrose rather than spread out, as they are today. There was the Silver Bullet, which was a bar for manly men. Nearby was Dirty Sally's, which attracted an older crowd, together with their "admirers," young guys from the edges of town looking for sugar daddies. The Old Plantation was a cavernous nightclub with multiple dance floors. It reminded me of Stonewall, with a mixed crowd of Mexicans, Blacks, and whites—though the bouncers had wide discretion to hassle anyone they wanted to keep out by imposing extra ID and security checks.

I wish I could say that our favorite places were full of both men and women, but unfortunately, they weren't. Lesbians had their own reasons to be careful and collected themselves around a bar known as Chances, where they could be safe from obscenity laws that deemed it illegal for women to wear pants with a zipper!

My favorite bar was the Copa. It was the size of half a city block and packed every night with a friendly crowd. On Saturdays, my friends and I would go shopping for new outfits and show them off when the Copa's dancefloor heated up. A DJ would play "freedom" music through dance sets. The Copa would hold its last call at two o'clock, a helpful rule for the working-class crowd, compared to New Orleans's twenty-four-hour temptations. On weekend nights, after the liquor ceased flowing, we could still enjoy each other's company in the Copa after-hours until 4:30 a.m. Through these adventures, I found my best battle buddies, Ramon Araiza and David Hernandez.

Ramon, David, and I have been close for over fifty years now. We met in 1970 at a party hosted by a gay guy who owned a couple of successful Dairy Queens. Ramon and David had known each other since the second grade, when they decided they were going to be lovebirds for life. They came from a working-class Mexican neighborhood that reminded me of my own Creole upbringing. Being so young, I thought their culture and mine were the same—and I was thrilled to find thousands of people who looked like me. Only later did I come to realize that Mexico had its own rich history, a civilization distinct from my small Gentilly world.

When we met, Ramon and David were only nineteen and twenty, to my twenty-four, and both lived with their parents. Ramon was the fluffier of the two, with big bones and a more outgoing personality. As the saying goes, nobody was a stranger to Ramon—just a friend he hadn't met yet. David's way of showing love was quieter. When we were hanging out at the apartment, he would always be in the kitchen, arranging the food and cleaning up afterward. He had a tender heart, and his sweet smile was welcoming to all. They fit well with each other. I liked that they were regular guys who didn't go around screaming "Mary!" Even better, they also worked at Foley's.

I had been drawn to Houston by its vibe, but I'd had no idea I'd find so many fellow queers at Foley's. Gays of all kinds were represented in every department, including management, even if we were all entirely in the closet. Even my boss was gay! Looking back, I was extremely lucky to have found a position that fit my festive personality, one I had lovingly adopted from my mother. I spent my days working the floor, supervising those who reported to me. I was responsible for personnel and inventory, as well as dealing with customers. I even got to hire my boyfriend of a few months to work in the stockroom of the Christmas division. His name was Randy, a broad-shouldered, blond-haired, blue-eyed, football-playing hunk of a man who had followed me from New Orleans.

With community building (fun parties, in other words) on my mind, I shopped around for an even bigger apartment, this time with two whole bedrooms. This, of course, required more money. I worked hard, and within a year I got four promotions. Soon, the entire first-floor hall of Foley's was my domain, with Greeting Cards and Seasonal Decorations filling out my portfolio in addition to Stationery and Festivities. But even as my job grew more and more impressive, I received only one raise.

David Hernandez and Ramon Araiza in Paris [1994]
COURTESY OF THE AUTHOR

After about eight months, I felt I was suffering a great injustice, and I decided to give "the Man" a piece of my mind. Before my shift, I looked in the mirror and put on a game face. I marched up the stairs to the manager's office, slammed my resume on the table, and gave him a choice. "I would like a $10,000 raise or you can stick this job up yours!"

The ultimatum didn't work. My two-weeks' notice with the department store began immediately. With a red face and an embarrassed step, I headed across the street to M. David Lowe, a placement agency. Once again, I threw my resume on the desk and demanded that they "find me a job! I have a degree!" Amused, the staffer smirked at me. "I like you! You're crazy—sit down." In short order, I came to learn that the tricks I'd learned on the streets of New Orleans weren't as universally applicable as I had hoped. Somehow I had missed that we were in the middle of a recession—and the placement agency had files and files full of people with master's degrees in addition to BAs. "Why don't you just try going back across the street to Foley's and get your job back." I had no intention of doing that.

What I didn't know, being young, was that I had actually lucked out with a competitive salary. Since Foley's had a diversity program, they were interested in my background. My initial salary was higher than normal in exchange for a pause on raises. I had no idea then, but over time I've learned how to ask the right questions.

With my Foley's experience, I soon found work at a Christmas store. This wasn't enough to cover bills and parties, so on a whim, I signed up to sell insurance part time. My route took me door to door, cold-calling in an array of tough and working-class neighborhoods.

The gig at the holiday store was seasonal, naturally, and at closing time on Christmas Eve, they told me that I could take whatever I wanted as a bonus. Just like that, I was a kid again, filling up my car with everything it could carry. With a big white Christmas tree strapped to the roof, I departed for New Orleans, feeling like Santa Claus.

During my first year away, and in all the years that followed, I returned home for every birthday and holiday. I could make that six-hour drive with my eyes closed. This time, I was up until midnight decorating, just as I had done every year since I was a boy. Mom and Dad were so thrilled to have their son back, and it wasn't two seconds after I finished with the lights and tinsel that it was time for Midnight Mass. As we were all getting ready, I let the news slip that I had, ahem, moved on from Foley's. Dad knew right away something was up, and when I told him about the ultimatum he wasn't surprised. He observed, with a chuckle, that I was "a guy who had to learn things the hard way." As we sang "Silent Night" at our church service, I brimmed with excitement for 1970, never dreaming that my part-time gig with Washington National Insurance would turn into a twenty-year career.

Back in Houston, Ramon, David, and I were inseparable. It was a joy getting to know Houston through the eyes of locals. They were both still living in their old barrio, El Dorado. Clear across town from Montrose, El Dorado had been established as a neighborhood where Mexican families could buy land through the GI Bill. Nestled against industrial lots, the brick homes in this "City of Gold" are low slung, with carports that face dusty streets and neat yards. The tight-knit community held festivals—just like the New Orleans ones I missed—for holidays like Cinco de Mayo and Día de los Muertos. Each festival was its own little carnival, with booths for street vendors built by local carpenters, reminding me of the plywood booths members of my own family had built for St. Peter Claver's parish festivals. Familiar games offered stuffed animals and goldfish as prizes for popping balloons with darts or tossing balls through hoops.

Ramon and David were well known in El Dorado, and they enjoyed the church fairs, despite the stir their sexuality caused. Growing up in such a macho culture, they were used to the bumps, scrapes, and rude remarks. Epithets of "¡maricón!" rained down on them. This negativity frankly surprised me, and I was left bothered and disappointed. El Dorado had known they were a couple since grammar school and somehow had yet to get over it. Ramon and David, however, were used to the abuse and still very much in love with their culture and each other.

But if you know me, you know that I wasn't going to let it stand. I was determined to plan revenge on all their haters in the most fabulous way possible. David was soon to turn twenty-one, and I hatched a delicious plan. It started when they came back to Montrose in the afternoon for what they thought was a quiet drink at my place. By then I had a new place with large picture windows and a patio that overlooked the whole neighborhood.

Soon enough, sirens began to wail! Quickly, Ramon and David darted downstairs, only to find out the commotion was for them! A long black stretch limousine was parked right out front, with Mexican and American flags on the antennas, just as I had ordered. When I contacted the limousine company the day before, I told them that a high-ranking Mexican diplomat was in town, and the flags were of the highest priority. From there, the three of us took a ride with a full police escort, surprising David with a trip to El Dorado. I wanted to show them off as valid and worthy friends of mine, despite whatever dumb prejudices they had grown up with. We only had the limo for an hour, so after a quick visit with Ramon's parents, and a few swings around the old neighborhood, we headed back to Montrose, where the scene had transformed from quiet tea-time to another huge rager!

I wasn't done making my point. I found just the right shiny, silver paper decorations and elegantly catered the affair with all sorts of food. Not only were many of our favorite pals in on the surprise, but many of Ramon and David's siblings, cousins, parents, aunts, and uncles were there, too. I wanted to honor my great friend David and his relationship, but I also wanted to show that gays weren't out to hurt anyone. We just wanted to have a good time—no different than anyone else. We were devils, but not the sort that some straights thought—and I wanted to punk the squares by showing how vibrant and colorful our lives were, and how much fun we had compared to them. Even then, with those family members, I had an agenda. David still brings up the party to me, decades later, as among his favorite memories of the time we spent together.

Above all, our parties were our way to build a family, and my mission was to spread those values far and wide. On my insurance sales routes, I had developed a habit of distributing toys to needy children over the holidays. And in a similar spirit, since I loved to spark childhood joy in everyone I met, I started holding an annual Christmas pajama party for my grown friends. We would dress like kids while partying like adults. I strove as always to gather a mix of people—men and women, gay and straight, all different colors. Rumors would swirl that a bunch of gay people in nighties couldn't be innocent. People speculated that it must be difficult to keep our pajamas on, and that what was nice must have turned naughty quickly. But those were just whispers brought on by the jealous. Ask anyone who went to my pajama parties, and they'll confirm that we were simply building our fun, diverse, happy-go-lucky chosen family.

Texas culture can be just as thoroughly Catholic as Louisiana's. Being a grown-up altar boy myself, I went to church regularly. I would try to attend Spanish Mass as often as possible, but being deaf in one ear makes it difficult for me to learn languages. Usually I would attend St. Anne Catholic Church on Westheimer. The mission cuts a striking figure on the street, with beautiful Colonial Revival architecture and a bell tower reminiscent of a small Sonoran village. Inside, the sanctuary had soaring arches, a vaulted ceiling framing an elegant altar, a grand organ, and stained-glass windows with an elaborate rosette. There was some irony to the Spanish architecture, since many of the parishioners were Anglos from the bourgeois River Oaks neighborhood next door.

One day, a storm of anxiety welled up within me, as it often does inside the minds and hearts of the formerly closeted. Again and again, to combat this anxiety, I had sought ways to reconcile my identity as a gay man with my Catholic faith—and on this day, I was motivated to make a confession that I was contrite about lots of things but *not* about being gay.

Inside the darkness of the booth, a screen slid open. "I'm not here to beg your forgiveness for being gay," I declared. "I just want to make penance like any other faithful!"

With a chuckle, a deep voice rang out. "You seem like an angry young man. Follow me outside." Dressed all in black with a white collar, a gorgeous man appeared. Tall, broad-chested, blond, and gay, this Father was beautiful! Sitting out in the open, he shared with me that St. Anne had a group for guys like us. The church hosted a branch of a national movement named Dignity where gay parishioners could gather for faith, fellowship, and snacks. This was the first time I had the gumption to come out to a priest, and lo and behold, I was soon meeting once a week in the church hall with other gay men.

It was a joy finding such a resource mere blocks from my house. Week in and week out, we talked about God, his love and plans for us, and how important it was for us to live good lives as gay men. It helped me grow spiritually, but alas, it was not to last. The archdiocese found out and had a fit. At first the archbishop wanted to cancel the local chapter. Perhaps a compromise was made—to meet here, not there, to talk about this, but not that—but by then I was done. I was already battling segregation as a man of color; I certainly didn't want to be segregated as a gay man by an institution that wanted to save me from hell. Given the very human nature of the Church, and its own complicated history with slavery and conquest, I still think Catholicism needs to get its act together. Not everyone can escape the Church's rigid, patriarchal dogma, and the resulting emotional conflict drives some people to take their own lives.

Yet I still attend Midnight Mass to this day. Catholicism is part of my culture, and I do love my culture. Thankfully, I believe God can be found anywhere, and the power of prayer is bigger than the failings of hierarchy. I also love finding God in the many Baptist churches I've been blessed to attend, and in the warm songs of Temple Sinai in New Orleans or the grand mosques of the Middle East. These experiences fuel my fervor and energize my quest for LGBTQ+ rights and equality.

Stonewall's riot lit the fire of a gay liberation movement that soon arrived in Houston. Starting in 1970 and in the years that followed, queer media and organizations began to spring up together with the many bars that would come to populate Montrose.

Pamphlets, newspapers, and radio programs were among the first ways gays and lesbians in Houston started to converse with one another. This included KPFT 90.1, founded in 1970, which offered a full slate of gay programming and which still operates today as a community radio station. The *Nuntius* was published by a couple of local characters—Phil Frank, who would go on to a career as a cartoonist, and Ray Houston (a nom-de-plume), who had published a short-lived, racier publication known as *Gayboy*.

In 1972 the Montrose Gaze began operation as a community center, and local festivals, conferences, and direct actions began to multiply. In 1973, local activists unsuccessfully pressed the Houston City Council to declare a Houston Pride Week in June. At the time such a notion was laughable. Many in the general public did not personally know any gay or lesbian people who were out of the closet, so the thought of taking pride in something that disgusted them sounded far-off and insane. Yet from this garden, in 1975, grew the organization known as the Houston Gay Political Caucus.

The GPC was formed by Pokey Anderson, Keith McGee, Bill Buie, and Hugh Crell as a classic political organization, with the aim of raising money, endorsing candidates, and bringing its constituency to the polls. The Houston GPC relied heavily for funding on well-connected, moneyed white interests, even if many of them were still in the closet and afraid to have their names and pictures published for the wider public. The first president of the GPC, Gary Van Ooteghem, looked and acted every bit like a young accountant, sporting a suit, mustache, and blond, thinning hair. Just months after moving to Houston for a job as Harris County comptroller, he was fired for presenting a resolution to the County Commissioners' Court that would protect gays and other minorities against job discrimination in the local government. After Van Ooteghem's term, Don

Hrachovy took over as GPC president. A full decade younger than Gary, Don had a strapping build, full head of hair, and a chestnut mustache. His primary contribution was a collection of 1,500 meticulously typed index cards featuring the names and addresses of gays across the area. Known as "The List," it grew into a database of fifteen thousand people and was the organization's greatest asset for raising money, registering voters, and electing preferred candidates. Early efforts included the endorsement for reelection of gay-friendly state representative Ron Waters and the successful reelection of mayor Fred Hofheinz in 1975. Soon, the GPC's model was replicated across Texas as the core group would often travel and make connections in San Antonio, Dallas, and more.

As much as I disdained their elite airs, the leaders of Houston's GPC had political skills that I coveted. They had built connections across the Montrose community and started whipping the neighborhood's eighteen voting precincts into shape by registering voters, holding events, publishing a newsletter, and raising money. They pushed to end police harassment, and their slate of political endorsements grew in influence. Within a few years of the GPC's 1975 founding, many in city politics were paying attention.

Gay life in the big city was often a frolic, with grand fiestas and warm friendships, and it could be easy to forget about the wide world beyond. But we couldn't ignore the forces around us forever.

In the years since Stonewall, gays had been flocking to America's cities, and as they got older, they changed the communities around them. Gays across the country, including me and many of my friends, had been traumatized by having homosexuality classified as a mental disorder. The medical community finally reversed its assessment in 1973. As we moved into our own communities, optimism was on the rise, and we were beginning to see gay representation in popular culture.

Miami was one of the most progressive cities in the US. Where once pamphlets had proliferated, warning the public about the danger of homosexuals, by the 1970s police raids were waning—and the 1972 Democratic National Convention even featured openly gay speakers. By early 1977, the Dade County Commission, which had jurisdiction over Miami, approved a law banning discrimination in social services, housing, and employment—which was apparently too much for one high-profile standard-bearer of the right.

Anita Bryant was a former teenage Oklahoma beauty queen who sang schmaltzy hits before being tapped as the spokeswoman for Florida orange juice. A devout Baptist, she was disturbed to learn about the Miami ordinance. She and her supporters mobilized a rowdy posse to oppose the vote—and even though the commissioners passed the ordinance, the backlash had begun. Soon, the Save Our Children organization was founded with Bryant at the helm to spread the ancient lie that gays, especially gay teachers, were on the hunt for children to recruit into homosexuality.

To proselytize for her cause, Bryant toured the country, urging the repeal of other cities' antidiscrimination laws. When she portrayed gay people as child molesters, she became the face of all the awful people who had rejected us for so many years. We were simply trying to date, live our lives, pursue our careers. While so much of gay life is costumes and cotillions, the nasty sludge of Bryant's message made it imperative that we come out of the closet and take a stand.

The Texas State Bar Association invited her to appear at their Houston convention on June 16, 1977. Her awful message galvanized us into action, and I participated in my first large-scale demonstration since high school. We were up all day and night organizing. We were expecting only a handful of dedicated people, but much to our surprise blocks and blocks of people—nearly ten thousand—arrived for the demonstration. Nuns and priests came out in their garb to demonstrate against hate. The police tried to confine us to the sidewalks, but our electricity couldn't be contained. Soon, even the local authorities gave up on keeping us off the street, and we massed closer and closer to the hotel where Bryant was speaking.

Anita Bryant protest, Houston [1977]
FILE COURTESY OF HOUSTONLGBTHISTORY.ORG

Anita Bryant protest, New Orleans [1977]

PHOTOGRAPH © OWEN MURPHY
COURTESY OF THE PHOTOGRAPHER

Again, a spirit came over me, the same spirit I found when I picketed the segregated department stores of Canal Street. I feel the same goosebumps today when I campaign for causes that I believe in.

The crowd of people was so large because it included many who weren't gay or lesbian. That means so much to me, even to this day. Liberty requires all of us for its protection, and after so many years of feeling alone, the presence of these allies felt like a breath of fresh air. Amid the pandemonium, high from the energy and excitement, I barely noticed a microphone creep into my face. A radio reporter was covering the scene and asked for my name and how I felt. Without thinking, I introduced myself as Larry Bagneris and cried, "As a gay man, I'm just elated! This is the most incredible experience of my life." The clip was on the radio in every hourly bulletin, and without realizing it, I had come out to the entire city.

Galvanized by the action in Houston, it was time to continue the pressure by following Anita Bryant to New Orleans. She was going to sing at the Municipal Auditorium two evenings after her visit to Houston, and a protest march was planned to begin at St. Louis Cathedral in Jackson Square. Ramon, David, and I just had to attend. We were familiar with the city, after all, and we had a place to stay.

Over the years, I had brought people home to see Mom, Dad, and my old neighborhood. I took Ramon and David back to my home regularly—but with the spirit of change in the air, I knew this time had to be different. Anita Bryant's assertions were so odious that we gays had to make a stand, and I decided this was the perfect time to bite my own bullet.

On the morning of the demonstration, June 18, 1977, my mother greeted us with a large breakfast. Just as she had done with every friend I've brought home, she rolled out the welcome mat and extended the embrace of Creole hospitality. Ramon and David were itching to get to the protest—but I asked them to give me a moment, and I sat down with my parents.

"May I have a word with you?" I gulped.

Sitting at the breakfast table, I told them the reason I had come home for the weekend. "Look," I stammered. "I'm gay, and we came here to march against Anita Bryant." Uncharacteristically, no one had anything to say. After a pause, Dad glanced over at Mom. "You know, this is your fault."

"And where did you get that?" both she and I shot back.

"I read it in a book! Let me go fetch it!" With that, Dad went and brought over an old, dusty textbook that looked like it hadn't been opened since it was published right after World War II. Our whole lives, we had been taught that homosexuality was a sickness, a psychological issue bred into young boys. There was no such thing as gay, back while I was growing up. Instead, there was "homosexuality," a disorder brought about by a domineering mother. Same-sex attraction could only lead to a barren life: no children, no family, and certainly no good job. Remember, back then, if you were gay you were mentally ill, perhaps even a child molester—that's what society thought, and that's what my dad's textbook had taught.

So it was Mom's fault. Even by 1970s standards, that sounded patently ridiculous. "Well, I've read some things in a book, too, and the books are wrong and they need to be updated," I said. With a tear and a bit of a smirk, I gave my mother a big hug and said, "You must get all the credit! I'm the happiest boy in the world."

Growing up in a Creole world, not quite white and not quite Black, it was important for every family to raise their children to feel accepted and loved. My community strove to reinforce those feelings. I still reflect today on the sacrifices my parents made to nourish me—and on their response when I finally came out to them the weekend of the Anita Bryant protest.

Maybe it wasn't instantaneous, but I could sense—even that morning—that acceptance was coming. "I've never been happier in my life," I told them. "I'm off to the demonstrations. Y'all deal with this now. Bye!" Once it was clear to my dad that I was pleased with my life, it became easy for him to shed society's outdated notions. For the rest of their lives, my parents would constantly remind me that they would always continue to love me.

Over the years there was no need to have any more conversations with my family about my sexuality. The thought never crossed their minds to try to change me. They accepted the fact that their son was gay and were eager to hear all about my activism. They would marvel at the home movies I'd show them, documenting my fun and diverse friends, our parties, and other facets of my life in Houston. They only needed reassurance that I was safe, healthy, and thriving.

Mom was always such a gracious host to the friends I brought home to New Orleans, welcoming them to stay in the two guest rooms at our family home in Gentilly. I wanted to connect my old roots to the brand-new life that was unfolding before me. Over and over again, I'd bring different friends from Houston, just enough to fill the extra bedroom at Mom's house: three at a time, usually David, Ramon, and another friend. My brother and I laugh today, because it's only after all this time that we realize how much work it must have been for Mom to accommodate all these people! She would always have fresh sheets, pillowcases, and bedspreads ready, which all had to be washed once we had spent the weekend and had our good time.

I understand now what I didn't quite understand then. I wanted my parents to see that I was no different from anyone else, and that my friends were just as normal as everybody else. They never complained and were always welcoming. My daddy would sit down and talk to everybody while my mother was in the kitchen. The first time Ramon and David came home with me, we had some car trouble and arrived at one in the morning. The first thing my mother said when we arrived was, "Thank God you're all right—what do you want to eat? I have some roast cooking, I have red beans and rice, I have fried chicken . . ." This is my mom!

It was only after I came out that she connected the dots: everyone I had brought home was gay! She had no idea—"WHAT?!"

I said, "Yeah, everybody's gay!" They were normal, decent young people, not like the crazy characters she saw on television, depicted as freaks. My friends, of course, had lots of fun living the wild and noisy stereotypes—but also knew enough manners to make pleasant company for my mom. In time, I would show Mom around Houston, taking her as my date to functions and affairs. She found out quickly that gay community life was nothing like the den of bunny rabbits she had imagined. She would also get to know my gay friends in New Orleans. She had met John, a police officer, and Walter, a caterer who lived on Burgundy in the Marigny. Walter even gave my sister a full spread for her wedding! It was my plan the whole time to show my family the full and varied lives led by gay people.

The movement I joined in Houston had really begun with a hippie named Ray Hill. With wavy hair and a bushy beard, he looked like a handsome, gay Kenny Rogers. Ray had a coterie of beautiful boyfriends and a carefree attitude. Having already been convicted of petty theft, he wasn't afraid of the cops or of public shaming. Everyone knew him, and he hosted a call-in show on the Pacifica radio network that focused on the current and formerly incarcerated. His aggressive style toward the authorities certainly earned him plenty of fans.

Ray's fearlessness led to a ton of attention, which he thrived on. Ten years older than me, he pretty much founded Houston's gay rights community, and whenever a bar was raided or a protest march was organized, he always found a way to get on television to represent us.

I admired Ray but I didn't like his approach to public relations one bit. Dressed in a trademark jumpsuit, he was adversarial and challenging, seemingly hellbent on shocking the public with his focus on sex. I might be forthright, but my Creole upbringing had instilled the value of good manners. I didn't like his presentation at all; he struck me as too much of a Texas redneck. I thought he needed a bit of finishing school.

We were bound to meet. He has his story, and I'm sticking to mine.

One day, I spotted Ray at a bar on Westheimer. I took a deep breath, walked over, and introduced myself. "Mr. Hill, I want to say hello, my name is Larry. I've noticed your activism and . . . you're doing it all wrong!"

"All wrong?" he was quick to reply. "Well, if I'm all wrong, why don't you show me how to do it, since you know better than I do?" And in my mind I thought, "I AM gonna show him how to do it."

Ray has since passed away. If he were still around and was asked about the story of our first encounter, he'd set the scene at one of the many drum circles he liked to organize. He'd have the whole crowd singing "Kumbaya" and "We Shall Overcome." And then he'd say he spotted me in a brand-new, gas-guzzling Mercury Marquis, yelling, "This is all wrong!" out the window.

Given how tight knit our community was, we eventually warmed up to each other. I still marvel at his organizing abilities. And the two of us laughed about our first encounter for years.

Ray played a vital role in the establishment of Town Meeting One, the Houston gay community's first big push to consolidate power. The year was 1978—a seminal year in gay activism. Pride celebrations were gaining momentum across the country, and Town Meeting One was envisioned as a political gathering to cap the city's first-ever Pride Week. Ray and the other organizers hoped to bring different elements of the community together to fight discrimination against gays, Blacks, Chicanos, and women. A date, June 25, was selected, and Ginny Apuzzo was appointed chair. With short hair and rectangular glasses, Ginny was a New Yorker and former nun who had risen in the ranks of lesbian activism to help lead the National Gay Task Force (now called the National LGBTQ Task Force). We hoped that her outside experience would wrangle us all together.

We knew we needed to take the pulse of the community to determine which issues to prioritize. The feminist and gay bookstore Wilde and Stein (named for Oscar and Gertrude, of course) hosted workshops and discussions. Draft proposals were published for the community to review, and Ray held things together as general project coordinator. Soon a keynote speaker had been selected, one with a most distinguished record of running for office and victory in public service.

Frances "Sissy" Farenthold, with tousled chestnut hair, came from a distinguished family of Texas lawyers. A 1949 graduate of the University of Texas School of Law—and one of just a handful of women in her class—she had risen quickly in Corpus Christi politics. In the 1960s, she was one of only a few women in the entire Texas House of Representatives. She challenged the state Democratic establishment with a run for governor in the early 1970s and established a national profile with her inclusive, positive campaign.

Although she was not queer herself, Farenthold lit up the gay community as a popular leader willing to take a stand on our right to exist. We grew particularly fond of her and wore green buttons with "Sissy!" (as we knew her) in bold type.

Today's queer movement celebrates, as best it can, all the colors of the rainbow. This includes all letters of lesbians, bisexuals, trans people, and more. But back then, the word was *gay*, and really only *gay*. And so, in the lead-up to Town Meeting One, Houston's Gay Political Caucus—its activism driven by a well-connected group of white boys—was guaranteed a big presence.

The GPC's president was Steve Shiflett. In his early thirties, Steve was slender, with thinning hair, a round face, and a steelworker's mustache. He and his friends tended to vote Republican on the national level, while seeking support and clout within the local and state Democratic establishment. I couldn't help but admire their political savvy. They were adept at touting their accomplishments—but it's fair to say that they had earned that self-regard. From their base in Montrose, the GPC pursued a political agenda with citywide impact.

In anticipation of Town Meeting One, I founded the Gay Chicano Caucus, a mixed group advocating for the rights of Mexican American gays, since no one was really speaking up for their community. The Black gays were already quite organized. Their leader was the charismatic Charles Law, an archivist at Texas Southern University. The broader Black

Steve Shiflett and Larry flank Howard Wells of the Metropolitan Community Church at a GPC press conference [1978]

PHOTOGRAPH BY JIM MCNAY
FROM *HOUSTON CHRONICLE*, © 1978 HEARST NEWSPAPERS, ALL RIGHTS RESERVED, USED UNDER LICENSE

Ray Hill at Town Meeting One [1978]

PHOTOGRAPH BY FRED BUNCH
FROM *HOUSTON CHRONICLE*, © 1978 HEARST NEWSPAPERS, ALL RIGHTS RESERVED, USED UNDER LICENSE; FILE COURTESY OF HOUSTON PUBLIC LIBRARY, HOUSTON HISTORY RESEARCH CENTER (RGD0006N-1978-2010-03)

Larry at a Houston Gay Pride Week organizational meeting [1979]
FILE COURTESY OF HOUSTONLGBTHISTORY.ORG

community was very socially conservative, leading many gay Black men to remain in the closet. Given my background, I had a different, more diverse group of friends, many of whom were Mexican American. Since I wanted to stand with them in solidarity, I decided to help them register an organization for Town Meeting One.

Mom and Dad, while of course supportive, had some blunt questions about my activism. My father sat me down in Houston one day and said, "Son, I just want to ask you, you realize you aren't Mexican, don't you?" Like one friend to another, I patted him on the shoulder and replied, "Of course. I just love the culture."

Our Caucus obviously needed a bilingual, Mexican president. As a Black (mixed, Creole, whatever) man, I was vice president. The treasurer was an Asian man, and the secretary was a Black woman. We would meet at my house, at 2001 Branard Street, to discuss the demands we planned to present at Town Meeting One.

Many of Houston's *hermanos*, and to some extent the *hermanas*, too, were treated roughly by police. We weren't so far past the days of Bull Connor–style cops, rough and rude when they found you somewhere they deemed improper for your kind. They certainly weren't polite, and they had a whole dictionary of slurs at their disposal.

Meanwhile, the so-called normal world was just as tough on gay men; lots of clean-cut adults thought we were sick. Perhaps even worse were the bar owners and bouncers in our own gay community, whose attitude I recognized quite well from my time in New Orleans. Many of Houston's gay bars weren't officially segregated, but they made it a hassle for anyone outside their preferred clientele to enjoy themselves. Doormen on power trips often demanded not one, but two or three IDs at the door. And if they let you inside, English was certainly the only language they wanted to hear you speak.

For this and a number of reasons, I had high hopes for Town Meeting One. And finally the last Sunday in June arrived, a sunny day, and the gavel banged shortly after noon. The Astro Arena was a concrete cavern with red plastic bucket seats, part of the larger Astrodome complex. Nearly four dozen community groups and upwards of 3,500 people were assembled—representatives from the sports leagues, the gay choruses, the health groups, and so many more. Large placards with spray-painted block letters identified each participating group, similar to the way state delegations are seated at a national political convention. Up front was a lectern flanked by large bouquets of flowers and a purple sign of interlocking male and female symbols, representing love and unity between the sexes. Anyone who supported the LGBTQ+ community could attend, but only residents of the Houston area could vote on the resolutions. Over the course of the day, delegates ironed out differences in competing resolutions, so that only one version per issue made it to the floor. Then, when it was time to call the question, we sat quietly and showed our badges as convention volunteers tallied the vote.

To set the scene, you have to remember that Town Meeting One took place at a time when simply being gay put you at risk. A statute in the Texas penal code—still on the books today, despite being ruled unconstitutional at the federal level in 2003—criminalized sodomy. As a result, many in the audience were perturbed by the presence of photographers, who were attempting to capture the event for posterity. The fear of being outed by a published photo, even if you only appeared as one in a crowd of thousands of friends and community members, was real. Some of the event's official photographers had their film stolen; very few photos of Town Meeting One survive.

Sissy Farenthold was a natural keynote speaker, born for the role with a fire in her belly. She was the big star, and we were all moved by her refrain: "None of us is free until all of us are free." As I stood in the arena that day, I sensed that this was the beginning of the movement I'd been waiting for since that day in high school when I stepped off a New Orleans streetcar and began to fight racism. I was inspired, at Town Meeting One, by my personal identity but also by my national identity. E pluribus unum—out of many, one. My community was coming together to forge a more perfect union.

By any measure, Town Meeting One was a success. The convention led directly to the expansion of health resources in the gay community, with the founding of the Montrose Counseling Center in 1978 and the Montrose Clinic in 1981. We stood united against the police who targeted our community for sport, or refused to act when our safety was concerned. Some issues would take longer to resolve, but we got the conversation started. Grievances were aired concerning the treatment of minorities within our community—and to this day, our embattled community strives to overcome our own prejudices and build a harmonious world for the abled and disabled, cis and trans people, and individuals of all races and ethnicities.

Everybody was moving to Houston in the '70s. Rocket City was becoming a gay mecca, light-years beyond what was going on elsewhere in the South. Every night was like Studio 54. While New Orleans still had Mardi Gras, Houston would lure Carnival crowds west the following weekend with the slogan "Let Us Entertain You." The GPC used the annual "LUEY" weekend to raise money—and since celebration ran through my blood, I knew we needed to organize the bars to achieve our collective goals.

I had spent my first few years in Houston building a family around me in Montrose, but now I was maturing into the political arena by getting to know all the bar owners and proprietors. Remember, bars are for the gay community what the church is for the Black community—a space where we can safely express ourselves and thereby develop collective strength.

Local activism, in Houston and beyond, bred national unity. Gay communities around the country were becoming intertwined. When one group was in trouble, all of us felt the duty to help. We had seen this phenomenon in 1977 with the Anita Bryant protests. And then, in 1978, a conservative California state representative named John Briggs drafted Proposition 6, an initiative asserting that any public demonstration of homosexual activity or conduct would render a schoolteacher unfit for service. Of course, being gay or lesbian has no bearing on how well (or how poorly) you can teach a grade school classroom, serve in the military, or heal the sick. But in 1978, too many Americans believed the lies preached by the Anita Bryants and John Briggses of the world. And so we fought for the tens of thousands of us whose careers would be threatened if our sexuality got out.

The national gay community mobilized to speak out against the Briggs Initiative, and I was on the board of the local "Stop the Briggs" committee. This was a good excuse to hold a Gay Chicano Caucus brunch as a fundraiser. Prominent gay Californians toured the country, including Troy Perry—before his mustache replaced his sideburns, but with his stern brow already established. He was a preacher, the founder of the Metropolitan Community Church, a religious community that welcomed gay members. Air Force Technical Sergeant Leonard Matlovich came, too, wearing a tidy mustache on his long, handsome face. A decorated veteran, Matlovich had been featured on the cover of *Time* in 1975 after coming out of the closet to challenge the military's ban on gay servicemen. His epitaph in DC's Congressional Cemetery would read, "When I was in the military they gave me a medal for killing two men and a discharge for loving one."

David Kopay was also there, with his flat nose, broad shoulders, and long brownish-blond hair. He had been a stellar NFL running back and, after retiring, the league's first athlete to come out. He was still a bit of a dumb jock. When he came over to the house for the brunch, he thought I was the help! Looking for a place to hang his garment bag, he came over to me—and without a word, but with a tip in hand, handed me the bag. "I'm not your boy!" I said. "Go hang it yourself!" Del Martin roared with laughter. Del had cofounded one of the first national organizations for lesbians, the Daughters of Bilitis, and she was nearly as built as the now sheepish David. She gave me a big hug and a kiss. "He's been a jackass this whole trip, and you're the first one to tell him off!" We became friends instantly.

Turns out, I had met the most impressive of the bunch the night before, when a bunch of us went to the Houston Hyatt to hear a little-known speaker named Harvey Milk, a San Francisco city supervisor. Harvey was a full-on extrovert, a people person, and full of joy. He was a Jewish man in his late forties, a half-generation older than me, who had spent his time, after a stint in the Navy, wandering around and falling in love. He had settled with a boyfriend in San Francisco, where he caught the organizing bug. He was charismatic—a natural—and he certainly left me in tears. When Milk came up to speak, he barely mentioned politics at all. His concerns were larger. He had lived our struggle, and with his famous slogan—"Come out, come out, wherever you are!"—he challenged us to come out of the closet. "They can't accept you until you accept you, until you accept yourself!"

Sitting in the front row, I must have been sniffling loudly. Harvey eventually asked about me, touched that I was moved; he had heard that I had organized the Chicano brunch to raise support for the Stop the Briggs Initiative campaign. Soon we met, and he was every bit the blunt New Yorker. He invited me to join him for a week at his office in City Hall to see him in action. I can't wait to tell you that story, a few chapters from now.

Inspired by Harvey and Town Meeting One, I was quietly trying to build my own political base within Houston's Gay Political Caucus. I encouraged members of the Gay Chicano Caucus to pay $15 for membership in the GPC. And I started paying better attention to representation, noticing that lesbians weren't part of GPC leadership. You could tell just by the group's name that lesbians were an afterthought. But women were beginning to join the GPC in large numbers and were a growing presence in the organization.

Elections for the GPC board were coming up and, naturally, I wanted to run for vice president. I wanted to challenge Steve Shiflett directly. See, I knew his type quite well. He was from Baton Rouge, originally. He had a firm idea of who counted and who didn't. In his mind, gay liberation really meant liberation for his bank account, and he was frank about who was worthy, about who was in or out of the tent. He hadn't grown up in a household that welcomed my kind of people, and our presence in his pet organization made him uncomfortable.

And yet, despite my personal misgivings, I wanted Steve to support me for vice president. I reminded him of all the new energy I was bringing into the GPC and offered him a deal: in exchange for his endorsement, my base and I would support his programs during his next two-year term as president. After that, he would support my bid for the presidency.

In Steve's mind, this arrangement would allow him to retain some control over me. He appreciated that I was bringing in paid contributors who were willing to put their money where their mouths were. So we shook hands, and I won the VP seat in February 1979.

We made the relationship work, despite our differences, and my profile began to rise not just locally but nationally. One evening in 1980 Steve and I were meeting at my home when I got the phone call telling me I'd been appointed to the board of the National Gay Task Force. Immediately after I hung up, a mutual friend from Oklahoma called to congratulate me.

"If Steve's there, let me holler at him," he said, so I handed Steve the phone. Perhaps Steve had grown too comfortable and forgot where he was. Chuckling, he joked about how they were "appointing niggers on the board now." I didn't gasp, didn't let out one breath of surprise. I knew that this was the same Steve I'd been dealing with all along. I chose to remain silent because I was learning things. It's hard to admit that I was enabling unsavory people, but I decided that as long as I was building my own tool kit, I would put up with his shit. He couldn't be saved, but I had a whole group of people to protect, advocate for, and defend—women and gay people of color who deserved every ounce of the GPC's power.

These events were just part of the massive mobilization underway in that era. The winds of the 1960s cultural awakening had finally reached the corridors of power. I was young, still in my early thirties, but I was privileged to be on hand as the political class awakened to the growing strength of the gay community. Sissy Farenthold helped us connect with the wider Hispanic, Mexican, and Chicano communities. State representative Ben Reyes and city controller Leonel Castillo stopped by the neighborhood to campaign. As I contemplated ways to build my own political career, I was gratified by my budding friendship with city councilor Judson Robinson Jr. He was a gregarious, down-to-earth person who looked quite Creole to me. He and his wife Margarette were simply wonderful people. My friends and I would visit their house often, introduce them to members of our community, and offer our support for his reelection campaigns. I very much enjoyed their sense of humor, and I really needed Judson's help at the time.

Not all of us gays were Democrats; some adopted the politics of their parents and voted Republican, not understanding that they were voting against their own interests. But the Democratic Party in Harris County was growing in power, and soon the Hispanic community called on us for support. Cesar Chavez, head of the United Farm Workers, was coming to town.

Famous for leading the UFW's grape boycott, Chavez was about as old as my parents. Born in Arizona, he came from an old Mexican family with strong ties to Texas. The Houston protest would publicize the effort to secure fair wages and better working conditions for workers. The gay community was already well versed in boycotts. We didn't like Anita Bryant, so we avoided Florida oranges. The Coors family donated heavily to antigay causes, so we drank other beer. It was no challenge to get us to support a boycott of grapes.

Meeting Chavez was a great honor; I found him to be quite humble. He was very religious and soft spoken, which belied his success in the political arena. He made great speeches, often mostly in Spanish. It was up to Dolores Huerta, cofounder of the union, to translate his speeches into English with an energetic style that complemented Chavez's quiet strength.

In addition to the boycotts in support of farmworkers, Chavez's followers in the Mexican-American community were doing activist work that paralleled ours in the gay community. We were happy to support their lawsuits toward the integration of Hispanic children into schools better funded than those traditionally designated for the Mexican community.

To my surprise, Chavez gifted me with a UFW flag, a red banner with a white circle that held a geometric, Aztec-style thunderbird. Today, the flag belongs to my friend Pablo Escamilla, a thank-you for traveling with me to Mexico City for my seventieth birthday.

I was GPC vice president under Steve Shiflett for two years. I learned a lot from him, including some unwelcome but valuable lessons about political hypocrisy. During the height of the Anita Bryant boycotts, he and I flew to Memphis for a convention. A friendly flight attendant came down the aisle to offer us a citrusy drink. "Excuse me, is this Florida orange juice?" I asked, and she replied, "Yes." Proudly, I exclaimed, "I don't drink Florida orange juice"—but Steve snapped back, "If you're not going to drink it, give it to me." I was so disappointed. I could see in that moment that the movement was just a way for him to feed his ego and raise his profile.

Politics was my great motivator, too, but I knew I needed a job, a career to fall back on, even as I prepared to run for higher office in the GPC. What had started as a part-time gig with the Washington National Insurance Company had turned into steady and often enjoyable work. The job kept me grounded when goings-on at the GPC proved destabilizing. You see, the longer I worked with Steve, the clearer it became that his heart wasn't really in the liberation aspects of the movement. And now I learned that he had decided to run for a third term as president.

Throughout the struggle for gay rights, minorities have had to fight to be included in the movement. Admitting African Americans into leadership positions took some arm-twisting. And it's fair to say that the gay establishment didn't learn from that experience, because it took us another couple of generations to welcome in our transgender community.

I wasn't all that surprised, in 1980, when Steve refused to honor the deal we'd made in 1978: "Naw, I think I'd like to stay," he said. His ego was large, and he preferred to ignore the demographic and societal changes afoot. Steve hadn't considered it a problem that more women and people of color were joining the GPC ranks, as long as no one questioned his authority and everyone was current on their dues. But the membership was growing dissatisfied with his leadership; although he was part of the aggrieved gay minority, his politics were ultimately conservative, revolving around money and power. Anticipating his double-cross, I had used my time as vice president to build coalitions—and to expand my own sense of who, and what, mattered.

Gay power was maturing hand in hand with women's liberation. I was inspired by the feminist activists I met, and I wanted them to bring their invigorating energy to the GPC. I had gotten to know many strong women when the National Women's Conference came to Houston in 1977, and these relationships deepened as we began to elect more women to state and local offices and caucused together at precinct meetings. As the 1980 GPC election approached, I sought the support of the women in the caucus. So much needed to be shaken up, both inside and outside the organization! It might seem unbelievable to younger readers today, but the GPC couldn't even register as a nonprofit organization with the IRS, as no one wanted to deal with "perverts" or outcasts. And so we were accountable to ourselves alone: we would raise funds and publish our expenses in the *Houston Chronicle* and the *Houston Post*.

Throughout the GPC election season, I felt optimistic about victory. But Steve had a trick up his sleeve. Just as I had taken advantage of open membership to tilt the numbers in my favor, Steve now did the same. When we convened at the Holiday Inn on North Main Street for the vote, I noticed many unfamiliar faces in the crowd of two hundred people. These were brand-new members. Steve had invited his friends from the GPC chapter in Dallas to register as Houston members and pay their fifteen dollars in dues. Thanks to their numbers, I lost the 1980 GPC election by eight votes.

I'll never forget that evening. In defeat, I went over to a country-and-western gay bar on Main Street to be with my supporters. I had the community with me, but Steve had the money. That night as I lay in bed, I didn't sleep. I just lay there with my eyes open, thinking, "What's going to become of me?"

After serving three months of his third term as president, Steve resigned from the GPC and started his own group, Citizens for Human Equality (CHE), which was mostly made up of gay Log Cabin Republicans. Conveniently, this group paid its officers a salary—unlike the GPC, where everyone was a volunteer. On the strength of Steve's connections, the CHE thrived. The competition was good for the GPC; it forced us to get better at political tactics. We'd hold rallies at Mary's, a popular gay hangout across from the Tower Theater, on Westheimer at Waugh Drive. We'd hand out cards to everyone who came, with the names of the candidates we were backing for office—people like Debra Danburg, who ran her first campaign for state legislature that fall of 1980, and championed gay causes for the next two decades. In this way, we kept the fight alive.

CHAPTER FIVE / *A Houston Parade*

Larry in the Houston Pride parade, in a car driven by Jimmy Armstrong Chavers [1986]
FILE COURTESY OF HOUSTONLGBTHISTORY.ORG

5

WHEN I FIRST MOVED TO HOUSTON, THE CITY HAD ONLY TWO PARADES OF NOTE: the Houston Rodeo parade, in February, and the annual Thanksgiving parade. It was always a joy when my family came to visit, and when my baby sister Gina was eight years old I brought her to Foley's answer to Macy's Thanksgiving spectacle. Having grown up in New Orleans, she was frankly unimpressed: "This is boring! No one is throwing anything!"

I was struck then with the revelation that we gays needed our own parade—a New Orleans–style, real parade! I had seen the creativity of the gay Mardi Gras balls in New Orleans, and I knew that a little bit of Mardi Gras was essential for the Houston community. The first Gay Pride parades—in New York, L.A., and Chicago—had been held in June 1970, to mark the first anniversary of the Stonewall riots. Other cities had picked up on the idea and staged subsequent demonstrations for gay rights. That was all well and good, but this Creole saw the promise in celebration. I wanted to have fun! I wanted to show off the gay community's ability to build floats and throw beads and celebrate properly.

And so, on the heels of Town Meeting One, I decided to organize the first Gay Pride parade in Houston for 1979. Our political power was growing, and a parade was a perfect way to organize, fundraise, and shine a spotlight on our movement. The parade would offer onlookers an opportunity to become aware of an array of organizations, from sports clubs to churches to bars with different vibes. It was also a way to increase both voter registration and turnout.

The plan was to stage two weeks of Pride programming, followed by a parade through the heart of our community—down Westheimer to Bagby Street—followed by a post-parade rally. We would draw everyone out, have a lot of fun, and I would get to show my friend Ray Hill that I could put on a spectacle as well as he did. The first order of business was obtaining a city permit.

Thanks to Congressman Mickey Leland and Councilman Judson Robinson, we arranged a meeting with the police chief on the matter of a parade permit. I had worked hard as vice president of the GPC to attend rallies for both Leland and Robinson, make speeches on their behalf, and garner both an endorsement from the GPC. I had even hosted a fundraiser at my home for my friend the councilman. This groundwork paid off, and they were happy to help us. Police chief Harry Caldwell, on the other hand, wanted nothing to do with the hassle and assigned his deputy, Fred Bankston, to sit down with us.

Old-school Texas police officers were a tough bunch. They were tasked with protecting the country club types, and their culture wasn't too far removed from that of the old runaway slave patrols or the KKK. They were vulgar, almost brutish, and invested with unquestioned power to enforce the status quo. This included enforcing a ban on new crowd permits in Montrose, which had originally been put in place to tamp down the riotous energy of the hippies. Knowing all this, I needed my own backup, my own deputy.

Her name was Carol Fennema, a talented professional whom I had known from working with the lesbians in the neighborhood. She had a traditional, corporate, ladylike look, with high heels, pencil skirt, ruffled blouse, and a briefcase—the uniform she wore to rise in the ranks of Houston's business world. We had worked together in the GPC on voter registration; I enjoyed her warm and generous spirit, and I knew she could lend her trusted and polished voice to our needs. She was a wonderful human being! The cops weren't focused on her professional attributes, however. They just enjoyed the eye candy clacking into the police headquarters.

We sat in Deputy Chief Bankston's office and got the answer we expected: even though he had the capacity to overturn the ordinance against marching in Montrose, he would not. I kept pressing my case. Turning to Carol, he softened up a tad, and asked her, "What's a nice Mexican boy like him doing, hanging around with this pot-of-shit gay community?"

Well, I had to pipe up. "I'm sorry, sir, I'm not Mexican, I'm Black." He responded, "You mean I got a nigger, a wetback, and a queer in my office?!" Tickled by his own clever assessment, he cackled as the phone rang, which bought us a few minutes to gather our thoughts as he answered the call.

With wide eyes, Carol looked like she was regretting wading into the matter. The chief was already in a poor mood—it was clear he was not interested in entertaining gay people. To get my attention and show that she was still with me, she dug her fingernails in my leg. I said, "I got this. No matter what it takes, I'm getting this permit."

And we did. Chief Bankston's short fuse was getting worn down to nothing, and as Carol continued to press our case, that fuse was ready to go off. Exasperated, he relented: "It's yours. Get out!"

I could have let it go there, but I wanted to make sure he knew what he was getting himself into. I didn't want to get pinned down on the day of the parade because of some technicality. "No, no, but wait a second!" I said. "We have a band. A sixty-three-piece marching band."

The chief tickled himself once more. "Oh, you guys blow on something other than each other?" Ignoring his needling, I simply said, "Yeah, and they're a good band." Truly impatient now, he made it clear that he just wanted us out of his office. Having seen and enjoyed a few riots in his day, he probably didn't think a few fairies were any threat—and he'd concluded that our gathering wouldn't amount to much.

"No, no! But wait a second. We have female impersonators."

"This is not San-Fran-Cisco!" he barked. "No, we are not having any drag queens in this parade. This is not San Francisco."

I just wanted to warn him ahead of time. I had seen the parades in New York and San Francisco, and they were messy and kind of gross, with participants gleefully pushing the envelope with all manner of acts and drunkenness. I wanted a parade, like the ones in New Orleans, that held up community standards. Montrose was a diverse neighborhood, and I wanted the parade to be fun for all—including families with children. For our gay community to thrive, I knew how important it was to represent ourselves well. I had learned this lesson during my time picketing segregated stores and lunch counters in New Orleans.

My Houston circle included a few good ol' boys here and there, so I knew exactly how to use the last trick up my sleeve. To pique the Chief's curiosity and secure the full permit I wanted, drag queens and all, I presented him with a challenge. I bet him five dollars—the cost of a round of beers—that Houston's finest drag performers would knock him out. They would look better than the women he saw every week at church, with bigger hair and beauty queen poise. There would be no beards or scruffy legs. His eyebrows rose as high as they could. He addressed Carol once again, asking, "Is that true?" She was caught off guard by my offer but, with a gulp, mustered a solid "pretty much!"

"Look," I offered, with five dollars in my hand. "Here's my proof. We'll let Carol hold the money, and on the day of the parade, we'll compare notes." With a quick squeak he pulled out five of his own dollars, and we left the office with a full permit in hand.

UPFRONT

MAY 16, 1979

Gay Pride Message From A Proud Gay

The Houston gay community has at last come into its own, taking its rightful place alongside New York and California as one of the most vital centers of the gay lifestyle in America. Gay Pride Week will be celebrated in Houston with one of the most diverse programs in the country.

This year, as opposed to past years, GPW will be a celebration, *NOT* a protest, and will feature as one of its main events a Gay Pride Parade on Sunday, July 1. Scheduled to begin at 3:00 P.M., the parade will feature floats, music, and marching units celebrating the pride of the gay community in Houston.

The Gay Pride Parade is seeking to proclaim and commemorate the diversity of life styles in Houston. Everyone is invited to come out and view the event that will gather national recognition for Houston's progressive attitudes toward its gay citizens.

The route of the parade, along Westheimer from Shepherd to Bagby, should provide a comfortable setting in the gay community for all Houstonians to come out and enjoy the pride and joy which your gay organizations and businesses bring to Gay Pride '79.

Larry Bagneris, Parade Chair

Larry's message to the community, from *Upfront* [1979]
FILE COURTESY OF HOUSTONLGBTHISTORY.ORG

I personally hung banners up and down Westheimer: "Welcome, Gay Pride Parade!" The signs weren't even that big, only two feet square, framed in American flag bunting. But the words made me a target. As I made my way along the busy thoroughfare, a few bus commuters screamed out their windows at me. One pedestrian saw what I was doing and called me a "wetback." With little patience, I replied, "No, asshole, I'm a nigger!" just to see the look on his face.

I had to keep going. I had to get over people's negativity. Some of the criticism came from within the community: people accused me of making the parade too bland. They wanted to freak out the uptight squares with the kind of spectacle seen in the bigger cities on the coasts. But I had been in New York City in 1971 for an early Stonewall remembrance, and what they had called a parade was a riotous protest. I had been in San Francisco in 1972 for their Pride parade, and I had been appalled—people on floats butt naked! That's not what I wanted my parade to be about. I wanted to fight for equal rights and full justice under the law, not just the right to show your pee pee in public.

Ultimately, I kept the distractions at bay by focusing on the job at hand. My philosophy was this: gays and lesbians needed to fight political injustice and cultural small-mindedness. But sometimes our community simply deserved to relax and celebrate. It all goes back to the Creole and New Orleans culture within which I grew up. Everything was worth celebrating—every birthday, every holiday, every Sunday afternoon.

The success of the plan hinged on the participation of the local bars. These establishments were raking in money—but we convinced them they'd make even more money if the parade was a success. We appealed to their competitive spirit. None of the professional float companies would touch us with a ten-foot pole, so we got the bars to sponsor and build their own floats.

The plan called for a big rally at the end of the parade, at Spotts Park, to thank the politicians who had supported us and to hand out trophies for best float, best display of creativity, best marching unit, and so on. I was putting so much of my ego and personality into this project—and, as you may have guessed by now, nothing I do is complete without fireworks. The cost of a big display was high, $10,000, so I hit the pavement again—and in the end, got twenty bars to put up $500 each. I had to call around before I found a fireworks company willing to take our money. The first six or seven said "no, thank you" when they learned the order was for a queer rally! But in the end, we found our fireworks—and the final piece of the puzzle was in place.

Finally, the big day arrived—July 1, 1979. We had a grand marshal—Thelma Hansel, better known as Disco Grandma—and a visiting dignitary: Harry Britt, the San Francisco city supervisor who had been appointed to Harvey Milk's former seat. While I was busy, bullhorn in hand, lining up the floats, Steve Shiflett—still president of the GPC at that point—made his way to Britt's car, right behind the grand marshal. Once again, Steve pissed me off: I had done all the work, and he just hopped in the convertible. In his smooth way, he presented the parade as a GPC function, which discounted the work of the parade committee.

But overall, the positives vastly outweighed the negatives. The parade route began at the Old Plantation bar on Kipling Street, turned onto Shepherd Drive, and proceeded down Westheimer for nearly two miles. The police department, having underestimated the turnout, only sent two police cars to the scene. As we got underway, one of their units was positioned at the front of the parade and the other at the back. When we rounded the corner on Westheimer, we saw that ten thousand people had shown up, just for the parade! Families, children, everywhere. It blew my mind. I'd been so busy setting affairs in order that it was a complete shock to turn that corner and see all those people, numbers beyond my wildest expectations. We took over all of Westheimer—and the police, who'd been counting on keeping one lane open, started trying to divert traffic. Since the police contingent had proven completely insufficient, it was up to me, as parade manager, to get out on the street and direct traffic. At one point

I even had to convince a city bus driver to back up and turn onto a side street off Westheimer.

I had ridden on a Carnival float when I was much younger. Mardi Gras was fun, but this first Pride parade left me feeling even more elated. Along the route were all manner of friends—including gays and lesbians who weren't quite out enough for us to meet regularly in the clubs—along with straight friends and family members and neighbors with their kids.

And the floats were enormous! All the bars had spent weeks on the job, each competing to out-fabulous the others by building the loudest and flashiest float. I invited representatives from one of the big float companies, Parades, Etc., to come out and see what our amateur builders had achieved. Rumor has it that the reps weren't expecting much more than a bunch of naked guys on flatbed trailers. Instead, to their surprise, they witnessed over thirty incredible floats built by the talented artists and carpenters of our own gay community. We earned their respect, and their company provided the floats the next year and every year after.

I was so careful about establishing a professional reputation for the parade that I upset a few people by playing warden up and down the route. Today's parades welcome all shapes, sizes, and gender presentations, but back then I felt that anyone who mixed beards and drag together would have to be a spectator, not a participant. And so I pulled a few people off the floats myself. It was too dangerous to break the commitment I had made to the deputy police chief. If I found someone wearing nothing but Speedo swimwear or leather chaps, I insisted that they put on a pair of jeans. I wanted to run a strict parade, with an eye toward securing a permit for a second Pride parade in 1980.

To lighten the mood, I insisted on throws—plastic beads and trinkets that brought joy to the crowd, just like in New Orleans. Tossing beads wasn't technically allowed, but we did it anyway, and by the time the second edition rolled the following year, we had used our political muscle to change the city's anti-throw ordinance.

Montrose Sports Association float in Houston Pride parade [1979]
PHOTOGRAPH BY LARRY BUTLER
FILE COURTESY OF HOUSTONLGBTHISTORY.ORG

When the parade reached the end of the route, at Bagby Street and Westheimer, we all went over to Spotts Park. The soundtrack, which I had personally arranged, opened with "The Star-Spangled Banner" and closed with "We Are Family," by Sister Sledge. It didn't take much to put me over the top. My heart was already touched that morning as the floats started rolling. I saw the creativity, dedication, blood, sweat, and tears of each float builder pouring forth. I sensed a change coming. I was already tired from running around for days and days, and I found my own spot at the top of the tallest hill in Spotts Park to catch the beginning of the fireworks display. I saw a kid out of the corner of my eye. He was with his mom, and he asked her, "Who are the fireworks for? It's not the Fourth of July," to which she said, "These are gay people's fireworks. They are celebrating their right to be free." I cried.

Today, forty-plus years later, Houston's Pride parade draws more than 700,000 spectators. It's the largest annual parade in Houston and the third-largest gay parade in the country. But that first parade carried extra significance. I still choke back tears of disbelief, thinking about those fireworks. That night in Spotts Park felt like a climax to a movement that had been growing for years, granting us the freedom to congregate openly with one another in love, passion, family, and friendship.

I've had friends say to me that they've gotten old, and they don't go to the Pride parade anymore. It's common to hear that it's too crowded and commercialized. The days are hot, and there's lots of walking. They ask, "Why do we need these anymore?"

We need Pride parades because the next generation must see the full smorgasbord of organizations that together form our community. The parade carries the spirit of Town Meeting One, a prism reflecting all the colors of the spectrum of sexuality. Maybe as you stand on the sidelines, a sports association will march past and catch your eye—or a band, or one of the handful of different churches that serve the LGBTQ+ community. Hopefully, you'll be inspired to join where you fit best, knowing that you can be yourself within the gay community in any way that suits you. This is how to build a new world, by exemplifying what positive, healthy, and well-adjusted LGBTQ+ life looks like. To our straight neighbors and allies: we welcome you to come and enjoy life with us. To the gay-bashers and pearl-clutching detractors: we don't need to put up with your crap.

That day in 1979, I made good on my promise to Chief Bankston, even though I never did collect my five-dollar bet. We were under a lot of pressure to keep things clean and avoid compromising any of the progress the movement had been making. We rose to the occasion. I would stay in the position of Pride chair, planning and managing the parade, for eight years.

Throughout my tenure, I always aimed to keep the focus on fun, and to serve the interests of the entire community—although sometimes it was impossible to keep politics out of the picture. For the 1982 edition, I nominated two of my biggest backers for grand marshal: a Republican woman named Marion Coleman, owner of the Kindred Spirits lesbian bar; and Andy Mills, a tall, skinny hippie with the biggest hands I've ever seen! Andy was the face of the community—the manager of Mary's bar and the director of the gay marching band. History repeats itself: at the last minute, Steve Shiflett tried to rally his CHE cohorts to throw the vote to his favored candidates. But not to worry: I called Andy and had him bring the entire marching band to the meeting where votes would be cast. We beat Steve at his own game. And to celebrate the victory, I tapped another New Orleans Carnival tradition. I commissioned a bunch of aluminum doubloon coins with Marion's and Andy's faces on one side, and the Pride Week theme ("A Part Of, Not Apart From") on the other.

Although it was a blow to lose the 1980 GPC election to Steve, my Pride responsibilities kept me busy, and I was still holding down a full-time job with Washington National. On top of all this, I was preparing to attend the Democratic National Convention in New York City as the first-ever openly gay delegate from Houston, Texas! I was holding fundraisers at my house to pay for my hotel room and putting together a booklet to share with my fellow delegates: "The Gay Community / The Democratic Party: Working Together." The format was a Q&A about some issues that might seem basic today but weren't back then. "What is a homosexual?" "What causes homosexuality?" "Are gay men and lesbians mentally ill?" "Can gays and lesbians be 'cured'?" "Are lesbians and gay men 'anti-family'?" There was also a page dedicated to the minority perspective, explaining how being a woman, Black, or Hispanic compounds the challenge.

I was excited to be a delegate because I wanted to push for the rights of gay and lesbian people. I thought there was power involved, and that I might wield a little. But I came to learn that the entire show is put together before you get there. The chair of the state delegation had been selected long before the convention—and it was his job, once we'd all gathered at the New York Sheraton on the eve of the kickoff, to run through the rules and coach the Texas team. As a first-timer, I had some learning to do.

"Excuse me," I asked the chair with a pout and an attitude. "Who are you and why are you speaking?" Granted, I should have known who the chair of the Democratic Party in Texas was, but I didn't.

It was gently explained to me that the power was in the platform, which was work we already had done. After presidential primary polls close, caucuses at the polling locations form and delegates are drawn from the many senatorial and state districts. Various interest groups have a chance to push and pull for their own delegates—friends of theirs, from their own circles. From there the delegates, many of whom have known each other for years, organize panels and iron out proposals. You have to go through the process. It's an easy way to make many, many friends, and it's how the Texas Democratic Party selected delegates at that time.

Fortunately, that process had resulted in my own selection as a delegate, and once I got over my pique I was thrilled to receive the credentials granting me access to Madison Square Garden. I even had invitations for my parents to see me in action! Since the Garden is so large, they had room for all manner of guests—and thanks to the tunnels of entrances and exits, it was easy to slip Mom and Dad into their seats. I was smiling from ear to ear. As a child, I had followed coverage of both the Republican and Democratic conventions on television and radio. Mom and Dad were delighted to be in New York—and only partly because of my convention debut. They wanted to see Broadway, where my brother, Vernel, was making a name for himself.

The national gay and lesbian caucus—which brought together representatives from various state delegations—saw an opportunity to press our issues by nominating Melvin Boozer, a Black gay man, to be vice president of the United States. He made a stirring speech about gay rights that few people noticed because his assigned time slot was midday, not prime time. Most delegates and power brokers were elsewhere: in hotel suites or hallways, in line for food, or inside convention meeting rooms, working to iron out that year's platform.

I was part of the Texas delegation that stood for Ted Kennedy. I didn't know, at the time, that challenging Jimmy Carter would imperil him in the general election. To me, Kennedy was more pro-gay, whereas Carter, as a born-again Christian, represented a constituency traditionally hostile to gay rights. To this day, I regret that I failed to put my emotions aside and prioritize party unity. It was great, however, to meet gay delegates from around the country—even if we eventually acknowledged that this wasn't the convention that would achieve the big changes so many of us had hoped for.

Jimmy Armstrong Chavers was the love of my life. I met him in 1980, on a crowded weekend night on Richmond Avenue in the heart of Montrose. It was springtime and, as usual, I was out cajoling bar owners for donations—in this case, funds for another fireworks display to cap the second edition of the Pride parade.

As I looked out on the dance floor, I swore I saw an angel. Jimmy was from the Cajun side of Louisiana, with his own Creole features suggesting Spanish and French descent. He was nicely built in all the right places without being too buff. He sported scruffy black hair with a cleanly shaved look, just my type, with almond eyes and an accent. Better yet, we matched in height perfectly.

I didn't try to pay attention to him. I was on business, but I guess I kept staring because he couldn't keep from glancing back. While concentrating on my main mission—wrangling a donation from the bar owner—I hatched a plan that had worked for me before. I wanted to keep an eye on Jimmy, but I didn't want the hassle of babysitting. So I introduced myself and introduced a friend of mine, Ramiro Marin, the chair of the Gay Chicano Caucus. He was single and I thought Jimmy suited him just fine, so I let them head off to the dance floor. Maybe they would hook up.

The music was loud, with colored lights flashing. Crowds of fashionable gays would wash in from one bar to the next. The dance floor would be empty at times, packed at times, a mix of fashion statements and dance routines. With business finished and closing time approaching, I went off to look for Jimmy and Ramiro and found them in line for the bathroom.

"It's 2 a.m., closing time. We have to go," I reminded everyone.

"I have to use the bathroom," responded Ramiro.

"Go use it then," I said in a reflex. Meanwhile, Jimmy had a strange look on his face as my friend took his turn in the stalls. He was disappointed that I hadn't spent any time with him, and he looked dejected. "I don't know what that look is for," I said. "Don't you like my friend?"

"No, I like you! I'd prefer to get to know you."

"Screw it," I said, and hurriedly steered Jimmy out the door and back to my home. By the time my friend emerged from the bathroom, we were gone.

Once upon a time, everything in the gay community was contained in that little neighborhood—and I didn't live more than a few blocks from the bar. Jimmy and I had a lovely first night together, but it didn't take much time in the morning sunlight for him to find out what he had done. "Wait, you're *Larry* Larry, aren't you?" I had been in Houston for some ten years by that point, spearheading various campaigns and making speeches. Jimmy had heard of me and my antics at the GPC. "You're him!"

Larry (far right, back to camera) and Jimmy Armstrong Chavers in Houston Pride parade [1982]
COURTESY OF THE AUTHOR

he exclaimed. He had only seen me from afar, and he was only in his twenties. He didn't know what he should do or act or say, but I reassured him that we could just "relax and take it one day at a time." He didn't need to worry about all the chatter in the newspaper or my run-ins with the police or interviews on television. And it didn't take us long to realize that we had found someone special in each other. Over the ten years that followed, we would share so much joy and so many good times.

Jimmy was ten years younger than me, and he had only just started exploring his sexuality. His family came from Mamou, a small town in the Cajun prairies northwest of Lafayette. He had a single mom who worked as a waitress; after separating from his father, she had moved herself, Jimmy, and his two brothers to North Houston.

Today's social media norms dictate that we define relationship statuses and share them with all. Thankfully, Jimmy and I didn't need to do that. We just kept dating, reconfirming how special we were to each other as we learned each other's hopes, dreams, and fears. Jimmy was only my second serious relationship. Before him, between 1974 and 1977, I had dated tall and handsome Desi Lopez. He took his movie star looks and ended up in the Air Force. The Montrose neighborhood was often a thick stew of hookups and exes, but no one could deny that Jimmy and I were a good fit.

We took it a day at a time. He was still living with his family in a packed apartment, but he'd come in to Montrose on the weekends. On my way to work on Monday mornings, I would drop him back home. My first challenge was to get to know and make friends with his mother, and get past any concerns she might have had about our age gap. I don't know that she truly understood the nature of our relationship for years. But she could see that I was making him happy. She also noticed that I gave him some direction, as he had begun looking for a better job to save up money to move out. Six months after meeting, we moved in together—and if I didn't think I knew him well enough beforehand, here was my chance. I loved Jimmy so much, but I soon learned that I'm not meant to live with others! I'm a neat freak with my space and need no roommates.

Week by week, year by year, we harvested the joys of togetherness. In 1981, he was my date to two of my favorite festivals—Fiesta, in San Antonio, and Mardi Gras, which he had never seen before. The following year, 1982, he was there with me when I served on the board of the National Gay Task Force. We would celebrate every holiday with romantic meals and moments at our favorite bars. My dream had come true, it really had. And he kept me honest! In 1983, we were on the train headed to Provincetown with a bunch of college kids, and I was bullshitting with them about being in college myself. He turned to me and said, "You keep up your bullshit while cruising, and I'll out your age."

Every autumn, we would attend the Texas-Oklahoma football game in Dallas, typically held the first weekend in October, when the state fair opens. Together we would watch the college bands in the parade in the morning, then head over to the fair, ride the ferris wheel, play the games, watch the Big Tex statue get all lit up outside Cotton Bowl Stadium, and then hit the bars—since gays all over Texas knew this was *the* weekend to go to Dallas.

In 1985, thanks to a $99 roundtrip airline deal, we decided to go to London. We toured the city and went to see the legendary Heaven nightclub. Diana Ross performed the night we were there! That same year, Jimmy was there when I brought Tina Turner to Houston for a GPC extravaganza to cap the year's Pride festivities.

Political meetings for the GPC doubled as parties and mixers, and no one wanted to miss out on the drama. It was like joining a special club: it was the place to be. We were building a community. Through the GPC, young gays and lesbians could make connections: join a sports league, find a church to attend, learn about social offerings at the Montrose Community Center. Everything revolved around the GPC. My brother—who found his community in New York, on Broadway—would joke that the whole system was just "queens looking for a husband," but for me it was reminiscent of the Creole world I had grown up in. Since New Orleans Creoles were mistreated by whites and not welcome by many Blacks, we kept close ranks. We built strong neighborhoods centered on local institutions: schools and churches that sustained one generation after another. I loved the self-contained world I found, and built, in Houston—and I can't help wondering what's been lost, today, as the LGBTQ+ community is absorbed more fully into heterosexual society.

Jimmy loved the lights, camera, and action of political meetings. But he loved me so much that he couldn't always handle the punches and counterpunches. It was common for people to challenge me about fundraising, endorsements, big races, little races, and more. Jimmy took every charge against me personally, even if my opponents and I were friends before and after our debates. It was touching to know that Jimmy cared for me, that he worried about me getting hurt. He really liked me! But I didn't like how angry and pent-up he became after a night of politics, so I insisted that he only come to the fun stuff—the galas and the parties.

Just a few months into our relationship, the Copa bar hosted an event in support of repealing section 21.06 of the Texas penal code, the anti-sodomy law. Those of us in the movement were feeling optimistic: the GPC-endorsed Democratic gubernatorial candidate, Mark White, had ended up winning the 1982 race. In Texas! In fact, Democrats had won all the top races that year. I was on tap to make a speech that evening at the Copa—and my aim was to encourage the gay community to keep pressuring the governor's office with phone calls and letters. I laugh now, thinking of the disparity between the seriousness of the stakes and the frivolity of the setting. We were essentially holding a political rally at a strip show! Our speeches were interspersed with comedy routines, strip acts, and dances. Having grown up in New Orleans, I knew how distracting a show could be, and I wondered to myself, "How do I grab the attention of these people?"

Once I got to the microphone, I quickly got to the point. "The sodomy statute makes it illegal for gay people to be gay people, period," I stated. "You need to contact the governor and tell him not to *fuck* with 21.06."

The gambit worked. The crowd, already worked up, met my words with roaring applause. However, when Jimmy came to greet me afterwards, he had a disdainful look. "Let's GO!" he said. I react poorly to being bossed around, and I asked him: "What do you mean?" Jimmy didn't offer an explanation; he was just adamant about leaving.

Once outside, I asked, "What's wrong with you?" He replied, solemnly, "I'm going to say something, and I'm going to say it once. You're president of the GPC, and it demeans the office to present yourself in that manner."

He recognized something that I had missed. The stature of my position called for respectability. I was embarrassed about being corrected—but even then, in the flush of the moment, I admired Jimmy for investing in my future, for calling me out and asking me to rise to a higher level. If I'd never left New Orleans, perhaps I'd never have learned this lesson. And so I made it my goal to carry myself as a professional. I've long cherished the New Orleans aspects of my personality. I live a life full of passion, and I call it as I see it. These qualities have served me well in life—but they needed some tempering, and for that, both Jimmy and Houston hold my gratitude.

Although I never brought it up again, I have always kept that conversation planted in my mind as I've striven to be a better person. Through activism, as Jimmy had reminded me, we create positive images for young gay people coming up and coming out. It's important to curate the images that a kid sees. Growing up in a solidly middle-class minority community, I was taught the value of keeping up appearances. And I'd modeled myself on early Black civil rights leaders, who encouraged us to protest wearing coats and ties.

While I grew into a fuller version of myself in Houston, a new gay political establishment was forming in New Orleans. The Louisiana Gay Political Action Caucus (LAGPAC) was founded in 1980—and other organizations, including the Forum for Equality, would follow later in the decade. One lifelong New Orleans activist who became a close friend was Roberts

Batson—a tall brunet, just a tad older than me, with a distinctly colorful wardrobe and working-class Yat accent. I was touched by his attendance at a vigil we held in the early 1980s after the GPC secretary, Fred Paez, was killed. Roberts was by my side, and as we marched, he whispered, "Would you consider coming back to New Orleans?"

Immediately, I cried "NEVER!" At that time in my life, everything was going perfectly. I was planning to run for office in Houston. I was riding high.

"I just want you to know," Roberts continued, "that there's a lot of work to do in New Orleans." I replied, "I'm in the middle of doing all this HERE, and I'm not giving this up!"

Why should I leave? Jimmy and I were happy at home, at 2001 Branard, in our wonderful apartment with big windows. I was pushing forty and thriving in my career at Washington National. As one of the best agents in the field, I was invited to lead trainings nationwide. While Jimmy held down the fort in Houston, I would travel from coast to coast, running sessions in Tucson, Arizona; Hackensack, New Jersey; Oakland, California . . . even Shreveport, Louisiana!

My job meant a lot to me, enough that I was willing to miss Mardi Gras one year for a training up in Evanston, in the north suburbs of Chicago. Wouldn't you know, it was snowing—of course!—and I had never driven in the snow before. So here I was driving slowly through the slop, hugging the middle lane, not caring if I had the whole town of Evanston backed up behind me. When I finally made it to the training site, my Washington National team must have sensed my blue mood. After all, Mardi Gras requires religious devotion, and I felt like a pilgrim with nowhere to go. So the team borrowed a pushcart from the hotel, decorated it with Mardi Gras colors, and pushed me through the classroom, as I showered them all with beads.

Working for Washington National brought benefits other than collegiality—namely, good healthcare. Once I had coverage, I debated doing something about the deafness in my left ear. My mom had always assured me that hearing loss wasn't a disability—and I was somewhat ambivalent about seeing a specialist because I had lived monaurally for so long. Indeed, I had taken my handicap and turned it into a political asset. If someone's words were awkward or upsetting, I could just turn my head and put them in my bad ear. I continue to do this, to this day. I'll just put you on mute and smile my head off.

Since New Orleans is a town full of musicians, many people lose their hearing occupationally. One of my brother's friends was in the music industry his whole life—and as his hearing deteriorated, he was always asking others to repeat themselves. But since I was born this way, I don't. If I can't hear you, forget it, I'm moving on. It must not have been important. You hear what you want to hear, as my mother had told me years ago.

Still, with my Washington National health plan, I took myself to the doctor, to see if I could learn anything new about my condition. When, after rounds of visits, the final specialist performed the "beep beep beep beep" test, the findings were underwhelming. I was still deaf in my left ear. It was 1986, and there really wasn't much they could do about conditions like mine—and I accepted that. Even today, a cochlear implant would do nothing to help the issue. All I know is that when I sleep on my right side, with my good ear on the pillow, I can sleep like a baby.

During my days running trainings for Washington National, it would have been helpful to hear in stereo. But I didn't have that option. To overcome my disability, rather than speak from a lectern, I would work the room and engage close-up with all the students. My only lasting heartbreak is that my poor hearing prevented me from learning Spanish, the language I love. However, in the end, my inability to hear out of one ear has become an intrinsic—and often useful—part of who I am.

The seed planted by Roberts Batson had continued to grow—and in my mind, New Orleans was starting to beckon. I was ready to hand off my responsibilities with Pride Week and the GPC. And not a moment too soon, because the sickness started to arrive in force in 1985.

Whispers had begun in the late 1970s, around the gay neighborhoods, of pneumonias and other strange maladies. We put two and two together quickly, that there was a sexual pattern in the incidents. What was first termed GRID, for Gay-Related Immune Deficiency, and is now known as AIDS, was declared an epidemic in 1981.

I wasn't terribly alarmed, at first. I was in a committed relationship with Jimmy, and I trusted him. I had also always preferred the cleanliness of protection. AIDS seemed to first affect the jet-set, New York and San Francisco types who could afford to fly from place to place to have their fun. It was happening to other people. Jimmy and I traveled as much as we could, and I was always on the road, but we tended to travel together. We felt safe.

Soon, the gay community began to connect more of the dots. This was no thanks to the Reagan administration, which wanted to keep things hush-hush. Since it was a gay disease, the argument went, we probably deserved it. Solving the problem was up to the gay community—and leaders like Larry Kramer, who organized the AIDS Coalition to Unleash Power (ACT UP), were soon steering the political agenda.

What was originally confined to the coasts soon arrived in Houston, and by 1983 and 1984, whenever Jimmy and I were on the road, disturbing news would greet us when we returned home. People began to die. Our community began to lose bartenders and artists. Some of my political allies and a few old boyfriends died. We lost people who worked on the parade, wrote in our newspaper, worshiped in our church . . . our community was decimated. The wave we had seen in New York, Los Angeles, and San Francisco just a few seasons before was now cresting and breaking on top of Houston.

By then, a steady stream of houseguests knocked on my door. I needed to help them grieve. People died and kept dying, for long stretches. Some of them were my best friends. But I had had enough grief. Arriving at middle age, I wanted to reorient my priorities, and I relished the idea of returning to New Orleans and spending more time with my family. I could work remotely: Washington National could fly me anywhere, so whether I was based in Houston or New Orleans was immaterial.

I saw this as my chance to jump ship, and in late 1986 I decided to move home. When I went back to Houston the following spring for Pride, a couple of people would tell me how disappointed they were in me for leaving. They'd had great expectations of what else I might have achieved there. But you know when you've had enough, and when you have an opportunity.

I guess, after seventeen years in Houston, I had accomplished everything I wanted. I had arrived after college and reached great heights in my career. I hadn't known a soul at first, but I had helped knit this community around me. I started a great tradition in Pride and parading, I got to represent my community in the DNC and, together with my boyfriend Jimmy, I could leave with my head held high. I'm proud of my generation for working to knit together an LGBTQ+ community in Houston, and I was blessed to have known such wonderful people. Today the GPC is known as the Houston LGBTQ+ Political Caucus and is the largest gay political organization in Texas. In 2019 the Pride Parade organized a fortieth anniversary reunion, and I got to meet the new board. We talked about some of the issues they're grappling with: things like inclusiveness, fundraising, team cohesion, crowd control. Some things change and some things don't. After telling them my story and listening to theirs, I received quite the honor: an invitation to ride with the board in the anniversary parade. Respectfully, I declined. I had noticed a group I could have more fun with: some New Orleans transplants who had taken our Louisiana Mardi Gras tradition and nurtured it in Houston. Their floats had more beads!

CHAPTER SIX / *Entrada a México*

Larry, Pablo Escamilla, and Charles Sydnor in Teotihuacán, Mexico [2016]
COURTESY OF THE AUTHOR

6

I'M ALMOST EMBARRASSED TO ADMIT THAT I DIDN'T KNOW MUCH ABOUT Mexico, a culture I've long admired, when I was growing up in the 1950s. Certainly, there was Speedy Gonzales on TV, but I was too immersed in my tight-knit Creole sphere to explore the interwoven histories of the US and Latin America. Later on, I learned not only that New Orleans was once a Spanish-owned territory but that Mexicans and Central Americans had a long history in my hometown. Thanks to the United Fruit Company, which once had its headquarters in New Orleans, Hondurans and other Central Americans had been steadily arriving in Louisiana since the turn of the twentieth century. This population included the ancestors of my maternal grandmother, Armantine Lumas, who was born in New Orleans to parents of Honduran and Guatemalan origin.

Many of those populations started to occupy the space between Canal Street and the New Basin Canal, the latter making way for the

Pontchartrain Expressway in my childhood. Today, there are still corners of New Orleans's Mid-City with thoroughly Central American populations, many of whom arrived after Hurricane Katrina to help us rebuild.

During my Seventh Ward childhood, however, I had no idea they were there! The city I grew up in was such a Black and white world that I had little exposure to Spanish speakers. Within the even more insular Creole world, where everyone knew each other's parents, we were concerned about and content with what few square blocks and institutions we had. Advocating for civil rights for Negroes was the order of the day. As I began to come out of the closet, I was more exposed to Greek culture than Hispanic culture due to the Greek bars near the port, on Decatur Street.

In fact, I was so naive when I arrived in Houston after college that—judging from their skin, their eyes, and their manners—I thought all the Mexicans I was meeting in Texas were Creoles like me! It was refreshing to find so many of my people: I had finally discovered where the rest of the Creoles were hiding! During my time in Houston, I made many Mexican and Chicano friends—and was always struck by how familiar their neighborhoods felt to me. I also had more than a few boyfriends from this community.

That sense of affinity has never diminished. I haven't yet made it to Honduras or other parts of Central America. But for the rest of my life, despite my inability to speak Spanish, I have always felt at home in Mexico, enraptured by its history, culture, and people.

My first time visiting Mexico was in 1970, soon after my move to Houston. Mexico had just hosted the Olympics, in 1968, and the World Cup earlier in 1970. The nation's economy had been booming since the 1950s, but inequality was growing along with the good fortune, and social strife and labor struggles were on the rise. I was only marginally aware of this larger context when James Schaffer, my former Xavier instructor, invited me to join him and a gay colleague of his on a trip.

Professor Schaffer was always the life of the party. He had a sense of drama—no surprise, considering his profession—and his hippie sensibilities sparked a love of travel. He and his friend had driven all the way from New Orleans to fetch me in Texas. It was still another six hours to the border, and soon the landscape transformed from the familiar swamps and bayous of home to something very different. The land started to get drier and drier, and the vivid colors of the desert started to bloom. No need for a passport in those days: it took only a flash of a driver's license to cross the Rio Grande into Mexico, and suddenly I was in my first foreign nation.

The professors were planning to drive all the way to the beaches of sunny Acapulco. We spent our first night on the road in the large desert city of Monterrey, where I woke up early for morning Mass, to thank the Lord for this trip. Then, after another long drive we ended up in Guadalajara, in the western state of Jalisco, where I decided to stay. Any visitor would understand why! Some say the city's atmosphere reminds them of San Francisco, while its weather reminds them of Los Angeles. Many Mexicans say it's the most Mexican city of them all, a less crowded and more comfortably paced alternative to Mexico City.

For a New Orleanian, the city seemed like the fullest possible expression of the French Quarter, with aging seventeenth-century architecture (older than Louisiana itself) set within the tight, square blocks of a terraced Spanish town. With another day's drive left for the professors, I decided I'd rather take in the verdant parks and mariachi bands of Guadalajara. After wishing my companions a good trip, it was time to find the gay bars. I hoped to meet a friend to show me the city.

Only scattered records survive to show how the precolonial civilizations of Mexico felt about homosexuality, but their attitudes appear to follow a familiar pattern. At times, they punished homosexuality with strict laws. Other times, those laws were ignored, particularly for the elite. The concept of lesbianism was known by ancient Mexican civilizations, and some cultures seem to have been supremely tolerant. It also appears that some

Indigenous groups in the area—like others across North America—recognized a "two-spirit" gender designation and considered these individuals to be shamans of a kind. Information on the subject is sparse, as much of what survives comes from the Spanish colonizers, who had their own agendas in reporting on the gays of the region.

Colonization and religion complicate the conception of same-sex attraction. Often, to this day, there's a "Mediterranean" notion that you're only gay if you're a bottom. Among Mexican elites of the nineteenth and early twentieth centuries, it was easier to adhere to the "dandy" model popular in New York, London, Paris, and other worldly cities—a model that tolerated ambiguously queer displays of wealth and fashion.

In 1901, during the reign of President Porfirio Díaz, a scandal—known as the Dance of the Forty-One—dominated tabloid headlines, and Mexicans still use the number *cuarenta y uno* as a slur against gays. Early one November night, a knock came at the door of a home in a well-to-do Mexico City neighborhood. Police barged in and found a dance going on; all the attendees were men, but some wore women's clothing. Although there was no law against this form of entertainment, the police took everyone to jail. While the names of the forty-one men arrested were never fully reported, the attendees were known to be well connected, which fed readers' appetite for horror and fascination. The rumor was that the president's own son-in-law was found at the party—the forty-second *maricón*—and let go.

Despite all the years of persecution, gays had never quite disappeared from Mexican society. By the time of my trip in 1970, activists like Nancy Cárdenas were writing and organizing, and the big cities—particularly Guadalajara—had become magnets for gays. From the Parque Revolución, in the ancient and timeless city center, it wasn't hard for me to find the cliques and gaggles of gay guys whose expressions I recognized from New Orleans. Near the park I found two gay bars of typical style, a seedy joint for hustling and another for dancing. The locations of cruising spots have always been spread by word of mouth or, at times, via mimeographed guides passed around by like-minded travelers. Lo and behold, the most popular Guadalajara cruising spot was a Denny's diner!

Despite the language barrier, it was easy to flirt, drink, and laugh with the locals. One handsome country boy in particular caught my eye. The feeling was mutual, and he wandered over to me and we did our best to get to know each other. I wanted to keep the vibe going, so I was ready to treat us both to lunch at Denny's—but when we approached the front door, I noticed he had disappeared behind me. Turns out, since he was of Indigenous origin, he was unwelcome at the diner! I took a peep inside the windows. A fairer set of gay Mexicans were sitting and glancing over, whispering to their waiter and doing everything in their power—with sneers and pointed fingers—to keep out the riffraff. It was a shock but not a surprise to find gays discriminating against one another. Having seen plenty of this at home in New Orleans, I'd come to consider this behavior unacceptable—and as an American tourist, I made a scene. Pissed off, I cried, "I'm an American! And this is my friend!" We were promptly seated, and *mi amor Indio* was certainly impressed. But my anger wasn't to be allayed. How disappointing to learn that the same stratification I'd known in Louisiana was just as present in Mexico, despite a different cast of characters.

The professors returned one week later, and we were off for a quick hop to Mexico City. By then, the holiday season was arriving, and you can be sure I enjoyed the Christmas displays the most. Mexican Navidad traditions and decorations are very similar to our own in New Orleans. In the end, despite witnessing a display of colorism in Mexico that I hadn't expected, the trip had been invaluable. Left to fend for myself in Guadalajara, my experience gave me confidence that I could hold my own and live life to the fullest, even outside of my home environment.

Just a few years later, my best friends Ramon and David proposed a trip to Mexico City. We decided to go for Mexican Independence Day—typically a two-day celebration, kicking off on September 15th, my birthday, another reason why I love Mexico! This trip would be a way for me to really drink up the culture while having fun with my dear friends. Ramon and David arranged visits to historical sites that highlighted Mexico's centuries of civilization. We were joined by our friend Mary Lopez, a slender lesbian from Houston with short black hair and glasses, who always reminded me of a Mexican Katie Couric.

As soon as we arrived, before even checking in at the nice hotel that Ramon and David had selected, we headed to the Zócalo, the central plaza of the Aztecs, seat of a Mesoamerican civilization. At the time, the square was pretty run down, but Ramon and David wanted Mary and me to see the very spot where they had professed their love when they were quite young, underneath the large flagpole. Their romance was wholesome and inspiring to me—Ramon looked like your typical Texas football player, while David was more of a twink, perfectly shaped for a cheerleader's outfit. Both were very proud to be Mexican, and the Zócalo marked the spot on the map where their heritage and their destinies crossed.

Ramon and David were firmly in charge of the itinerary. They both knew Mexico City quite well and served as wonderful tour guides. But I couldn't resist returning to the Zona Rosa, which I'd visited briefly on my earlier trip, with the professors. Mexico City's largest and most historic gay neighborhood sits in a somewhat secluded section of Colonia Juárez, between the city center and the hills of the large Chapultepec Park. Home of the famous Angel of Independence, it's a gay neighborhood whose history follows a trajectory similar to that of many of the world's great pink zones. Home to large mansions built in the early twentieth century, it became known as the American Zone for its population of affluent expats. The revolution put a check on the decadent foreigners—but the neighborhood remained a trendy spot for boutiques and coffee shops until it became just run-down enough to attract a new generation of beatniks, artists, and activists, many of whom added murals and sculptures to the streetscapes. Soon, as Mexico City grew busier, the barrio's exclusivity declined, making it fertile ground for gay businesses and cruisy bars.

It was around this time the neighborhood earned the name Zona Rosa. Later, as the economic crises of the 1980s and '90s arrived, the area grew quite seedy, but it continued to attract gays of all kinds to its clubs. Some settled in the neighborhood and, as is typical, fixed up just enough homes to make the area a target for gentrification.

Traveling with Ramon and David, I found myself inspired by the whole sweep of Mexican history. One special landmark, not far from the Zona Rosa, was Chapultepec Castle. Sitting on a majestic hill, the castle was originally built in the eighteenth century for the Spanish viceroy, Bernardo de Gálvez, right after his stint as governor of Louisiana. Gálvez was another one of those links between my Louisiana heritage and my Mexican affinities. At just thirty, he had been selected to govern the vast territory stretching from New Orleans up to Illinois and beyond. Thanks to military success, he was promoted to replace his late father as administrator of New Spain—today's Mexico and much of the southwestern United States.

Long after Spanish rule, Chapultepec Castle remained a landmark in Mexico City. In the 1860s it became the seat of the Emperor Maximilian, an Austrian archduke installed by European powers to govern Mexico, and it later served as the country's presidential mansion. Today it serves the people at large, as the National Museum of History. To reach the castle, one must pass through the park grounds—home to formal gardens, various other museums, and a zoo.

What a sight! The castle was the most complete expression of the Creole spirit I've found anywhere, dripping with neoclassical and neo-Gothic details that mix European habits with New World styles. The epic murals, grand staircases and hallway, and decorative elements—plaster medallions, ornate wallpaper and lamps—remind me of an Uptown New Orleans mansion, instilled with the full force of Empire. The castle's stained-glass windows filter natural light upon marble floors, framing a majestic view of Mexico City below.

Chapultepec Castle was just one of the cultural wonders I got to explore in Mexico. Ramon, David, Mary, and I might visit the murals of Diego

Rivera by day—and then, at night, catch the Ballet Folklórico, performing in a theater graced by a multistory Tiffany glass curtain. In between, we would dine on the forty-first floor of the Torre Latinoamericana. We raised our glasses and toasted the wide valley of Mexico below, with its magical mix of Indigenous, African, and European peoples.

Because ours was a mixed group, we didn't spend as much time as I might have liked in the gay bars. Instead, Ramon, David, and Mary liked to eat! Their favorite restaurant was the historic La Gruta, a grand dining room set in volcanic caves outside of town. Having no sense of smell, I was never a foodie, but I did learn to love rich, dark, chocolate mole sauce. Even though we had to watch what we ate as we acclimated to the altitude, I couldn't get enough of the mole sauce. I had it all over my face!

I was lucky to live in Texas for all those years, with its large Hispanic population. As often as possible, I would head out to San Antonio for Fiesta. San Antonio and New Orleans are birthday twins, both founded in 1718. On my first visit, in 1972, I arrived on a Sunday afternoon in April, not knowing a thing about Fiesta, which had just ended that morning. What I saw on that brief work junket gave me enough of a taste that I wanted to return and celebrate properly.

While Fiesta San Antonio is over a hundred years old, the festival always finds a way to renew itself. It is San Antonio's largest event of the year and commemorates the Battle of the Alamo and the Battle of San Jacinto, the latter of which gave Texas its liberation from Mexico. Akin to Carnival in New Orleans, there's a whole weekend's worth of parades, with flower-bedecked floats and bands and dance troupes in floral skirts in the Mexican style. They even select and honor monarchs every year, just like we do!

The site of the action was always the Menger Hotel, across from the Alamo, where it's impossible to miss the preening gays showing off outside. The hotel bar was a popular spot for cruising and, whether management liked it or not, served as the headquarters for all manner of Texas steers and queers. Not too far away, mostly between the historic Alamo and the glitzy River Walk, were a number of gay bars—including the Country, which had large rooms in which to hang out and chill. There were other gay bars downtown on North Main Avenue, among them the Saint, which featured drag shows; the Pegasus, still in operation today, where go-go dancers performed; and the Silver Dollar, a country-and-western bar that hosted line dances. My favorite time to go to the Silver Dollar was on the nights they played traditional Mexican music.

Every year, I would ring up the Menger Hotel and get two rooms. I'd make up some story about arriving in town with my wife and requiring a separate room for my traveling secretary. Every year, my wife and secretary would magically be unavailable and, voilà—I would have two whole rooms for parties and reunions. You can imagine what the Daughters of the Republic of Texas, caretakers of the Alamo (at that time), thought of us streaming in and out of the lobby as they were having their cotillion!

Sometimes the best places are just holes in the wall. Outside the city limits, on I-35, stood an aluminum warehouse known as the Ponderosa. Can you imagine a gay bar out in the middle of the dusty expanse of Texas brush? It was about half an hour from downtown and it took an effort to get down there.

Just when it started to feel like you were on your way to Laredo, lo and behold, like a fairy tale, you would arrive at the Ponderosa—and it would be packed! Before the internet, when it was risky to run a gay business, the Ponderosa's reputation spread widely through word of mouth alone. Attracting a mix of gays, lesbians, Blacks, Anglos, and Mexicans, the Ponderosa was famous for its "Academy Awards" drag show, with queens trotting out to 45-rpm records playing on a sound system that would often break.

To this day, I try to return to San Antonio as often as I can in the spring. It's a beautiful time of year in Texas, when wildflowers bloom along the highway. And back in the day, to make sure all the queers from miles around would feel welcome, we would decorate the busiest highway rest stops with flowers and signs welcoming them to Fiesta, pointing them in the right direction.

Many years later, in 2003, I had the opportunity to see a new side of Mexico on a visit to Yucatán with a pair of Tulane professors. Despite a full beard that made him look a bit like Fidel Castro, Mark Thomas was known to friends and more than a few students as Guadalupe. On this trip, he was joined by his colleague Gene Cizek and Gene's boyfriend, Lloyd Sensat, who served as our tour guide to the Maya architectural sites that were our destination.

From the minute we stepped off the plane in Mérida, I was transported to paradise. The streets formed the same strict squares that you can find in Spanish towns all over the Americas, similar to the grid of New Orleans's French Quarter. However, these streets weren't paved, and downtown Mérida was as lush as a jungle. Conveniently, we spent our first night across the street from a popular gay watering hole.

Thus began a two-week adventure spent with a bus full of students and, thanks to Mark, great camaraderie. The monuments of a pre-Columbian age filled me with reverence for ancient civilizations. I was already well versed in colonial styles of architecture, from previous trips to Mexico and from my childhood in New Orleans. But the masonry and grand stone temples of the Maya impressed upon me the depth and achievement of Mesoamerican culture.

There was plenty of time for hijinks along the way, and team spirit built over the course of the trip. For instance, in the small town of San Cristóbal de las Casas, the itinerary called for a day of rest between visits to major Maya sites. As true New Orleanians, we spent the day splitting two cases of beer among ourselves.

When it came time to switch to something harder, we wandered into a bar that turned out to be an active movie set for a quite lewd film featuring a farmer's daughter! The experience of delving into the history and culture of the region was made even richer by the relationships we formed on the bus. I enjoyed being silly and cutting up with the students, and by the end of the trip we had grown into a family.

Little aspects of the countryside kept reminding me of Texas and Louisiana, particularly the Spanish fort of San José el Alto, in Campeche. And we were all lucky to have the tour end with a bang in the port city of Veracruz. Now over five hundred years old, Veracruz is an oceanside, sun-bleached city that serves as a vital link to the sea for the mountainous region inland. We arrived right during the big Independence Day celebration—which, as I've mentioned, happened to be my birthday! The whole town filled the streets: girls in bright, embroidered dresses, mariachi bands supporting virtuosic harp players, and rodeo shows with horses and bulls.

Upon nightfall, the party continued into the bars. I wanted to witness the big fireworks show, so I convinced a few of us to press on. Mark was there with his big beard, and I was sporting an NYPD t-shirt, since this was relatively soon after 9/11. Also with us was a student whose platinum blond hair made him look like a Backstreet Boy crossed with Ricky Martin. This was enough for the bouncers to start whispering among themselves. Soon, a decision was made. Escorted by two large men, we were seated right up front! Apparently the bouncers thought the blond student was a famous American singer, accompanied by his manager and security. Imagine that—they thought we were VIPs! As all the drag kings and queens in the club checked us out, I reflected on how wonderful this trip had been.

Something about Mexico awakens me. In all its variety, it's my happy place. The warmth of the people makes me feel at home, like I'm a kid in the safety of my Creole neighborhood all over again. Mexico City and Monterrey are hustle-and-bustle places with tall buildings like New York, whereas Guadalajara is much more laid back. And the Yucatán is a place apart—its own world, even as tourism seeps in. There's so much to love. The music is filled with passion; the Spanish, Aztec, and Maya architecture

Larry in Guadalajara, Mexico [1970]
COURTESY OF THE AUTHOR

Larry's Mexican sweetheart [1970]
COURTESY OF THE AUTHOR

is grand and impressive; and the landscapes are breathtaking, with soaring mountains, green jungles, and wide-open seas.

Mexico recalls for me the familiar patterns of my childhood. So much is the same: the pull of the church, the strength of the family, the heartiness of the food. Unfortunately, not all of the similarities are pleasant. The more time I spent in Mexico, the more I saw the same prejudice I knew so well from back home: the lighter and more affluent people looked down upon the darker-skinned and Indigenous peoples who had come down from the mountains. Native Mexicans have endured centuries of maltreatment by Spanish society: an old refrain that rhymes word for word with our experience in New Orleans. As an American tourist, it was all too easy to find myself in positions of unwarranted and unwanted privilege. Fortunately, my observations of racial prejudice only inspired me to learn more, to dig deeper. My awe in the presence of vast and intricate Maya ruins, my joy in the exuberance of Independence Day celebrations—I owe it all to the rich bedrock of culture formed by all the different colors of Mexican people.

All of these reflections swirled through my head in 2016, when I returned to Mexico City for my seventieth birthday. I had Pablo Escamilla and Charles Sydnor, great friends of mine from Houston, to thank for planning the trip. Pablo and I had been introduced by Annise Parker, the city's mayor from 2010 to 2016, during my period of activism in Houston. As I got to know Pablo, I learned that—like the best lawyers—he had the patience for arcane details and the tenacity to power through setbacks. Our politics are the same, and his steady pace is one of the big reasons he's been part of my life for so long. His sweetness is an extension of his reliability. We just click.

On this seventieth-birthday trip, we stayed at the St. Regis, not too far from the Angel of Independence monument. I got reacquainted with Chapultepec Castle, and we traipsed about the Zona Rosa, exploring the crowded alleys between the gay bars. Much remained familiar from earlier visits, but spaces once filled with young locals were now swarming with rich American queens, prime targets for the big muscle boys who could sniff out foreigners and trick them into a good time.

¡Dong! The clock struck midnight in the plaza, and I was snapped out of my contemplative mood. ¡Dong! The fireworks blasted. ¡Dong! "¡Viva Mexico!" we toasted. What a way to celebrate seventy years of life—with great friends, enfolded by the culture I so admire. I want to thank Mexico for continuing to be my paradise and inspiration. I still have so much to look forward to. Maybe one day, despite my bad ear, I might even learn to speak the Spanish language!

CHAPTER SEVEN / *Windy Times, Windy City*

Chicago brownstones [1941]

PHOTOGRAPH BY RUSSELL LEE
LIBRARY OF CONGRESS, PRINTS & PHOTOGRAPHS DIVISION, FARM SECURITY ADMINISTRATION / OFFICE OF WAR INFORMATION BLACK-AND-WHITE NEGATIVES

7

NEW ORLEANS AND CHICAGO, AS DIFFERENT AS THEY MAY SEEM, ARE TWO points on the same line. As much as I love the steamy heat of home, I've been lucky to spend many years in and out of the stiff Lake Michigan breezes of Chicago. Given Chicago's schizophrenic split between its endless Black plain in the South and its lily-white expanses to the north, it's nice to remember that Chicago's first non-Indigenous settler was Jean-Baptiste Pointe DuSable, a Haitian Black man who made his way north from New Orleans.

The area, which takes its name from the native word for wild garlic, had been known to European traders for some time when DuSable decided to settle a plot where the Chicago River meets Lake Michigan—not far from the bustle of the many Native American tribes who had traded vigorously with one another since antiquity. Many, many years later, Chicago had become a magnet for Black families. At the turn of the twentieth century,

Chicago's meatpacking plants, factories, and railroads were a big draw for sharecroppers fleeing tough conditions in the rural South. Another great migration would follow in the decades after the Second World War. Cultural opportunities, not just economic opportunities, attracted many of Louisiana's most talented figures: Louis Armstrong, Mahalia Jackson, the list goes on and on. In Chicago, ambitious New Orleanians could find a world of Black people who had created educational, cultural, and business institutions.

My first visit to Chicago, in the summer of 1960, came as John F. Kennedy was engaged in his quest for the presidency. As Catholics, we were excited by his youth and optimism. I sat in the back seat with my brother and sister as our family arrived in the shadow of the city's skyscrapers. Dad had driven straight through, as it wasn't really safe for Blacks to stop anywhere, and those motels that were available were below my mother's standards. Thus, it was a great relief to arrive at my cousin's house on the south side of Chicago.

Our cousin Vernel Fournier—he and my brother shared a first name—was a drummer with the famous Ahmad Jamal Trio, featured on their hit version of the jazz standard "Poinciana." Born in New Orleans, he was about my father's age, in his thirties. He had ventured north because everyone knew that the most talented New Orleans musicians were paid very well in racially integrated Chicago. He was a relative on Daddy's side of the family—his sister's child, part of the Fournier branch whose members often served as godparents to my line. Vernel had done really well for himself and lived in a brownstone, a stark contrast with the wooden shotgun houses back home. From the moment we pulled up at his house, I knew I had arrived in a different world! I had never met anyone like Vernel's Black neighbors, who spoke with the clearest diction and the widest vocabulary. I was amazed by the symphony of words one of his neighbors used to curse at a cat tearing up one of the gardens on that block of brownstones.

In celebration of our visit, Vernel's wife served a whole spread, real New Orleans food swimming in the richest butter and flavored by the hottest spices. It was common for the young men of the neighborhood, Pullman porters, to supply the entire South Side with the freshest bushels of iced Louisiana seafood, vegetables, Vaucresson sausage from the Seventh Ward, and other ingredients, thus ensuring that their gumbo tasted (almost) as good as ours did in the Tremé.

I felt like I was on some distant planet, where instead of fog there was clarity, and instead of black and white, there were colors. To start, we went to a large amusement park, with rides and adventures more thrilling and impressive than those at Pontchartrain Beach, the whites-only amusement park in New Orleans—and we were allowed in, no problem! To show Mom a good time and to educate the family, Dad took us all to a fancy restaurant on Lakeshore Boulevard where we were seated right away by the maître d'. Apart from Dad, who had served in France, it was our first time in an integrated restaurant. I had never eaten so close to that many fancy white diners! At the Chicago department stores, the salespeople would insist we try on all manner of outfits. At the museums, the docents would bend down and entertain the bored kids of every color. And we would spend every twilit evening running around Buckingham Fountain, with no one grimacing, inching away, or calling us "nigger"!

A new idea about race awoke within me. I was thirteen years old. If I could drink from any water fountain, ride in any seat, pee in any toilet, try on any shirt, and ride the most thrilling roller coasters here in Chicago, why couldn't I do that in New Orleans?

An environment like that can do wonders for your ego. There's nothing like the feeling that there's nothing wrong with you—that you're a human being, a somebody. The trip planted a seed that grew inside me, made me a believer, and brought me a powerful burst of energy and sense of dignity. It was an ideal time to visit that wonderful place—just as I was getting ready to enter high school. Thanks to that visit, I reoriented my aspirations toward equality and liberation. New plans and ideas took root within me.

In college I met some friendly white midwestern boys who spent the summer helping us at Xavier with an Upward Bound program. Liberal-minded, with a zeal for integration, they were more than happy to save the Negroes with support from the federal government. Their enthusiasm took them to the sugarcane fields out in the parishes around New Iberia and Lafayette. They would tutor youngsters to make sure they could thrive at Xavier, and we repaid their kindness with hospitality. They returned this hospitality when I visited Chicago a second time, in 1966.

Now a young man, I traveled by myself, on the train, looking forward to seeing Chicago again and meeting up with local civil rights leaders. Can you imagine my thoughts when, on the street outside my lodgings at a YMCA near North Halsted, I saw a smattering of drag queens? I had to double-check that I hadn't mixed up my reservation! It was my first experience of Chicago's Boystown. I had never seen drag queens so comfortable on the street and had no idea that the YMCA was popular with gay men.

The trip was otherwise wholesome, with waterskiing on Lake Michigan and American flags flying all along Michigan Avenue. It turned out that one of the friendly Chicago boys who had volunteered with the Upward Bound program was the son of a great, big industrialist, a state senator—and he had found the keys to his parents' lake house. He was quite generous, and I spent a wonderful summer weekend up north.

It had taken a while to grow into my skin as a gay man. Houston gays were quite a bit more sophisticated than New Orleans ones, and in Houston I had my first gay bosses. The Washington National Insurance job, initially supposed to last only a few weeks, had solidified into a career, providing me with a cushy lifestyle—and confidence in my ability to navigate a wide range of social and professional settings.

My job as a trainer took me all across the country and allowed me to revel in the unique characteristics of disparate gay communities. I soaked up the minutest of details and took pleasure in the endless variety of life: from the Italian *ragazzos* of Hackensack, New Jersey, to the *hombres* of

Riverside, California, to the mountain men of Allentown, Pennsylvania. Being the charmer that I am, I had enlisted the office secretaries in my secret mission. We figured out in advance where the festivals with the cutest boys would take place, and when. By some magic, my training schedule always aligned with the hot gay gatherings!

I did most of my traveling from my home base of Houston. But in the summer and fall of 1983, I settled in at the corporate seat, in Evanston, as an employee and guest of Washington National. My previous visits hadn't taught me much about the bars of Boystown, but this extended stay gave me a chance to explore the gayborhood on weekends. While AIDS stalked the land, Chicago had thus far been spared the worst of the nightmare striking the bigger circuit scenes of New York, San Francisco, or Los Angeles. As a result, I was able to experience Chicago in its fullness without worrying about being exposed to this virus.

Back in the Roaring Twenties, rising rents had pushed gays out of their enclave near the Water Tower and into the empty wilds along North Halsted Street. Lakeview and Wrigleyville had also attracted a large and active gay community starting in the 1960s; and thanks to a liberalizing trend in Illinois law, gay nightclubs were increasingly able to operate without fear of raids. The club scene grew and grew—and by the time I was exploring the city in the early '80s, highlights included Sidetrack, three times the size of any club in New Orleans, and many smaller, more intimate places where you could talk without screaming. Little Jim's was a leather bar popular with upper-middle-class Midwesterners who flocked to Boystown to escape the alienation of the suburbs. After the corporate workday was over, they would change from their suits into jeans, flannel, and leather. Their secret charm was making me forget I wasn't in my twenties any longer. Around the corner from Little Jim's was a trio of Latin-owned gay bars, sign of the city's growing Puerto Rican population.

Happily, the boys back then didn't have too much glitz. The neighborhood as a whole was humble and working class, and most of its denizens had rolled in from smaller towns, just happy to find a place of their own.

But there were fewer Black gays and lesbians than there should have been. The same "old time religion" that gave southern Blacks the strength to migrate from the Deep South often carried with it an unfortunately conservative outlook. You could find plenty of gay people in the church choir, but few of them were fully out. Black gays, at that time, looked upon the bar scene as a den of sin, just as they'd been taught in Sunday school. You could see the courage to stand up to religious judgment on the faces (and in the outfits) of the few African Americans you did find in Boystown at the time.

Like so many gay neighborhoods, in so many cities, Boystown eventually got too expensive for working-class gays. Now rechristened Northalsted, even the local bathhouse is as high-end as the new condos. That said, boys from all over town—some from the South Side, some Mexican, some Polish, some even Uzbek—can be found in the 'hood, bundled up in heavy coats on winter weeknights or on display in short shorts when the longest days of summer arrive. Thanks to many generations, one can literally retrace history while ambling up and down the avenue past the bars, pubs, theaters, and clubs of Northalsted.

Can you believe I didn't stroll the Miracle Mile on my own until I was thirty-five? Thirty-five! Chicago always has something more for me to discover. It is a beautiful city with great landscaping and grand skyscrapers. I just wish the people had as much snap! Although it's a cosmopolitan city, Chicago still attracts many from its own backyard—and I'll never get used to the Midwestern habit of avoiding loud, showy, or contentious communication. That's not exactly how I grew up.

I'm an explorer, and I pride myself on the ability to blend in, wherever I go. But Chicago tested me. The city is large and segregated—so divided into neighborhoods, each with its own ethnic identity, that a New Orleans–style gumbo never forms. In the heart of gay Chicago, my color, style, and texture struck many as seductive—but once I left the comforts of Boystown, I stood out so much, it got uncomfortable.

I found Evanston to be friendlier than Chicago. Even back then, it was a progressive sort of place—and in 2021, it would be the first city in the nation to pay reparations to qualified Black residents. Many of the Evanston friends I made in the '80s were Jewish. I would meet them in the stores, at the company headquarters, at the hotel—and we instantly formed a bond. They were survivors!

In the end, I never felt tempted to settle in Chicago: a continental winter is far different than a coastal one, with a cold that can last from July to July, and a near-hurricane-force breeze that forms thirty-foot-tall snowdrifts. In the depths of winter, everyone is bundled up and busy, everyone's a stranger, and no one says hi. In the summer, it's wonderful to see so many thousands of people out and about, enjoying their few days of relief from the cold-ass weather. But even then, there are fewer opportunities for serendipitous encounters. When good weather is rare, why share it with strangers?

However, Chicago remains a special place for me—a witness to the full arc of my growth. As a child, I loved Chicago. As an activist, I loved the energy, the protests, the freedom. As a young executive, the city filled me with confidence, for Chicago was my career headquarters. As a lover, I felt the warm embrace of Chicago's hospitality. And I'm grateful for the friends I still have in Chicago. In 2009, in town to celebrate Halloween, I strolled the Loop and reflected on the nearly half-century since my first visit. As the waters of the Chicago River flowed beneath me, memories flooded back—and I was transformed into a thirteen-year-old boy, marveling at the tall skyscrapers and taking their dare to straighten my back, lift up my chin, and take a deep breath. Chicago does that to me every time.

CHAPTER EIGHT / *California, Here I Come*

Larry (second from right) with friends at San Francisco's Civic Center Plaza during Gay Pride weekend [1972]
COURTESY OF THE AUTHOR

8

THE SPANISH IMPRINT ON LOUISIANA, THOUGH LESS PUBLICIZED THAN THE French, is strong. We were a Spanish colony for four decades, and following the Louisiana Purchase, we became the southwestern border of the young American republic, adjoining Spanish Texas across a wild "neutral ground."

During the same era that Louisiana was a Spanish colony, the Roman Catholic Church was building a network of missions up and down the California coast. Across Latin America, the Spanish Inquisition had a mandate to root out perversity—and the English-speaking administrations that followed brought similar intolerant attitudes, bolstering and enforcing laws that criminalized homosexual acts. Whether these laws would be enforced by the US government remained to be seen; the remote frontier, deserts, mountains, and plains of California might as well have been on a different planet.

At the start of the gold rush, in 1848, San Francisco's population hovered around 1,000. But within a few months, the city doubled in size, then doubled again, expanding so quickly that within two winters, the population had reached 25,000. The Forty-Niners lived on the decks of old ships and in tents and shanties of all shapes and sizes. In this flood of young men, animated in equal parts by anticipation, greed, and desperation, you can imagine that anything went.

The massive influx of newly arrived strangers—overwhelmingly men, far away from their past lives—made it easy for those who wished to, to assume the role of women, cross-dress, find boyfriends, and live with new names. Soon, same-sex households and masquerade balls proliferated. Those few women who joined the migration sometimes took advantage of the chaos to dress as men to fit in. With literal boatloads of strangers arriving every hour, day and night, rules were broken and rewritten. And so the world's most famous gay capital was birthed.

Over the course of the next century, authorities would strain to reestablish the norms of the old world. Crusades for decency and calls for cleansing were commonplace in San Francisco, with its plethora of nasty little bars along the Barbary Coast. The pattern may sound familiar to anyone familiar with the history of Storyville and the French Quarter of New Orleans. City government, beholden to upright citizens but covetous of adult-industry tax dollars, issued ever-shifting rules, cycling between enforcement and permissiveness, crackdown and decadence. During World War II, the feds cleaned up the Barbary Coast businesses in an effort to control sexually transmitted diseases among servicemen. By the mid-twentieth century, much of the city's gay activity had drifted into the North Beach and Chinatown neighborhoods overlooking the Bay to the east. The end of World War II would bring a fresh wave of boys with nowhere to go and no particular rush to get moving. For those who sought release, San Francisco offered a growing world of LGBTQ+ neighborhoods, networks, and lovers welcoming them in with open arms.

War's end brought thousands of men back from overseas, and many found their way to the seedy streets of the Tenderloin. Toward the water was the famous Black Cat Bar, home of beatniks and nonconformists. On the other side was Polk Street, the original fashionable track for the "blue slip" crowd of discharged military soldiers. It was from this neighborhood that José Sarria, a drag queen, first ran for the city's Board of Supervisors in 1961—shocking the establishment by winning 6,000 votes. It was on these streets that Virginia Prince, now living as a woman, distributed her *Transvestia* magazine. And it was here that the infamous police raids took place—targeting the Daughters of Bilitis, the Mattachine Society, and more throughout the early 1960s. The community celebrated when trans women fought back against police at Compton's Cafeteria, in 1966. These events all predated Stonewall—and while all were prompted by repression, and all resulted in pain, the collective imagination was sparked by a new sense of promise.

After a few years of making regular money, in 1972 I set out for San Francisco to attend my very first Pride parade. Nothing will ever match the excitement of arriving in downtown San Francisco and checking into the Hotel Californian in the Tenderloin, at 403 Taylor Street. Boy, was the Tenderloin seedy! Named after the famous district in New York and tucked in a valley between other San Francisco attractions, the neighborhood has been a den of gambling and sin since the Gold Rush. I found the performers and hustlers quite friendly, with an atmosphere that rivaled the French Quarter, even if the architecture could not. The Tenderloin not only held restaurants, halls, and gay bars, but a diverse population as well. The cheap rent had attracted multiple waves of Asian immigrants and refugees—and as I walked the streets I felt a familiar flush of curiosity. Such diverse people, all enjoying one another's company, inspired visions of a new world. Although most of the hippies were over in Haight-Ashbury, the entire city had a touch of that Flower Power spirit. I'd only been in California a day, and I loved it already.

As I was settling in, who did I bump into? A Purple Knight! So far from St. Augustine High School, and yet here was one of my brother's friends, who had graduated three years after I did. Tyrone had always been very comfortable with his sexuality and was doing quite well on the West Coast. He had even been lucky enough to bag one of the most illustrious drag queens on the scene. A wedding was imminent. What an unheard-of idea! They were to be my first gay "married" couple, and they were living life to the fullest. But first it was time to celebrate Pride '72, and together we headed to the Castro!

As bustling Market Street descends from the soaring, ferry-side skyscrapers of the Financial District, the thoroughfare passes through the rough Tenderloin, then rises gently until it turns crooked at the morning side of the saddle between the Twin Peaks. There lies the Castro, the world's most famous gay and lesbian neighborhood.

Eureka is the name of the valley the Castro sits in, a touch above the historically Spanish-speaking Mission District. Back when the Castro was still countryside, its first plots were occupied by Scandinavian settlers, with Finnish sailors establishing taverns. Italians, Irish, and other ethnic whites moved in as the neighborhood was built up—and then, as they took flight for the suburbs, the gays began to take root.

By the 1960s, word had spread of free love, cheap drugs, and cheaper housing in and around Eureka. Gays spotted an opportunity to fix up homes and grow their own communal family—and they found solidarity with the sexually liberated, antiwar, and anti-establishment leanings of the early hippies nearby in the Haight. Soon the neighborhood was anchored by a gay watering hole, the Missouri Mule, and galvanized by activists like the lesbian pioneers Del Martin and Phyllis Lyon.

And now here I was, standing with my friends at the corner of Castro and Market, the heart of the gay community. I could hardly believe it. With Pride celebrations underway, the city was buzzing with gay men looking for romance. Thankfully, I wasn't a stranger! I was part of the

Gay wedding ceremony, San Francisco [1972]
COURTESY OF THE AUTHOR

grand entourage of one of the most imitated drag queens in the city. We went from bar to bar as cherished guests, making friends old and new, and it wasn't long before I had set my sights on a certain someone. Before the end of the evening we were a festival couple, and my schedule was set for the next six days.

My timing was great: on Friday, Tyrone and his husband-to-be took me up to the Haight to play, visit, and gawk at the last of the hippies. The next day, Saturday, they headed to Golden Gate Park to make their love a show for the world to see. They had rented eight limousines, with eight drag queen bridesmaids in gowns and eight groomsmen in full tuxedos. Their marriage certainly wasn't legal, but it didn't matter. This wasn't the first time I'd seen two men so in love that they wanted to spend their whole lives together. But it was the first time I had grasped the idea that two men could marry—each other!

Sunday was the big Pride parade, and then on Monday night, after a ferry ride to Sausalito, the couple held a ball back in San Francisco, at the Fairmont. The gay drag court system is filled with grandeur and pettiness—a culture so intricate that I sometimes swore they'd copied the whole routine off our Gay Mardi Gras krewes. Since I never travel without a white suit, I was assigned to be one queen's escort the whole night. I was a perfect gentleman.

After the public reception, we returned to the Castro and partied until four in the morning, when the bars closed. Just as my Creole community had its rituals and superstitions, I could see that an alternative liturgy of traditions was growing up in California. Here, united by our queerness, we could share ties with family of all different shades and backgrounds. What a wonderful introduction to San Francisco, with memories to savor upon my return to Houston.

After World War II, members of my own extended family had felt the calling to go west, leaving New Orleans for Los Angeles. We kept in touch by mail and phone calls, as they settled into a nice suburban life—and while they paid the occasional visit home to Louisiana, my parents had never made it out to the West Coast, themselves.

That all changed in 1973. I had just started to hit my stride with Washington National when I was invited to Las Vegas for the Western Territorial Sales Conference, at the Sands Hotel. This was a milestone for me—and a testament to my parents, who had nurtured in me the strength to confront the world. And so I surprised my mom, dad, and baby sister Gina with a free trip to California, making sure the tickets would arrive by mail on June 21, my sister's tenth birthday. They would have a chance to visit the California side of the family, and then—while Gina stayed with the cousins—my parents and I would enjoy Las Vegas together.

It all went off like clockwork. My boss and office manager, A. J. Massey, had become good friends with my parents when they visited Houston. He made all the Vegas arrangements and made sure they had seats at the convention's keynote event: a Wayne Newton concert in the hotel's Copa Room. Following the convention, the three of us flew back to Los Angeles together—but not before creating one final Vegas memory. My mother hit the jackpot on a slot machine in the terminal and boarded the plane with piles of quarters pouched in her skirt!

The family reunion meant the world to my parents, and it also gave me a chance to explore Southern California's gay capital for the first time. It was fascinating to compare the gay bars of L.A. and the ones I had seen in San Francisco, Houston, and New Orleans. I was surprised how much they all had in common, despite the geographic divides.

Los Angeles plays an outsize role in gay history. It was the original home of the Mattachine Society, an early activist and benevolent society that later spread to well-to-do, white enclaves of other big cities. The pioneering, gay-affirming Metropolitan Community Church was born in Los Angeles—founded by Troy Perry, later to become one of my dearest friends. But all things considered, I find L.A. a bit too spread out. And so, while I enjoyed catching up with my cousins, the city's geography made it hard to spend time with my family of choice, the gay community.

My second trip to San Francisco came in September 1978. I had an appointment with the great Harvey Milk, the country's highest-ranking openly gay elected official. I had met Harvey just a few months earlier, in June, in Houston, when he came to raise money for his "No on Six" campaign to combat the Briggs Initiative.

Harvey's vital message to the movement was that we had to come out and show everyone the fullness of our lives in order to achieve equality. His exhortation to live one's truth still moves me today—and at that banquet in Houston he had noticed the tears in my eyes. Through Ray Hill, he reached out to me, and we giggled over the progress of our gay lives, careers, and romances. Because of our shared resolve in the fight, he invited me to join his office for a weeklong internship.

It was bound to be a great learning experience, but it was also an excuse to see the country. I was growing older, and part of finding myself was finding connections among dispersed gay communities. And so I took some time off the insurance beat, found a travel companion in my old teacher, Professor Schaffer, and we set off on an eight-week journey in my Mercury Marquis. Both of us were galvanized by the activism occurring all over the country, and we wanted to explore the state of gay rights across the land. As the gay movement gained steam, conservative forces were pushing back with efforts across the country to root out gay teachers—open or closeted—from their jobs. Referendums had already been passed in places like Florida and Eugene, Oregon. That fire had raged into California.

Professor Schaffer and I started by traveling to Albuquerque, and then saw the Painted Desert, the Grand Canyon, Las Vegas, Pueblo, and Denver before continuing on to Salt Lake City, where we visited the Mormon complexes. This was the first time I had seen much of the American West by road, and we were sure to stop in every gay bar we could find. We drove on to Boise and Seattle, and even made a deviation to Vancouver, British Columbia. In our travels, we observed not only the terrain but also the whole tapestry of gay life in the Western part of the continent, in small towns and in large cities.

Once we arrived in Canada, our plan was to trace scenic Highway 101 down the coast. Professor Schaffer had his own plans to visit wine country, while I drove on to San Francisco. The first time I had gazed upon San Francisco's City Hall was during the Pride March of 1972; now, in the fall of 1978, I was invited inside that magnificent building.

No one ever forgets the first time they see City Hall. Built in the aftermath of the infamous fire of 1906, it opened in 1915. Its dome soars even taller than that of the US Capitol in Washington, DC, and drips with gold leaf. Inside, staircases of marble amplify shouts and whispers alike, and large windows overlook the hilly city. The sound of cackles and giggles led me through the corridors to Harvey's office and the wonderful sight of Harvey being himself! His office had a view of the parking lot, and he was surrounded by piles and piles of paper. It was exhilarating to watch him work the phones and coach his staff. He was abundantly real, and comfortable with himself, although some aspects of the scene were shocking to my Creole sensibilities! One office guest, clearly a favorite of his, was a kind of woman I had never seen before, let alone in a government office: a woman clad head to toe in motorcycle leather, with long, blonde hair spilling out from under her helmet. She joined the parade of local characters who would march in and out of the building, often escorted by Harvey's boyfriend and campaign manager, Scott Smith. I now look back on this era as tragically innocent. There was little security between us and the street.

Harvey was excited to take me on a tour of the Castro. In just the few years since my first visit, the neighborhood had grown gayer and teemed with new businesses. Harvey's Castro Camera store was, of course, the first stop. It was the headquarters of his whole operation. All manner of neighbors and characters streamed in and out, just like they did at City Hall. From there, we stopped by the Midnight Sun on the same block, the original Toad Hall the next block over, and Nothing Special across the street. Wherever he went, Harvey was greeted as a rock star, and in return he would present his constituents with special City Hall proclamations inscribed with each owner's and bar manager's name. It was easy for Harvey to arrange these honors, as he knew all the right secretaries and had the backing of Mayor George Moscone. Yet for people who were used to being illegal, used to running seedy, blacked-out holes, and used to negotiating with the mafia for financing and with the police on raids, nothing felt better than even the most token recognition of their contributions to the community. I would borrow this idea from Harvey years later, when working in New Orleans city government, and I would bestow recognition upon community leaders in the French Quarter and beyond. The looks on recipients' faces were always the same: eyes wide with a mix of surprise and gratitude.

This wasn't the only tactic I learned from Harvey Milk. One morning we were heading out of the building in a rush when he spotted a pile of dog poop. He asked me to take note of it, which I found bewildering. Later that day, he was scheduled to issue a proclamation—which, I soon found out, was concerned with street cleaning. He made sure the press was on hand to witness his trotting off, after delivering the proclamation, right into the puppy waste! He lifted the sole of his shoe in the direction of the press, as if by accident, to underscore his point. When I say he was a natural, I mean it was clear he had the game down in the womb!

Harvey had the kind of touch that made everyone feel that he had known them for years. Larger than life, he was also quite down to earth, a man both charismatic and relatable. He represented all of us. Together with Troy Perry of the Metropolitan Community Church, he had provided inspirational leadership for groups around the country fighting the heinous Briggs Initiative. As a young man with political aspirations, I couldn't have asked for a better role model. My weeklong internship ended, and it was time for me to get back on the road, but the lessons I learned from Harvey Milk have stuck with me for a lifetime.

Later that fall, the Briggs Initiative would be put to a vote and would fail, even in its sponsor's own Orange County. Even Ronald Reagan,

Larry with Harvey Milk, San Francisco City Hall [1978]
COURTESY OF THE AUTHOR

the conservative former governor and future president, opposed it. Nationwide, the gay community breathed a sigh of relief. That relief, however, would soon turn to tears.

Dan White was a retired US Army sergeant who had worked briefly as a cop and a fireman. He came to represent a conservative, Catholic, primarily Irish and Italian district as a member of the city's Board of Supervisors—where he established himself as an opponent of his fellow supervisor, Harvey Milk. Among other complaints, White was unhappy that a halfway house for juvenile offenders, promoted by Milk and the mayor, was being built in his neighborhood. He was dissatisfied with city politics in general and gay liberation tactics in particular.

In November 1978, White submitted his resignation from the board—but then, having changed his mind, he slipped back into City Hall, avoiding the metal detectors, and pleaded with Mayor Moscone to let him back on the board. By then it was too late. An argument ensued, and while the mayor lit a cigarette and poured a pair of drinks, White took out a revolver, shot, and pierced Moscone's lung. With the mayor dead behind him, White sought out Milk, whom he invited into an office for a chat. It is there that Milk was murdered with five bullets, the first in his wrist as he defended himself, the last in his skull.

White turned himself in hours later. At trial he claimed that on the day he shot the men, he couldn't think clearly due to emotional duress. A sympathetic jury found him guilty of voluntary manslaughter instead of murder, and White was given a sentence of less than eight years for killing Moscone and Milk. The gay community in San Francisco gathered by City Hall to mourn that night, and when police attacked them with billy clubs, they fought back. After that scene was brought under control, a group of police officers retaliated by rampaging in the Castro District.

When the news of Milk's death broke, I was in Houston. I took it personally! I was sad and scared and retraumatized. All the old feelings I thought I'd put behind me—of being in the closet and of being bashed—came flooding back. I was inconsolable. Thank goodness, my mom was there to answer my call! I had convinced myself that I would go to the memorial in San Francisco—but knowing how out of control I get when I am angry, she talked me out of it. She reminded me that I was needed in Houston, as a vigil was forming. So in my grief, as mourners began to file into Houston's City Hall plaza, I invited a friend with a guitar to play "Imagine" by John Lennon while I gave the best speech I could to my neighbors in the community.

Through all of this—the murder, the riots, the marches—Harvey Milk was still both a saint and an ordinary man in my eyes. This was so when he was alive but also after he died, even as my grief continued to unfold moment by moment, each day an eternity. Neither I nor anyone I knew could have imagined a future in which these stories would be written in history books and made the subject of big Hollywood productions. Looking back, I feel very thankful to be part of that history. But that's the funny thing about the people who inspire you and the work you push, wholeheartedly and sleeplessly and without guarantee of success—history only feels like history after it becomes History.

In the years after Harvey Milk's assassination I would return often to San Francisco: to reunite with comrades over drinks and memories, to attend National Pride meetings, and to work with fellow Democrats to birth a new gay caucus within our party. It was organizational meetings held in San Francisco that made each March on Washington—in 1979, 1987, and 1993—so well attended by the LGBTQ+ community from coast to coast.

When it was cheap, the city was home to all manner of gays, from barefoot to buttoned-up. Castro was the sun, but many satellites existed in each corner of the fog-swept peninsula. You could have a complete gay experience in the rough-and-tumble Tenderloin in the company of sailors and beatniks. The famous (and famously nasty) Folsom Street Fair would take place in the South of Market district. Leather bars had stemmed from the old military bars on the Embarcadero, and the leather scene was already quite established as early as the late 1950s and early 1960s.

Like fireflies, the push and pull of housing, neighbors, and communities oscillates slowly until in the blink of an eye, the rents rise, and generations of friends wake up in a world no longer theirs. Always a gold rush town, San Francisco has attracted successive waves of tech companies since the 1990s, with astronomically salaried kids happy to hand over exorbitant rents for crowded and dilapidated housing. Your world is split and split again, with buyers willing to pay any price, in cash, with added zeros, and old landlords ready to cash out. Or even older landlords, out of touch with long-gone handymen, afraid to sell, for there is nowhere left to buy. Children of the elite impose a new order of life handled entirely through convenient but impersonal apps. When change happens quickly, no one is ever taught the courtesy of checking in with the elders and their grandkids. I mourn for the systems and traditions that nurtured the formerly fertile, artistic, and loved patches of land.

Today gays can live almost anywhere, and queers are even more widespread. We're more a spectrum than a village. I suppose it's what I fought for. The younger LGBTQ+ communities melt into their own shades and scenes, indistinguishable from the straights. Grindr, founded in West Hollywood, makes cruising possible and "convenient" everywhere. One thing, however, that unites the entire spectrum is the high cost of living. You can be anything you want, provided that you're compensated well, which usually requires a good degree and better connections. From there you can go goth or Harajuku and beyond. No longer can San Francisco be a magnet to the poor GI or the small-town fairy, willing to sweep floors and clean toilets in the day just to strike fierce lewks and fall in love at night. Maybe Modesto is still affordable. Maybe remote work will eventually clear the city out or calcify its residents.

Despite it all, the California Dream remains golden. There is a poetry in the misty vineyards and sunny peaks that beckons to lost souls. We follow the sun all the way to the end of its route and find a place—thanks to the warmth of its weather and the illusion of empty land—where rules seem flexible and the hangups of the East Coast and Old Europe can be forgotten. No matter that the dream remains but a dream, and reality washes in and out with the tides, California remains an open promise.

Often, in my mind, I imagine myself in Mission Dolores Park. When the mists of the morning clear up, I reunite with true comrades who span the seasons of my life and bring along a new date from the night before. We cart out our wicker basket, lay a blanket on the grass, drink champagne in plastic flutes, with dollops of caviar, and pass around generously rolled joints. We look on and smile at the sight of the children of our community as they gallop and frolic in their freedom under the California sun.

CHAPTER NINE / *Yankee Doodle Dandy*

Larry and Susan Clade, March on Washington [1987]
COURTESY OF THE AUTHOR

9

NEW ORLEANS REVELS IN ITS HAUGHTY ATTITUDE AS IT STANDS APART from Anglo-Protestant America. We presume that if we outlasted the French and the Spanish, perhaps we will outlast America, too. But New Orleanians can be provincial—and I've been fortunate to have expanded my own perspective through travels in the Northeast, an old land with its own lineages and contradictions, influenced by both the worldly fashions of Europe and the Victorian mores of England. It is home to the oldest lines of commerce, privilege, and society in the US, as well as large, anonymous cities of immigrants funneling in and out. It is a busy place, with important responsibilities and down-low hustles, yet also a place for artists ambitious to carve a life apart from, against, and within the old power structures.

My travels in the Northeast renewed my civic awareness by allowing me to commune with the most profound symbols of our enlightened republic.

When it was time for fun, I was happy to visit seaside towns, which line the coast like little buttons on a shirtfront, from Provincetown to Fire Island to Asbury Park. These towns came into being as escapes from a society that kept queer communities tight-laced. Here, before we had words to describe gays and lesbians, men and women stepped away from the hustle and bustle, put on shorts and bathing suits, and faced the salty Atlantic, ready to fall in love.

My experiences in this part of the world granted historical perspective to my activism. The Northeast has been the stage for many of the LGBTQ+ community's grandest triumphs and starkest defeats; coming from the South, I needed to shuttle up and down this corridor to learn its history before I could write my own.

In the popular imagination, the colonial era is full of Puritans, decked out in sober garb, doing their best to crimp everyone's style. But the story is more complicated than that. The historical record reveals more radical forms of expression—sects organized around the tenets of pansexuality and interracial free love—as well as warm and emotional, if not explicitly romantic, correspondence among all manner of Founding Fathers. One of our nation's revolutionary heroes, Baron Friedrich Wilhelm von Steuben, has been adopted by many as an early gay hero. A Prussian, the baron was recruited to the US by Ben Franklin himself, who admired his martial confidence and waved away rumors of his dalliances. Von Steuben arrived in America at the age of forty-seven, accompanied by a young male secretary thirty years his junior, and got right to work whipping the Continental Army into shape. Known for his flamboyance and his gallantry, he modernized the American approach to warfare and sanitation. He was a tough commander who let nothing slip, drilling his troops with a keen eye for any missteps. The same uncompromising attitude followed him as he inspected soldiers' quarters to ensure that they were clean and well kept, knowing that he could not stand to lose the next battle due to pestilence and disease.

Finally, when night fell and everything was in order, this soldier's soldier was more than happy to socialize with men from the whole chain of command, whom he invited to parties in his tent. In time, he adopted two of his favorites, officers in their twenties, ensuring—in a time when sodomy was illegal and widely considered repugnant—that his favorite lovers would be taken care of by his estate.

It has taken a long time for this hidden history to surface. The notion that gays and lesbians contributed to building this country, despite being confined to the closet, is still controversial for many people. The United States was built on the ideals of equality, liberty, and unity. To achieve the promise of our national motto—E pluribus unum—in our fallible world, we must fight together for more inclusive institutions, norms, and laws.

By participating in the process of government, I am reaffirming my rights, under the Bill of Rights and the Constitution, to include myself as an equal citizen, both as a Black man and as a gay man. Quietly, our closeted gay and lesbian forebears provided a road map for those of us who have followed. An abundance of senators, vice presidents, at least one chief executive, and many Daughters of the Revolution helped build a foundation for civic participation—even if who they loved had to remain a secret.

With a life of public service ahead, eager to affirm my citizenship as a proud gay American, I embarked on my first trip to Philadelphia in 1972. I wanted to see the Liberty Bell, the Constitution, the Bill of Rights, and Independence Hall. The 1960s had been a tumultuous time as the country lurched past the spasms of civil rights, antiwar activism, women's rights, and gay rights. I wanted to see if I could find myself relating to the emergencies the Founding Fathers had faced. I thoroughly enjoyed playing tourist and hearing stories of the hot, sloppy summers and frigid, miraculous battles of the Revolution.

I was fortunate to have a pair of lesbian friends, Marian and Janet, to show me around Philly, where I was struck by the mix of Anglos, Italians, Puerto Ricans, and Blacks. In the Philadelphia Freedom days of the early gay rights struggle in the 1960s, everyone seemed to blend together well, and I found the city's intimate, gritty, working-class mix to be among the more diverse I had found on the East Coast. My friends also let me in on the word-of-mouth gay beaches of Atlantic City, with our kind cruising above and under the boardwalk.

Gay Philadelphia centered around the artsy corners and theaters of Center City, though segregation left Black gays to attend their own private parties on the north and west sides of town. The Gayborhood grew out of Rittenhouse Square, with its beatnik crowd, and toward the flashy theaters, bars, and fashion houses of Washington Square West. I enjoyed wandering around these parts and admiring the colonial architecture. Even before Stonewall, Philadelphia's gays and lesbians had been in the forefront of the liberation movement, and I couldn't help attributing the city's spirit of tolerance to the early influence of the Quakers.

Stonewall had sparked a widespread desire for collective action—and the idea for a National March on Washington for Lesbian and Gay Rights was born at a 1973 meeting in Urbana-Champaign. Momentum built over the course of the decade, but the power brokers in New York and San Francisco couldn't agree on anything. Eventually, the parties agreed to hold a planning meeting at a neutral location, and what better location than the birthplace of liberty? So in February 1979—in the wake of Harvey Milk's assassination—the national steering committee met in Philadelphia.

Steve Shiflett represented our Houston contingent in Philly. He found comfort in the company of the West Coast delegates, a well-to-do professional crowd with high-culture aspirations. That's right—contrary to what one might expect, many of the California attendees were conservative! The East Coast delegates, in contrast, were what we'd now call woke: veteran hippies who pushed for a more radical agenda. With some details left unresolved in Philadelphia, Houston—another geographically neutral site—was selected to host a July 1979 meeting to smooth out differences.

At that July meeting, the Third World Committee—a group of gay activists of color—rose in prominence. Unhappy with the white-led activism of the gay Republican contingent, this counterforce grew to include Black and brown gays and lesbians. The Third World Committee was adamant about leading the march, and they threatened to walk out if their demands weren't met. I found their logic unimpeachable. Many LGBTQ+ people live in countries where it's even more dangerous to be out than it is in America—and outreach to those populations was essential. The Third World members wanted visibility because their representation mattered. They wanted to show that gays were everywhere. Ray Hill asked me to organize this new group, ensure they were unified in their demands, and broadcast the messages they agreed upon.

While the minority activists ultimately won, it took some effort for me to persuade Steve Shiflett and the other Houston delegates of the legitimacy of their cause. Many white delegates operated under the assumption that we already lived in a fair democracy, so it was only natural for Alabama, at the start of the alphabet, to lead the procession. The Third World Committee, however, wisely intuited that a mass of queer people of color, spanning many continents, was waiting to be activated. Because the key to our strategy was getting numbers in the streets, we needed to fill our ranks with women, trans people, and Black and brown people. So determined were we to expand the movement that we invited a white trans woman, Phyllis Frye, to give rousing speeches about why women and people of color were vital to our movement. Many years later, Frye was appointed by Mayor Annise Parker to serve as a Houston municipal judge.

After six years of planning, the time had come for the March on Washington. On a frigid evening in October 1979, I checked into a Holiday Inn in DC with my fellow queer Texans. Like an invading army, we raised the Lone Star flag to let the world know we had arrived and headed over to the DC Eagle bar. Marching in with a Texas flag, we were greeted by

Mayor Marion Barry himself. The atmosphere was electric! Years of nurturing the roots of the movement had finally resulted in a blooming flower.

The next day, I offered up a quiet personal prayer at the Washington National Cathedral, and then caught up with my friends to make our way to the opening party. The site was rich in symbolism: the Daughters of the American Revolution Constitution Hall, on C Street, just off the National Mall and across the street from the Department of the Interior. In 1939, the DAR had refused to let soprano Marian Anderson perform at their hall—and now, forty years later, we purposefully selected a masterful Black lesbian activist from San Francisco named Pat Norman to emcee the function.

For such a history-laden location, I was surprised by how pedestrian the hall was. It reminded me of a Schwegmann's grocery store. Wit and high spirits tempered the solemnity of the occasion. As my friends in the Louisiana delegation marched into the hall behind a banner depicting the Pelican in Her Piety, I heard some gays behind me ask, catty as ever, "Now, which state has that mosquito on their flag?"

The chilly weather was no deterrent as the city filled with a hundred thousand gay people, in every color of the rainbow, ready to meet old and new friends. As Sunday, October 14, dawned, there was my tribe, as far as the eye could see. Surrounded by friends in the bright, forty-degree sunshine, we marched with fifty Texas state flags, another one of my festive ideas, to make us look like the biggest delegation around.

Honestly, the speakers that weekend could have said anything, and I would have been thrilled. There were so many of us, finally out of the closet, forming the largest gathering of gay people in world history. The size of the crowd made us feel invincible, like we were finally on the winning side. So many touching and silly moments happened that weekend. My dear friend the Reverend Troy Perry brought a contingent of gays to tour the Carter White House. The Christian papers, of course, made a big stink about the cowboy who wore leather chaps on the tour—and their coverage attempted to downplay the size of our crowd. So forever more,

Larry with Texas delegation, March on Washington [1979]
FILE COURTESY OF HOUSTONLGBTHISTORY.ORG

Larry with friends, March on Washington [1979]
COURTESY OF THE AUTHOR

I say a million of us were there! No matter how many actually attended, each one of us carried four or more of our friends in spirit. I claim the right to blow up our numbers as much as our opponents have tried to diminish our crowd. On that day, it didn't matter. We were all there, together and unstoppable, and so we cried: "We're here, we're queer! Get used to it!"

The gay history of Washington, DC, long predates the 1979 march. Many historians have speculated that President James Buchanan, the only bachelor president in US history, was gay—even though strong homosocial friendships were not terribly unusual in his day. His writings and estate stay mum. The city's leading LGBTQ+ health clinic, Whitman-Walker, pays tribute to the queer and healing identities of two other nineteenth-century pioneers—famous author Walt Whitman, a transplant to Washington and a Civil War medic, and Dr. Mary Edwards Walker, a Civil War surgeon.

Gay life in Washington bloomed in the twentieth century, only to wither and then bloom once more. Just as the two world wars brought thousands of young men to ports like New York or San Francisco, thousands of new government workers came to DC as the New Deal expanded the size of the federal government. Gays and lesbians found a welcoming environment: the city was home to some of the earliest lesbian bars and gay bookstores, and despite segregation, some of the oldest African American gay bars—the latter serving an affluent Black middle class that grew up in DC after the Civil War. Indeed, in 1991 DC would host the nation's first-ever Black Pride event, a tribute to the strength of the community.

But in the postwar years, it was still illegal to be gay—and as politics is a routinely brutal game, those angling for power needed to climb upon a few heads and shoulders to further their rise. Thus, the Lavender Scare, in the wake of the Red Scare, was the ideal excuse to purge gays and lesbians from government—and for many, there was no difference between communists and perverts. Lafayette Square, in front of the White House, was a popular gay cruising spot. One day in 1953, a nervous nerd perked up at the sight of a buff young man taking interest in him, only to discover that he was a cop. Busted for solicitation, that young man turned out to be the son of a US senator. While the case was quietly thrown out, the senator's political enemies found out and threatened to publicize the situation. Senator Lester C. Hunt ended up shooting himself in his Capitol Hill office, overwhelmed by disgrace.

Over the years, I would come to know many of the men and women affected by the Lavender Scare. In the 1980s I served on the board of the National Gay and Lesbian Task Force with Frank Kameny, who in 1957 was fired from the Army Map Service because he was gay. He was the first person to make a civil rights claim in the US courts based on sexual orientation, and he played a key role in convincing the American Psychiatric Association to drop homosexuality from its manual of mental disorders. I met other pioneers who had organized the first picket lines of federal workers in the 1950s, and succeeding generations who protested and violently pushed back against government inaction on AIDS.

I was proud to participate in the 1979 march, but what felt then like the start of something inevitable would come, over time, to feel more halting. No matter—I continued to take pleasure in each visit to Washington. I always loved visiting the monuments, including new installations like the Martin Luther King Jr. memorial on the Tidal Basin. The city's nightlife expanded in lockstep with its growing gay and lesbian population. The professional types would gather in the bars and restaurants around Dupont Circle, like JR's, although I always preferred the DC Eagle, downtown, for its welcoming, laid-back vibe. In the city's southwest and southeast sectors you could find all manner of lesbian bars. Despite the risk of harassment from the nearby Marine barracks, large, popular clubs attracted gays from all over to these waterfront neighborhoods.

The founding of the Human Rights Campaign, or HRC, in 1980 seemed to herald an era of new political clout for gay activism. The tragedies that followed—the drug and AIDS epidemics of the 1980s—were compounded by the reemergence, following the election of Ronald Reagan, of the Anita

Bryant crowd we thought we had defeated for good. Grit and gravity, not jubilation, were the dominant notes of the second March on Washington, in 1987. Thanks to the government's silence on AIDS and its dismissal of our community, so many comrades from our first march were gone by the second.

The neighborhood around the convention center, full of welcoming bars in 1979, seemed emptier now, and the city felt a bit more dangerous. We had to stick together, and I stuck with my tribe—this time around, members of the New Orleans delegation. Despite overtones of sadness, I was blessed to see old friends. One night, I reconnected in Georgetown with Steve Endean, founder of the HRC, and my old friend the Reverend Troy Perry. We laughed about old boyfriends and silly acquaintances over a steak dinner.

The pendulum always swings back, however, and in 1992 we fought hard to elect Bill Clinton. Finally we had a president friendly to gay people—or so we thought. As part of Clinton's inauguration, in January 1993, we even held the first-ever Gay and Lesbian Inaugural Ball, in the grand hall of the National Press Club.

What wonderful energy! Our generation of activists were now approaching our forties—and for the many attendees who had skipped high school prom, this was one hundred times better. We were certainly dressed much better than anything we could have cobbled together in high school. My date was Joan Ladnier, my biggest supporter and one of the first lesbians appointed by New Orleans Mayor Marc Morial as a gay community liaison. She would soon ascend to lead LAGPAC, the Louisiana Lesbian and Gay Political Action Caucus.

The event was well organized by the HRC, with none of the missing coat checks and cheap tablecloths found at many other inaugural balls. Best of all, it was down to earth, with a DJ playing disco all night. It was unprecedented to have the leader of the free world and his administration acknowledge just how hard the LGBTQ+ community had worked for ourselves, for our party, and for a more joyful future.

To this day, on my wall at home, hangs a framed sign from the gala: a presidential seal, with the words "Gay and Lesbian Inaugural Ball, 1993" in gold ink. I thought it would make a great souvenir so I brought it home with me from DC, but the shop where I took it to be framed made the mistake of cutting it down to size. Cropped out of the picture was an arrow and a caption informing attendees, "This Way to the Bathroom."

The glories of gay marches and reunions always grind up against the vulgar realities of political wheeling and dealing in Washington. The cyclical display of the growing AIDS quilt on the National Mall served as a powerful reminder that our plague was a result of the failures of the Reagan and first Bush presidential administrations. We worried that even our friends could turn their backs on us in service to political expediency. The joy of the 1993 Innaugural Ball was crushed later that year when President Clinton issued his Don't Ask, Don't Tell policy, backpedaling from his campaign promise to end the ban on gays serving in the military. In 1996 the Republican-controlled Congress passed the Defense of Marriage Act (DOMA), further obstructing our full rights as citizens, and signed into law by President Clinton himself.

Subsequent marches on Washington allowed generations of gay leadership to gather together, a particularly important function when the AIDS crisis required political coordination. It gave us a network of faces and names we could trust. In 1990, ACT UP had marched on the National Institutes of Health to yell and scream at Dr. Anthony Fauci to do more to keep us from dying. Loved ones were dumping the ashes of their relatives on the White House lawn to make the deepest of statements. We were still burying our friends daily, not just due to AIDS but due to poor medications, like AZT, for which we had no alternative.

Thanks to continued struggle, and despite concerted opposition—such as the use of gay marriage as a wedge issue—the movement has kept going. Just over the course of my lifetime, gay art and activism has resulted in freer LGBTQ+ youth. Each political victory—against sodomy laws, against firing and discrimination, for gay marriage and military service—was the result of broad-based organizing, but it all came together on the steps of the Supreme Court and in the halls of Congress. Don't Ask, Don't Tell lasted through nearly three presidential administrations before its 2010 repeal. For a spell, numerous Republicans who had once supported DOMA joined Democrats to protect gay families—until it once again became politically inconvenient for them to do so. All the awful legislation now bubbling up, affecting trans youth and LGBTQ+ adoption, reminds us that we can't ever let the pendulum swing back.

Today's Washington, DC, is a thriving place, where many gays and lesbians rise up in activism—or otherwise engage in public life—while pursuing good careers and falling in love. The city is cleaner and richer than in the past and the LGBTQ+ community is increasingly affluent and accepted—but I miss the old fixtures that once defined the community. Although Mid-Atlantic Leather Weekend still happens in January, sometimes overlapping with the presidential inauguration, nearly all the historic LGBTQ+ bookstores, lesbian bars, and Black-owned bars have closed.

Nonetheless, I have great hope for the many, many dedicated government workers, activists, policymakers, servicemembers, artists, and native Washingtonians of color. Members of this community lift their heads high and contribute to their nation, able to pursue their careers and follow their hearts in ways unimaginable to past generations.

Already, in the US Congress, there are openly gay and lesbian representatives and a bisexual senator. Maybe one day the District of Columbia, perhaps renamed the Douglass Commonwealth, will be represented by a trans senator serving with a Black president. I fought my whole life for people to feel what I was lucky to be raised with—the knowledge that anything is possible. Perhaps this young vanguard will grow up to become as distinguished as the pioneering Congresswoman Barbara Jordan, and they won't represent just one or two of their own identities. Instead, fulfilling the words that founded our republic, they'll ascend as far as their ambitions and talents will take them to build a more joyful world for all.

CHAPTER TEN / *Return to New Orleans*

Larry, Vernel, Gina, and Joanne Bagneris with their parents, Lawrence and Gloria [1990]
LARRY BAGNERIS PAPERS, AMISTAD RESEARCH CENTER, NEW ORLEANS, LA

10

JIMMY AND I OFTEN RETURNED TO NEW ORLEANS FOR THE HOLIDAYS, BUT AS 1986 came to a close we were planning a Christmas surprise for my family: we were moving back to Louisiana! We had scouted apartments on a September trip and, from Houston, signed a lease to start in November.

A few members of my Illinois-based training team came down to Houston to help with the move—inspired in equal parts by generosity and by curiosity about the cost and quality of housing in the South, compared to Chicago. After finishing packing up at 2001 Branard we went to Jimmy's house to load his boxes, covered in cat hair despite my allergies. And then we set off in our U-Haul, headed east on I-10 with all our worldly possessions.

We had a big reveal in mind—and so, for a few weeks, my brother Vernel helped us keep the secret of our French Quarter residency from the rest of the family. We always came home for the holidays, so my parents had no reason to be suspicious when we joined them on Christmas Eve. We attended to our familiar family traditions, including a celebration of Midnight Mass at St. Peter Claver. Usually, we'd then return to the family home, where my grandmother would be ready for her annual midnight shot of whiskey. "If I'm here next year," she'd always toast, "we'll have another!" However, this year was different. We concocted a ruse to convince the family to have holiday drinks in the Quarter instead. They were envisioning Pat O'Brien's or some other humming holiday room, but their expectations were overturned as we headed instead toward a quieter part of the Quarter. They didn't know what to think when we pulled behind a strange gate and into a parking patio adjacent to an L-shaped building with two stories of Colonial Revival condos atop brick pillars. They did, however, start to get the picture as we took the back staircase to the top floor. When I opened the door, they gazed upon a fully furnished apartment decked out in holiday splendor. Jimmy and I yelled, "Surprise!"

This was our new home: the Chalet Dauphine. My baby sister, my mom, my dad, my grandmother—we all packed the apartment as I announced that I had moved back home to New Orleans! They thought I was playing. "No!" I said, "Here's all my furniture! Don't you remember all these chairs from Houston?"

"Boy, how did you do that?" they remarked, full of excitement. Thanks to the nature of my job with Washington National, I explained, I could live anywhere I wanted. By the end of the evening, Mom was in tears, as a mother always is when her babies move home. She embraced Jimmy, who could finally attend our official Sunday family dinners as a resident of New Orleans, not a visitor from faraway Texas. My mom was happy we were both here together and pledged to take care of him, the first time she had ever acknowledged any boyfriend of mine as a member of her family. Life was pretty perfect.

Mom was a reserved woman who conserved her energy for her family. Dad was more comfortable with groups of people, better at shaking hands and cracking jokes. However, thanks to my activism, Mom had grown more open over the years, as I had demonstrated that my LGBTQ+ brothers and sisters were like a family to me. Two of my lesbian friends had met my mother and, not long after, asked her for a hug. They had not hugged their own mothers for years, and the thought that she could provide such affection brought her to tears. She finally absorbed the true meaning of the unity between my old and new families, even if she was still a bit too shy to march with PFLAG.

It felt so good to be home again in New Orleans. When I first left for Texas, I had no intention of returning. I had built a life for myself in Houston, full of friends and a rewarding career. I was even preparing to run for Houston City Council with the connections I had made over the course of nearly two decades. Unfortunately, the crisis arrived. AIDS was a horror to the gay community, and it was reaching fever pitch in Texas. The emergency affected all of us in different ways. For me, I just wanted to surround myself with family and loved ones. This was my priority. I decided to leave my political life behind and settle peacefully in Louisiana.

For the next few years, I continued to travel widely for work, while returning to Texas often enough to maintain old friendships. I provided sales trainings across the US and Canada—Detroit, Reno, Toronto, and more—while always taking time to explore each new city. In Atlanta, one of my visits coincided with the Hotlanta River Expo. It had only been twenty years since Stonewall, and I could still be caught off guard by the wonderful sight of so many gays and lesbians frolicking openly in a conservative Southern state like Georgia. I could thank my job at Washington National for all of these travel experiences—not just the trainings but the conventions, typically held in beautiful locales, to which Jimmy came along as company. But corporate life was still just that, corporate. And as you can imagine, I had to deal with all kinds of personalities.

Right before my move to New Orleans, I was promoted to the training division at Washington National. Once a month, they held a training school for new agents just outside of Evanston, at the Skokie Hilton. I had to conduct trainings with Rudy, a colleague who wasn't used to the whole gay lifestyle. While he usually kept his negative attitude to himself, I was still conscious of his disapproval. Another trainer, Bill, was even more negative than Rudy, and he didn't keep his feelings to himself. He would make a point of scolding me for bringing up "all that kind of gay shit," though I hadn't brought any of it up.

One day in Skokie, Bill got his digs in while instructors and trainees were socializing over lunch in the hotel ballroom. To the delight of my table, I piped up: "Bill, if your mouth is not where I'm sticking my business, then it's no concern of yours what I do with it!" The quip was met with a hearty round of laughs, oohs, aahs, and "I guess he told you!" Those from the younger crowd had been to gay bars and knew how we strike. I never had any trouble with Bill after that.

Employees of Washington National had known since 1985 that change was afoot. The parent company was going to be sold, and major divisions merged or remolded. For my department, it took a full five years for the transition to unfold. During this period, my life outside the office had evolved, and the move to New Orleans had opened up new arenas for my activism—a story I'll tell in full in another chapter. One day in 1990, a superior of mine at the Evanston headquarters called me into his office. Put delicately, he had always been "fond" of me. As soon as I walked in, he closed the door and handed me that day's *USA Today* and asked, "Have you seen today's newspaper?" I replied that I hadn't, and thought to myself, "Uh oh, this can't be good." My colleague drew my attention to a bold headline in the scuttlebutt section: "New Orleans: Openly Gay Candidate Larry Bagneris Runs for City Council."

"Everybody's going to know!" he warned me, to which I responded, "I don't care." I challenged him to come out of the closet, himself. "I can't do that!" he instinctively replied. Just as readily, I replied, "You're missing a lot in life, because I! Don't! Care!"

I was lucky to have this attitude. I was proud to have survived a racist environment, first in New Orleans and then in Houston. Being gay, I needed to have control over my self, my life, and my feelings, or I wouldn't have gained success as an activist. During my years as an agent for Washington National, I simply didn't care who found out about my sexuality. This posture became a habit for me. After I did my first television interview as president of the Gay Political Caucus in Houston, Jimmy asked, "What are you going to do when they find out on the job?" I just said that I would deal with it in the morning. Despite my confidence, the interview did cause a bit of a stir. When I arrived at the office the next day, all the secretaries, former beauty queens with bouffant hairdos, gasped in near unison, "We saw you on TV last night!"

Although I thought about flipping them off, I replied with my trademark swag: "Didn't I look good? Didn't I speak well?" Internally, I was a bit worried about how the other agents would respond—but they were used to me by this point, and because I had never acted any way but as myself, the controversy was minimal. In fact, one of the sweeter Texas housewives at the office invited me to a barbecue, way out in the country where there were far more steers than queers. I decided to make it fun by bringing some friends of mine. I loaded my Mercury Marquis with my usual gang—Ramon and David, along with my favorite Black sister, Adrienne—and together we drove to the barbecue. It was exactly what we expected in some respects, with cowboys, proud rednecks, and ten-gallon hats. Almost giggling, I instructed my crew to be on their best behavior. "We're here to educate these fools!" But to our surprise, everyone took us in with warm hospitality! We all had such a fun day of dancing, drinking, and eating. It's so important to expose different cultures to one another in the name of fun—and in our case, everyone came out better for it.

Part of the joy of returning to New Orleans was the promotion of my relationship with Jimmy. By the time we pulled up stakes in Houston, I was forty and he was thirty. Together, we had chosen to return to Louisiana rather than start a new life closer to my company's headquarters in Illinois. As I had ascended the corporate ladder, I spent more and more time on the road. Often, Jimmy and I would only see each other on weekends. We decided to elevate our relationship by moving in together, even if, neat freak that I am, cohabitation required some adjustment on my part. We settled right in; Jimmy had always loved New Orleans, particularly when a celebration was happening—and as everyone knows, there's no scarcity of reasons to party in New Orleans.

A pretty boy from the Texas sticks with Cajun blood, Jimmy dreamed of modeling, bartending, and earning his GED, which he did after we moved to New Orleans. He meant the world to me. Back then, to maintain a degree of independence, gays might refer to another man not as a "partner" but a "lover." But when we called each other "boyfriends," we really meant "husbands." The nature of our commitment really was nobody's business, but anyone who knew me and Jimmy could see that we looked after each other. And as the old adage goes, part of the attraction lay in the many ways we were opposites.

From the day we met, Jimmy impressed me as a very open and curious person. However, like most people with these traits, he liked to party and was always looking for the next thrill. I didn't discourage him. In our quiet moments, we would giggle and smile together and play elaborate pranks on each other. Even if he liked bright lights and dancefloors, he was honestly more of an introvert than an extrovert, which he didn't let most people know. I was lucky to see the real Jimmy at home, as he loved to read and listen to his music. Together with the latest Madonna hits, he loved Billie Holiday, even if I thought her music was depressing.

I've learned from my family that the secrets to a happy relationship are separate spaces and separate bathrooms. I famously keep minimal furnishings, in black and white, but Jimmy was far less disciplined. While he respected our common areas, he had his own room, nested with clutter. And yet despite these surface differences, I really loved how he lived in the present—and spending time with him was like a vacation from my constant planning. At the end of the day, Jimmy had a good heart and paid his bills. His independent streak was one of the reasons why I had encouraged him, early in our relationship, to move out of his mother's house and—rather than settle in with me—get his own apartment in Texas. This was an experience he had never had, and it helped him gain confidence for living in the real world. So young when we first met, he had grown in so many ways.

When we arrived in New Orleans, I tried to get Jimmy to contact his father, who had left the family many years earlier. Inspired by Harvey Milk, I believed that coming out was the finest thing a gay man could do. I thought it was a gate we all had to pass through, and I was living proof that a gay man could be loved by his dad. However, Jimmy's redneck father was religious and unaccepting. The attempted reconciliation didn't go well and may have even started Jimmy's downward spiral. Whereas I was my own father's buddy and son, his dad had no need for a fag in his life, and I learned the hard lesson that not everyone's family was as supportive as mine.

Jimmy could trust others easily and he inspired trust easily in turn, as he came across as innocent as a puppy dog. Messy room aside, he was otherwise thoughtful and very compassionate, both qualities that made him good in bed. However, his trusting attitude also resulted in his hanging out with a less disciplined crowd. He'd stay up all night and chase the latest highs. I came to understand that young people can have hard heads and don't like to be told what to do. My experience with my first boyfriend, Desi Lopez, had taught me not to play Daddy: there was only so much I could do to salvage another person's life without sacrificing my own wellbeing. I was starting to learn similar lessons with Jimmy.

While we grew closer to each other and to my family, Jimmy struggled to reconcile two facets of his personality: the part of him determined to earn a GED and move up in life, and the part that preferred the easy joy of a new New Orleans thrill. Either you manage your thrills or they manage you.

All my life, I had a chip on my shoulder about my disabilities. Today, they call it imposter syndrome, where no matter what a person accomplishes, they feel like a fraud at risk of being found out at every turn. Fortunately, during this period of transition—as I made a new home for myself and Jimmy in New Orleans—I was able to take advantage of top-notch services offered by Washington National. As the company reorganized, it wasn't just offering buyouts to executives, it was also helping us to find new careers. Now, I had always hated exams, but I took a career aptitude test and somehow scored ninety-nine out of a hundred on the diagnostic for public leadership skills. At first I was shocked, but then I remembered all of the qualities I had worked so hard to perfect: my sense of humor, my oral communication, an ease with numbers, my street smarts, and my formal education. No one should really need a test to affirm their self-actualization, but after all those years of being Black in America, gay in the corporate world, and deaf in front of audiences of hundreds, it took me until this moment to say "screw it!" to all those labels. I had carried this burden my whole life, but the aptitude test reminded me that even with all my challenges, there was still more I could build with my life.

The career seminar that accompanied the test was also a blessing. It continued to assess my personality and encouraged me to establish achievable goals, while providing recommendations on paths that might lead to success. While many around me at Washington National took the career development and life strategies seminar to map out their ascent up different corporate ladders, I was looking to sharpen my political game.

My twenty years of service to Washington National earned me a generous financial package that allowed me to buy the apartment I'd been renting at the Chalet Dauphine. I still count my years with the company as a blessing. The job gave me a great foundation for professional growth, while allowing me to travel extensively and socialize with gay communities worldwide. Can you imagine all this for a little Black boy from the Seventh Ward? Life was perfect, or so I thought.

The constant travel had taken its toll, though. Despite our best intentions, the pattern of seeing each other only on weekends followed me and Jimmy from Houston to New Orleans. By 1988, our relationship was showing signs of falling apart. While I was traveling for work, Jimmy was working as a bartender, a job where you can meet all kinds of tempting and unsavory characters. Soon he began to look unwell from drinking—and while there was ample cocaine and pot, it was the booze that made him unravel. He spent most of his nights, whether on or off his shift, chasing the cheap thrills of tourists—and his days hung over, shut in, withdrawn into music. His life was going down the drain, and nothing I tried to do was working. This was the love of my life, and I couldn't help him.

So we had to break up. I couldn't be Jimmy's caretaker; it was time for him to be his own person. When you love someone, you share losses as well as wins—but you can't possess each other. We all have to be our own adult selves.

Jimmy stuck around the apartment through 1989, grappling with the desire to do something drastic to reset his storyline. His mom, now in Tennessee, counseled caution. She thought our relationship could still do him some good—but we all knew that New Orleans had too many temptations to keep him on the straight and narrow. In time, he settled on San Diego—a place he knew well, having split his time growing up between California and Texas. He wanted to return to a familiar place with warm weather.

Fortunately, we weren't angry with each other. We could still sit down and talk through anything. I made sure he knew that I had plenty of heart left for him and would help provide whatever he needed to move on. One morning, he flew away. He took his clothes but left a lot of stuff with me, even his heavy stereo, but he paid that little mind. By this point, Jimmy just needed to start over.

Through long-distance calls, I made sure to check on him in San Diego. Things went well for the first six months. He was looking for a job, found a place to live, and made friends. Then one day, he stopped answering the phone. He stopped communicating not only with me but with his mother, who grew so worried she reached out to me. Without thinking twice, I knew I had to fly out to San Diego. Getting there was easy enough, but once I landed I had no idea how or where to search for him. I can still close my eyes today and remember the drab airport car rental stand in an unfamiliar city. Fortunately, the boy who rented me the car was in the family. We traded notes on the entire gay landscape of Southern California. And since everyone in our community keeps track of one another, I decided to ask about Jimmy. "Jimmy from New Orleans?" the rental agent replied.

Turns out Jimmy was working at a Subway—and he was properly pissed that I had tracked him down. We caught up, and he gave me a tour of all the San Diego bars. I loved him deeply, but by now the romantic spark had expired. He offered to show me Tijuana, but my flight home was already set.

Having suffered this breakup, this investment of love and vulnerability, I had a mountain of pent-up energy that I could choose to spend either negatively or positively. I decided to use that energy by running for public office.

Jimmy Armstrong Chavers [1980]
COURTESY OF THE AUTHOR

CHAPTER ELEVEN / *Running and Running*

Larry with family at the Maison Dupuy Hotel on the evening of the runoff [1990]
LARRY BAGNERIS PAPERS, AMISTAD RESEARCH CENTER, NEW ORLEANS, LA

11

DESPITE ITS REPUTATION FOR PERMISSIVENESS, IN MANY WAYS NEW Orleans has always been somewhat backward in its embrace of gay life, possibly due to the strong hold of the Catholic Church. However, the 1989 Pride Festival in Washington Square Park on Elysian Fields, my first in New Orleans, inspired me. Roberts Batson, Bob to his friends, was a New Orleanian who had known about my work in Houston, and now he began to introduce me to members of the local community. I'd been in New Orleans for a few years by this point—but because my work had me flying all over the country, I hadn't met many of the movers and shakers.

Bob had long had faith in my ability as a candidate, dating back to my days in Houston—and now he began to float the notion of my running for a seat on the New Orleans City Council. Some of my cousins were starting to find success in public life, and the Bagneris name was becoming more famous in town. But my path promised to be a little harder: no openly gay man had ever run for Council. Nonetheless, when I was approached about a run, I thought, "Hell, I'm looking for a job, anyway. Let's do this!"

I'll never forget the day Bob came over to my parents' house and we spread a city map on the dining room table. "This is the district. District C!" I exclaimed as I showed the map to my mother and father. "Dad says the whole family lives in District C," I noted to my mother. Piping up, my dad joked that if I didn't run, he would.

Although I hadn't yet officially entered the race, in August 1989 I got to work making signs and campaigning informally. In early September Jimmy came back from California for a short visit. The fact that it was Southern Decadence—the city's annual gay festival—had a lot to do with the timing, but he seemed eager to hit the town together and grateful for the warm welcome he received at the old barrooms and parties. However, the energy had changed, and I could see that he was in a much more serious mood. After the big weekend, he revealed to me that he wasn't here to party. He had tested positive for HIV, and we were both devastated.

There was no time to grieve, however, as I officially launched my campaign the weekend after Labor Day and plunged into an active fight. Perhaps I used the campaign to mourn for Jimmy, for our life together, for the many friends I'd lost to this plague, and for the avalanche our whole community still strained to hold back.

New Orleans is split into five geographic council districts. With two at-large members, the city council operates as a board of seven. District A contains the farther reaches of Uptown and extends to Lakeview. District B is the portion of Uptown that includes Central City, the Irish Channel, and the Garden District, while District D is a Creole seat that covers Gentilly. District E includes the outlying areas of New Orleans East and the Lower Ninth Ward. What's left is District C, my district, which combines the increasingly gentrified but always gay French Quarter and Marigny neighborhoods on the east bank of the Mississippi with the working-class expanse of Algiers on the west bank.

Mike Early had served as councilman for District C since the mid-1970s and was ready to move on. The West Bank's conservativism had traditionally overwhelmed the East Bank's progressivism—but as the gay community became increasingly empowered, the balance of power in the district was changing. A few years earlier, in the 1980s, Councilman Early had voted against a gay rights ordinance offering protection from job firings, housing discrimination, and the refusal of public accommodation. This didn't sit well with my community, and it angered me. After a lifetime, I had finally found full comfort in being gay. My parents and my whole family were supportive, and I had grown accustomed to Texas queer life. I expected the climate in New Orleans to be the same, but its cultural politics were ten years behind those of Houston! As far as I was concerned, time was up. It had been two decades since Stonewall, a decade since the 1979 March on Washington—and my hometown needed to catch up.

In Louisiana, we have open primaries: if any one candidate earns a majority, they win outright, but if no one reaches that mark, the two candidates with the highest vote totals enter a runoff election. With eighteen candidates in the race for District C, I needed to earn my way into a runoff against Jackie Clarkson, the hand-picked successor of Mike Early and his West Bank power base. The primary was scheduled for February 1990, the runoff—if I was lucky enough to make it—for March.

I was proud to be the first openly gay candidate for the New Orleans City Council, but like all pioneers in any field, I didn't want that one trait to define me. I adopted all the issues my neighbors urged me to promote—not just the gay issues—for the overall betterment of our community. The French Quarter has always struggled with historic preservation, housing, and zoning. I spoke to those issues. But too many people were dying from the HIV/AIDS crisis, so community health had to be a fixture of my campaign.

Since District C is so large, I did my best to represent the concerns of each of its constituencies. In 1968 the city had erected a freeway overpass above North Claiborne Avenue, tearing through the heart of historic

African American Tremé. With my family background, it was easy to find ways to hang with those in the community and brainstorm about ways the city council could respond. On the West Bank, billboards were popping up like mushrooms on General De Gaulle Drive—and, having just seen massive signage gobble up the San Antonio and Houston landscape, I wanted to fight for appropriately sized billboards in New Orleans, to fit the look of each neighborhood. Historic preservation is a familiar issue in the French Quarter, which struggles to balance the needs of tourists and locals. To this day, we have intricate rules about the appearance of buildings in the historic district and limits on residential parking so that locals can park close to home. After twenty years in corporate America, I was eager to apply my understanding of finance, budgeting, and investment to the local scene. But everyone ignored my business experience. They wanted to talk about one thing: being gay, gay, gay, gay . . . gay!

As a newcomer to the local political scene, I was lucky to have a campaign manager, in Bob Batson, who knew the ropes. Any new candidate—whether in New Orleans or elsewhere—needs to meet the local political icons, people like former mayor Moon Landrieu or then–US senator John Breaux. Kissing the rings of the Democratic Party establishment was a necessity—but it wasn't easy. I was an outsider who had done all my gay rights work in Houston. No one knew that history, and no one really cared.

But Bob was familiar with all the personalities. He had been active in the community for decades, as an organizer of the anti–Anita Bryant march in 1977 and one of the founders of LAGPAC in 1980. He knew all the heads of the Black political organizations—the alphabet soup of COUP, SOUL, and BOLD—and he introduced me to their leadership. He knew gay and straight, Black and white, and young and old influencers. He was also instrumental in earning me an early endorsement from LAGPAC and the Louisiana Forum for Equality, even if some of those leaders thought they should have run instead of me. Even though trusting others has always been hard for me, fond as I am of setting my own agenda and goals, I knew that Bob was someone to trust implicitly.

It was important to put both "Lawrence" and "Larry" on my campaign signs to unite the people who knew me both before and after my time in Houston. Once I overheard people at a bar arguing over whether Lawrence and Larry were the same person or not! I also had to clarify that in Houston, my name was pronounced "Bon-ya-RIS," with a silent g, whereas in New Orleans, my name was pronounced "Bag-NA-ris," with a hard g.

I was still working weekdays for Washington National at the very start of my campaign, but on weekends I would meet with neighborhood groups in the French Quarter, Marigny, and Bywater. I didn't reach out much to the West Bank until later—I needed to get my base in line first before heading across the river. Our official kickoff event, at the Sheraton Hotel, served as my first fundraiser. My brother, Vernel, helped by holding an entire performance of *One Mo' Time* to draw people into the ballroom. I was so lucky, as a gay man, to have my parents, siblings, cousins, many of the aunties from the house on St. Ann and Galvez, and even my 89-year-old grandmother Armantine, my Mami, in attendance and in support of my campaign.

With the election two months away and counting down, it was Bob who decided to hold a New Year's Eve party on behalf of my campaign to welcome in the 1990s. We selected the perfect location—the Esplanade and Gov. Nicholls Street wharves, overlooking the city's festivities along the river. Imagine if you can a warehouse, normally filled with cargo, now packed with revelers—their cars safely stashed behind police barricades. We had a DJ, food, and lots to drink. At the stroke of midnight, the city's fireworks lit up the sky, with boom after boom, until one loud noise came not from the sky but from the warehouse next door. A transformer had exploded, and soon the whole space was dark! With a flash of genius, Bob got all the cars turned in the same direction with their lights on, so people could see where they were going. Between the fireworks, the crowd, and the drama, it was an evening that still ranks among my favorite memories.

The morning after, however, brought back the reality that I still had a race to win. Jackie Clarkson and I were polling at the top of the field of eighteen. The February 3 primary would determine who would make it to the runoff.

The day before the election, WWL-TV called for an interview. The call came while I was at my campaign headquarters on Esplanade and Rampart, and I wasn't having it at all. I refused to do yet another election interview that would surely focus on my being the first openly gay candidate. This time it was my dad who sat me down, talked sense, and rescued me. He had been just as dedicated to my campaign as any one of my volunteers—and it had been his idea to round up the nieces and nephews to canvass door-to-door on my behalf. After lowering my temperature, he convinced me to invite the cameras into our headquarters, patting my back and urging me to "come on, son." In the throes of frustration, I repeated, "man oh man, I'm not doing this, I'm just not doing it. I'm sick of it."

We walked back to my apartment, just around the corner, to do some housecleaning as a distraction—and as we sat in my living room, my dad said, "Look, there's just one more day in this campaign, let's just go ahead and do this." He was right. So I cleaned up, put on a fresh coat and tie, and went back to headquarters. The crew from Channel 4 arrived, and I'll never forget this: with lights set up and wires strung everywhere, the reporter asked—with a straight face, with my campaign staff behind me, still reeling from my earlier explosion—"How does it feel, running as the first openly gay candidate?" I nearly lost my shit right there! Thank God for my dad, who quickly stepped in.

"Excuse me, let me answer that. My son feels no different from anybody else running for public office. Listen to what this young man has to say about the different issues that affect our city and the ideas he's come up with for our district, the most diverse district in the city. He reflects that diversity." My dad was never one for toasts or speeches, but the eloquence of what he said touches me to this day.

Dad was active not only in his support but also in his protection. He took a great risk taking my nieces and nephews out to knock on doors. When people found out that little Juan and Miguel had a gay uncle, they caught hell in high school. Their classmates teased them about me, telling them that I was a queer, a sissy, and other nasty things. I never knew any of this at the time and only found out years later.

Making it to the runoff wasn't a lock. On the night of the February primary, I was way behind when the returns started coming in. Sensing my anxiety, Vernel soothed me by reminding me, over and over, "We've got way more relatives in that district than they're coming up with on that television—you are going to be just fine." And whether it was blood relatives or the gay community, he was right! We garnered enough votes for the number two spot, and now we were in a runoff!

Jackie Clarkson and I squared off one Sunday morning on local TV, where my cousin Warren Bell hosted a political affairs program. Right off the bat, Clarkson went straight for the red meat, bringing up my "lifestyle" over and over again. Normally, this would have bothered me into paralysis—but perhaps because I had family sitting between us, it was easy for me to reply, "You know, my private life has nothing to do with how effective I would be as a city councilperson."

I remained calm on air that morning, but it was no secret that I was nervous. After months of campaigning, I was physically exhausted, and tired of the relentless focus on gay, gay, gay, gay, gay, gay . . . gay! It was a torrent of gay news headlines, gay questions from journalists, even gay interviews from gay supporters talking about how gay I was! Many gays volunteered for my campaign and noticed my huffing and puffing. Some grew upset that I was less bothered about being referred to as a Black candidate than about being labeled a gay candidate. But I kept thinking of the Creole saying that "if you put too much filé in the gumbo, you ruin it": I couldn't let one of my flavors overwhelm the others. I felt I was more than just the gay candidate—and that the media and community were ignoring my ideas concerning the multitude of issues that affected District C. Everyone was only interested in talking about the gay issues.

One on one, at my endorsement interviews, I did get to share my thoughts on a whole range of ideas, and for this I'm thankful. I earned a spectrum of endorsements, from the *Times-Picayune*, *Gambit*, the Alliance for Good Government, the Community Organization for Urban Politics, the Crescent City Democratic Association, the Forum for Equality, the Independent Women's Organization, the Regular Democratic Organization, and of course LAGPAC. I was also endorsed by over a hundred civic activists and business and professional leaders who lived in the district.

In the end, Jackie Clarkson won the runoff. I earned big majorities in the French Quarter, my home turf, and even garnered a respectable number of votes across the river—but it wasn't enough. We had gathered at the Maison Dupuy Hotel, at 1001 Toulouse Street in the Quarter, to watch the returns coming in. Disappointed though I was, I could still recall the joy of making the runoff, one month earlier, and these memories buoyed me as I gave an exclusive interview to one of the gay reporters. I told him, "I'm speaking to you not as a gay man or a Black man, but just as a human being. I thank everyone for their support." That's truly how I felt. Looking back, I suppose being gay may have helped me stand out in a crowded field. Maybe if I had just been a straight Joe, I wouldn't have been able to get in a runoff with Jackie. After all these years, I've taken to this new way of looking at things.

Plus, I was touched by witnessing the power of the gay community coming together. That alone made this race worth it. I can still picture my supporters at the election night party. I'll never forget how hard we worked. I'll also be forever grateful to LAGPAC and the Forum for Equality for the massive support they lent my campaign. I owe a special thank you to Roberts Batson for his vision and artful management of both the campaign and me. That election night, despite our defeat, it became clear what we had the power to accomplish together as a community.

Today, the Bagneris name is famous in New Orleans politics. My cousin Michael Bagneris, who would later become a civil district court judge and would run for mayor, supported my 1990 campaign tremendously by finding donors, talking with voters, and attending functions. I didn't know it at the time, but he was sympathetic to my struggle because he had a gay daughter of his own. I am grateful for Michael's support and that of other extended family members, but I did not benefit directly from relatives with political connections. My experience with the GPC in Houston had familiarized me with the democratic process and allowed me to practice my political skills. The 1980 Democratic National Convention also made for great preparation—not only the experience of working with other delegates to push an inclusive party platform, but also the process of writing and distributing a booklet about gay people in the Democratic Party. I'm almost embarrassed about how primitive the booklet seems now, but it was an earnest attempt to effect change by personalizing the gay experience—and I will forever encourage leadership opportunities for groups of people that don't normally have a voice.

I had lost this round, but I was bitten by the bug. This would not be my last race. I would run for the state legislature three times, in 1991, 1995, and 1999. And although I wasn't ultimately elected, I achieved my larger goal of normalizing the idea of a gay candidate. There were still ancient attitudes about gays and lesbians that needed to change, even among my own beloved Black community, and especially in the churches. I'm still surprised, however, by how eagerly some lay parishioners supported my campaigns out of the love they had for their gay relatives. There is always hope for a better future.

With the loss to Jackie Clarkson behind me, my old life began to seep back. I called Jimmy's mom and learned that he was planning to return to Fayetteville—south of Nashville—so that she could care for him. As

Larry (center) and his father (front seat) in the St. Patrick's Day parade, New Orleans, during race for state representative [1991]
COURTESY OF THE AUTHOR

LARRY

much as I wanted to help, Jimmy was proud and independent, and I knew I needed to keep my distance. But burning inside me was the deep wish to make sure he traveled safely back to his family.

Given Jimmy's pride, he couldn't know that I was checking on him. So, I found out which flights he was taking from California to Tennessee, and I flew to Houston to try to glimpse him as he transferred planes there. Having witnessed the AIDS crisis in Houston, I knew how quickly patients could deteriorate—but it broke my heart to see what the disease and medication had done to him. Sitting in the terminal, peeking from behind a newspaper, I witnessed Jimmy's physical decline. He was pale and emaciated. Once he was on his final Southwest flight, my tension gave way. I hid in a bathroom stall and cried, cried, cried, until it was time to take my own flight back to New Orleans. After composing myself back at my apartment, I called his mom. She reported that Jimmy was fine, and she was happy to have him home.

That Christmas, I visited them in Tennessee. On Jimmy's better days in the country, we would go buy fireworks and shoot them off. Afterward, we would share a meal at Bennigan's, where he was ID'd for looking too young to drink, which flattered him.

He wanted to see New Orleans one last time, so we welcomed the arrival of 1992 by spending New Year's Eve together. Jimmy was staying with me, and I held a party of nearly forty people, including some of Jimmy's oldest friends, my mom and dad, and Terry Harris, our best friend from the Houston GPC. Then, approaching midnight, the party ventured out of the apartment. All of us carried champagne in Schwegmann's grocery bags down to Jackson Square. We gathered by the doorway of the St. Louis Cathedral, our favorite spot to watch the fireworks that signaled the New Year. Then we returned to Dauphine Street, our old home. Despite our love affair, this couldn't be a romantic moment between lovers, but a caring moment between friends.

I went back to Tennessee one more time to see Jimmy for his birthday. Although it was mid-March, it was still snowing there. He didn't have much longer to live—but his mom and I had made sure that over thirty people were on hand to celebrate with him. We gossiped and talked about so many things: what his life had been like, how much he missed New Orleans, and how much he missed our life together. We shared a lot of memories—us being messy in Europe, and in Boston, where we had found a frat house and had a good time. On September 25, 1992, he died.

The tragedy was that it wasn't the disease but the medicine that had killed him. The AZT that was prescribed to Jimmy was too strong for his body, a fate many other AIDS patients shared. Unfortunately, it was the only treatment available until Dr. Fauci convinced the federal health authorities to fiddle with other medicines to find the right cocktail. These days, HIV infection can be prevented by PrEP—and with proper medicine, HIV can be rendered undetectable in a positive patient, making the virus untransmissible. These treatments, however, came many years after Jimmy died.

In the end, Jimmy wanted his ashes to be spread in New Orleans—and so, along with Terry Harris, I traveled to collect his ashes in Nashville. After consoling Jimmy's mother and sharing tears of grief and laughter as we commiserated, I took the ashes back home. Glancing at the urn in the rearview mirror, I knew how much I missed and loved him. I saw him in everything, in every joke and bump in the road. Back in New Orleans, Rev. Shelley Hamilton from the local Metropolitan Community Church gave the service by the river, with my brother Vernel's gospel friends performing and my entire family there. I was touched that they knew how much he meant to me. And at sunset on September 30, we sent Jimmy home on the riverfront steps by the Mississippi.

CHAPTER TWELVE / *Local NO/AIDS Work*

Larry with NO/AIDS Task Force educational poster [1990s]
LARRY BAGNERIS PAPERS, AMISTAD RESEARCH CENTER, NEW ORLEANS, LA

12

THE NO/AIDS TASK FORCE GOT STARTED IN 1983, IN A BOURBON STREET living room, as the AIDS crisis began to reach New Orleans. It was founded by a handful of people deeply concerned about the spread of HIV and AIDS. What started small—as a project to pass condoms out by hand—grew larger and larger. Today it is known as CrescentCare and occupies a modern, beautiful headquarters on Elysian Fields. It is a full-service community health center, providing everything from dentistry to psychiatry—to, yes, condoms and lubrication.

My introduction to the organization, in 1990, came at a time when the relationship between community activism and city government was evolving. I'd lost my own race for city council, but I saw hopeful signs that civic leaders were growing closer to the gay community. Councilwoman Dorothy Mae Taylor, for one, was more than tolerant: she was supportive and had pushed legislation. And Mayor Sidney Barthelemy, an enlightened and positive spirit who had been elected in 1986, was developing programs that would soon coalesce as the city's inaugural Human Relations Commission.

Jeff Campbell, the executive director of the Task Force, was the person who recruited me as director of community affairs—but I had met the entire board through my campaigns and my community work. They knew me as a good trouper. Grant funding would pay my salary, while I continued to draw from my severance package from Washington National.

By some measures, I wasn't a natural fit for the Task Force. I had been traumatized by watching people on their deathbeds in Houston. I didn't have the endurance to provide hands-on care. So I contributed other forms of care: my apartment was open nearly all the time for friends and families to gather and commiserate about the trauma they endured. Sometimes people would stay with me for a few nights—because when some men died, their families would kick their lovers out of their home. I had seen all that ugliness, and I didn't want to go through it again. But NO/AIDS was fighting in the halls of hospitals and the halls of power, and they needed someone with community organizing experience. I knew I could help. Plus, I needed a day job!

As director of community affairs, I fought the stigma, denial, misconceptions, and despair that marginalize gay and Black communities in particular. I provided education on safer sex, held workshops, and walked the streets, teaching people how to reduce harm, get tested and treated, and keep others safe, even when you're positive. We had a variety of tactics, from silly to somber, to fit every audience and venue.

Unfortunately, we faced the same abundance of discomfort found in every epidemic. So little was known about the disease, and people out there were scared. The general public only saw what was sensationalized on TV, frightening images of hollowed-out patients with growing sores. But it was not enough for people to believe that AIDS was real. As a city, and as a nation, we needed to develop the political will to fight for change rooted in compassion for those suffering.

Some people wouldn't even touch those afflicted with AIDS—and for the sick seeking care, it was like wearing the scarlet letter. People would drop off the radar after a positive diagnosis; they'd be shunned, just at the time they most needed care. And the care was expensive and unguaranteed, with sickening side effects. Many people, gays as well as straights, bristled at the thought of using protection; they convinced themselves that someone else, not them, would catch the disease.

Our whole lives, we had been stigmatized: first considered sinners, then criminals, and now diseased. The post-Stonewall years had brought a glimmer of hope, but not enough to overcome the effects of lifelong oppression. As AIDS decimated our family of choice, many gays began to internalize the hatred—to feel that they themselves were responsible, it was their fault for being sick, and they should accept their fate. So many of us had taken refuge in the closet when bar raids and public outing were the primary threats. Now, a generation later, the parade of funerals sent people deeper into the closet. This phenomenon was particularly acute within the African American community: Black churches, conservative as a rule, stayed quiet even as half their choirs would die of "pneumonia."

These were the obstacles that our task force confronted: not just the threat of disease, but the debilitating realities of shame and denial. But I had a knack for connecting with people, wherever they were. I had always been a fan of protection. I thought it was more sanitary. It was now my job to break out the bananas and offer condom training: checking the expiration date, pinching the tip, and letting it roll. So much morality and judgment gets tangled up with how people approach sex. In that regard, all humans make mistakes.

For the record, HIV is passed through specific bodily fluids. It can be transmitted not only through seminal, vaginal, and rectal fluids but also by blood and breastmilk. Kissing can even spread HIV if the case is untreated and there is blood in the spit. In an atmosphere of fear, denial, and apathy, it wasn't surprising that drinking and drugs would come into play. If you're not protected when nature calls, it's easy to get infected, and if you're drunk or high, you're much less likely to pause for the protection of a condom. My outreach to the local gay community had to factor these realities into the picture.

Nationally, it was ACT UP that led the charge to demand more action from the government, more research from the NIH, and more engagement from the public. They held confrontational protests such as a takeover of the FDA building, in 1988, and a huge die-in protest at New York's St. Patrick's Cathedral, in 1989, to counter the silence and anti–birth control message of the Catholic church. The government remained mostly mum, except for one Dr. Anthony Fauci, who had the courage—after being educated, himself, by the passion of gay activists—to give us straight information. ACT UP pushed the message that HIV wasn't only spread through sexual contact. Heterosexuals who had blood transfusions, intravenous drug users who shared needles, and babies born to HIV-positive mothers were also afflicted. None of this information was new, but the more it was emphasized—the more the general public truly absorbed the fact that AIDS wasn't just a gay disease—the greater the chance of political action at the highest levels.

AIDS organizations nationwide fought hard for research that would lead to a vaccine, but scientists were finding that the virus mutated so quickly that it could evade vaccines. The first treatment that showed any promise was an antiretroviral drug named AZT. It was the only medication available and was rushed out quickly. AZT was expensive, so rich people were the first to access it. Sometimes when patients died, their leftover pills would be redistributed to the needy. In those early days, the dosages were quite high, and the side effects were so severe that many people died from the medicine. This is what had happened to Jimmy. People often took AZT despite the risks, willing to gamble that it would prolong their life until new therapies could be found. There was no surviving AIDS without medicine.

During the first half of 1990 I was out organizing with the community, doing outreach, hanging banners across Bourbon Street, and more. Despite the circumstances, the work was a lot of fun. One banner that graced the French Quarter during Mardi Gras was a play on the slogan "Laissez les Bons Temps Roulez": "Let the Good Times Unroll," spoken by a cartoon condom. I'd give out souvenir plastic go-cups with "wear a condom, play it safe" printed on the sides. I hung huge posters in each gay bar and in the bathrooms, promoting the NO/AIDS Task Force as a trustworthy resource. The posters reminded people to practice safer sex, in language sensual enough to attract attention but clean enough to post in public. Borrowing from a certain cartoon, I created the Care Bears, young gay men who would volunteer during big holidays to give out condoms. Young people were usually a lot less shy than members of my generation when it came to talking about how the disease is transmitted.

In those days, technology didn't fit in your pocket! I would lug an overhead projector around town to give presentations. I would furiously make and keep appointments with bar owners, recalling the days when I was seeking campaign donations. I even established a bartender training program—and over the years, many people have come up to me in gay bars and sweetly told me I saved their lives through my insistence that they shut up and listen to what I had to say.

One night, when the AIDS crisis was peaking and people were dropping like flies, my work brought me to The Club, a bathhouse on Toulouse Street in the Quarter. For my first official visit as a NO/AIDS educator, I was loaded up with posters and filmstrips when some commotion stopped me in my tracks. Police cars were everywhere!

I reported to the officer in command that I was there to do a training. "Well, you're gonna have to wait until after the investigation," the officer replied. Someone had died of a heart attack, and inhalants had been found nearby.

Still in investigation mode, the police officer looked me up and down, and said, "You look like you work out here." With a smirk, I said, "No, but

I do work out." That was enough for me to keep him chatting, and I soon discovered that he was completely clueless. "Now," the officer posed, sincerely perplexed, "Why do they got them rooms upstairs?"

"Well, officer, the rooms are for changing. People are very private about changing, so they change in their private rooms." The officer furrowed his brow, not completely convinced, which I took as an invitation to keep going. "And hey, if they want to take a nap after a night's drinking, they can, because this is New Orleans!" Finally a sergeant appeared, knowing full well by the look on both of our faces that I was playing joker and the police officer was playing fool. The sergeant chuckled him out of his command: "Get out of here, you're busy, resume your patrol elsewhere."

I'm not convinced the sergeant knew what I was getting after, either. There are so many signs and secrets gays keep to themselves. Some of this culture is slowly evaporating—fun quirks and inside jokes that we were happy to keep away from the mainstream, away from the vanilla world.

For some people, the bathhouse was almost a religion. Just as bars were our safe spaces for exploration and acceptance, so too were bathhouses—a welcome respite from the outside world of buttoned-up expectations. Just ask my friend Bob, the owner of Midtowne Spa and a number of bathhouses. He had them registered as religious congregations to take advantage of the tax deduction!

The opportunity to feel welcome at home is something LGBTQ+ youth can't take for granted. NO/AIDS featured a drop-in center on Rampart Street whose outreach included the many gay kids left homeless when their families rejected them. Many of these young people came from small, rural communities; they had been thrown out of their homes and had nowhere to go. Tumbling into New Orleans, young and barely educated, they would often turn to the typical pattern of hustling for sugar daddies. They were thankful that we provided laundry facilities, space to secure their belongings, and a break from the grind. All grown up, I made a point of looking presentable, with a tie. They knew me as "Mr. Larry," and they were more than respectful—unless they weren't, in which case I had to demand their attention.

Rampart Street forms the back end of the French Quarter. Away from the busy port and the stately mansions in the middle, Rampart Street is a back door, a wide strip that separates the Quarter from Tremé and the rest of the city. Unfortunately, the hustlers liked to hang out in the dark corners, and graffiti started to proliferate. As a resident of the neighborhood, I was incensed. So, one day at the center, before the youth could get their daily meal and lockers, I called everyone together. They had no idea I had it in me—but my emotions weren't far from the surface. Pouting just a bit, I said, "Look. Next time I see some damn graffiti on a wall in the Quarter, I'm heading straight to y'all. I'll be checking your fingernails for paint. If you check out, I'm sending you right to jail!"

I got a burst of laughter in exchange, but graffiti diminished in the neighborhood. In the end, my well-to-do neighbors in the French Quarter appreciated what NO/AIDS was doing to take care of our gay family's less fortunate relations.

CHAPTER THIRTEEN / *Lobbying in Baton Rouge*

State Capitol, Baton Rouge [2000]

PHOTOGRAPH BY WILLIAM KARAM JR.
HNOC, GIFT OF WILLIAM KARAM JR., 2018.0308.2

13

ULTIMATELY, THERE WAS ONLY SO MUCH WE COULD DO TO STOP AIDS IN THE community. A well-ordered society requires good governance, and the fight to legitimize our personhood had to take place in Baton Rouge. At the state level, due to the hysteria around AIDS and the so-called culture wars, conservatives whipped up bad legislation like a wave that we had to hold back. One legislator proposed that HIV-positive people be tattooed, so they couldn't lie to prospective partners in the bedroom. And that was just the tip of the iceberg.

Fortunately, I knew a lobbyist in Baton Rouge who looked like he had been sent from central casting. Russell Henderson had tousled hair, a loose tie, and wrinkles steamed into his starched white shirts from all of his running around. As a straight ally, he was excited to hear about our idea to connect the NO/AIDS Task Force with other community-based organizations across Louisiana. I couldn't stop bad bills alone. The rest of the state has always been jealous of New Orleans, and sometimes the legislature would spike good bills just to spite us. We needed to educate legislators all over the state that human dignity—achieved through more humane health policies—could be a popular and cost-effective strategy for all of Louisiana's sixty-four parishes. I had a vision of what we needed in Baton Rouge, and when I shared my ideas with my good friend Jeff Campbell, the NO/AIDS director, he encouraged me to go for it. I was off to be a lobbyist.

I traveled the whole state, setting up networks of HIV organizations. Were people all over the state affected with HIV/AIDS? Yes. Even in rural areas? Oh, yes! While a lot of prejudice remains, the death of a child changes the whole world of a grieving parent. Since so many families had lost a member to AIDS, many people had changed their outlook and had chosen to fight to prevent further suffering. Help from state and federal government was inadequate, but a grassroots coalition was building. Within the LGBTQ+ community, at the local level, AIDS advocacy made inroads against traditional gender segregation. Gays would welcome lesbians with open arms and equip them with the tools to help us in our struggle.

There were no cell phones back then and barely any email. The work of organizing required old-fashioned mailers and answering machines, printed newsletters and newspaper ad campaigns. We had a telephone tree that knit everyone together in case some odious bill was making its rounds through the legislature. When it came time to make the call, the message was sent quickly, and we would man the barricades and barrage newspaper editors and local politicians.

Effective politicking required integrating ourselves into the complex and technicolor culture of Louisiana. Krewe du Vieux, a New Orleans Mardi Gras organization, is a bastion of white liberals with a naughty and subversive edge. For their parade in 1992, we made a long snaking condom and bounced it down the street like a Chinese dragon. Afterward, we collected ourselves at the ball, took the same condom, and fooled around with the crowd to really make it a party. We also partnered with them that season by hosting a pub crawl, named the "Trash Bar Tour," where we dressed in full costume, distributed petitions, and shared safe sex information on the raucous Lundi Gras night before Fat Tuesday.

Back when I was running trainings for Washington National, I had traveled the country—and as a lobbyist, I traveled the state to meet locals where they were and build cohesion. I would go to town, visit a bar or two, and see what level of knowledge the community had about HIV/AIDS. Perhaps because of our ostracization, there were far more gay bars in Louisiana a quarter century ago then there are today. There were three in Lafayette, two in Lake Charles, two in Houma, three in Alexandria, five in Baton Rouge, and four in Shreveport. After getting a good overview of the existing landscape, I could bring the right information to the local meeting. I would begin the conversation with my impressions of the community's needs, and then lead into the bigger picture of what we were doing across the state. Most important, I would demonstrate that I was there to serve them, not to demand their compliance with some agenda created in Baton Rouge.

For every ally we gained, the opposition just dug in deeper. I remember driving down the highway one night trying to figure out how our state legislature could foment such stupidity. Looking down those lonely, North Louisiana highways, I had an epiphany. The poles had no cable television lines, only telephone lines! "Aha! I know why these people are so ignorant! They don't have cable!" Looking back, I have to laugh that I once thought cable TV was the path to enlightenment.

I racked my brain over and again, wondering what drove people to racism and homophobia. On one trip to Shreveport, as I pulled up to a red light on a Tuesday afternoon, there were three guys in Ku Klux Klan outfits, handing out leaflets for a rally. Spooked, I decided to play dumb. I innocently asked, "Is this for Mardi Gras?" "No, it's not," they replied, "but we're having a rally tonight. You should come!" I guess that since I looked Hispanic, I passed their admissions requirements.

One of the worst bills introduced during this time was House Bill 290, classifying the murder of HIV-positive individuals as justifiable homicide. Sponsored by a representative from Shreveport, the bill affirmed that if you believed someone to be HIV positive and you felt threatened by them, you could kill them in self-defense. With such dangerous legislation on the way, I had to play spy.

Up in Baton Rouge, I removed my NO/AIDS ribbon and posed as a constituent from Bossier City. I walked up to the sponsoring representative and voiced my wholehearted support for the bill. It still managed to shock me, how many of these legislators came off as nice guys on first blush. But I was fishing for information, so I continued to chat in a friendly manner. When I casually brought up the number of African Americans that were dying from AIDS, he showed his true colors by responding, "Fuck those niggers if they can't afford a five-cent condom." His honesty was, frankly, helpful: it showed us not to waste our time cultivating a relationship with his office. We had to kill his bill in the House Judicial Committee, and we did. That bill lost by one vote.

After the win, I went up to that same representative, who was sitting in committee chambers in the state capitol, this time with a gleaming NO/AIDS ribbon pinned proudly on my lapel. "Excuse me, Mr. Representative," I said, "I'm one of those niggers you were talking about, and that's why your bill died." I had quite the blast!

For the most part, however, I had to be sparing with my dramatics. I had navigated political arenas to achieve my goals in the past—and I knew when to speak up and when to keep my mouth shut. As a lobbyist, I wasn't putting my own face forward. I needed to be a coordinator, not a leader of this movement. So I supplied community-based organizations around the state with the information they needed to persuade their own representatives that antigay bills were unnecessary. Getting all the pieces to fall into place required orchestration, not spectacle. The last thing I wanted was national or local media attention focused on me personally; I wanted to solve the problem and fix the system!

Of course, I wasn't completely muted. One time, a legislator and his whole "Christian" gang found me in the elevator and declared that they were going to heal me from sin. A Christian lobbyist in that elevator was moved to lay her hands upon me and pray for my salvation. I said, "Lady, if you lay your hands on me, you're going to lose them and find them up somewhere unpleasant!" They learned that this alligator had a bite. Remember, the culture wars were intense. Over in Florida, for instance, people were burning the computer of a young AIDS victim because the boy's hysterical family was convinced they could catch the virus through a machine. The panic was so extreme that it was international news when figures like Barbara Bush and Princess Diana cradled HIV-positive babies.

Fortunately, our NO/AIDS network drew strength from friends and relatives of those affected by the disease. And as for me, personally, I was happy to have much of my large New Orleans family on my side. My cousin Michael, whom I've already mentioned, had supported my campaign. His brother Dennis—who rose to be a state senator and later a judge on the Louisiana Fourth Circuit Court of Appeal—was extremely helpful during my time as a lobbyist. Dennis and I had grown up in the same circles and were the same age, but he palled around more with my younger brother Vernel than with me. Many people knew and respected Dennis, and he helped me understand, by example, not just how the state budget operated in a financial sense but how to maneuver around the various personalities.

One year, our lobby finally got the state to commit $10 million for HIV education—only to see it struck out of the budget by the legislature. This called for a visit to the governor. Mike Foster, the grandson of a former governor, had been born in Shreveport and raised in Franklin, planting roots from the top to the bottom of the state. An LSU grad, Governor Foster was a business-friendly good ol' boy with a country mustache and a bowling-ball head. Although he was Republican, he had bipartisan inclinations, and I was hopeful he would help replace the item in the budget.

To arrange a meeting, I called Andy Kopplin, the governor's policy director, whom I had known for quite some time. He helped me strategize my visit with a little role-playing.

"Good afternoon, Governor, I'm related to Dennis Bagneris," I ventured. "Don't use that," Andy replied. "Madlyn Bagneris is working for the governor, use Madlyn's name." I hadn't even known my cousin Michael's wife worked in Governor Foster's administration! The family still makes fun of her for working for a Republican.

I was learning how relationships worked in the system. I went to meet with the governor, prepared to argue my case that the number of people dying was intolerable! Before I even had time to launch into the speech I had practiced, he waved me off and said, "Nah, don't worry about it. I'm going to put that money back in the budget, we need that for medication." Thank goodness! But I didn't let it go at that. "By the way, Governor, didn't you promise me $2 million for education? The $10 million you just pledged to me was for medicine, but the legislators cut $10 million for education." Without missing a beat, he replied, "Now, you know you just got $10 million out of me! You better get your ass out of my office!" I laughed and choked and scuttled out. Governor Foster was about my favorite type of guy to work with. He called it the way he saw it and moved on. He recognized the seriousness of the AIDS crisis, and I'm still grateful for his realism. That $10 million ended up being spent on AZT and on education; it was spread among community-based organizations around the state, including NO/AIDS.

Unfortunately, even in the best of organizations, operations ebb and flow. As the economy heated up, nonprofits were competing for prominence. In 1997, NO/AIDS decided to hire a splashy new director whose fame inspired the organization to offer triple the salary of the old director. To make room, they had to let five of us go. I was fired on October 9, 1997, the first and last time I'd ever been fired from a job. It was time for me to live on my credit cards and find something new.

AIDS Candlelight March in Baton Rouge, with Larry at front right in ball cap [1991]

PHOTOGRAPH BY PAULA KREISSLER
LARRY BAGNERIS PAPERS, AMISTAD RESEARCH CENTER, NEW ORLEANS, LA

CHAPTER FOURTEEN / *The Oldest World*

Larry by the Dead Sea [1996]
COURTESY OF THE AUTHOR

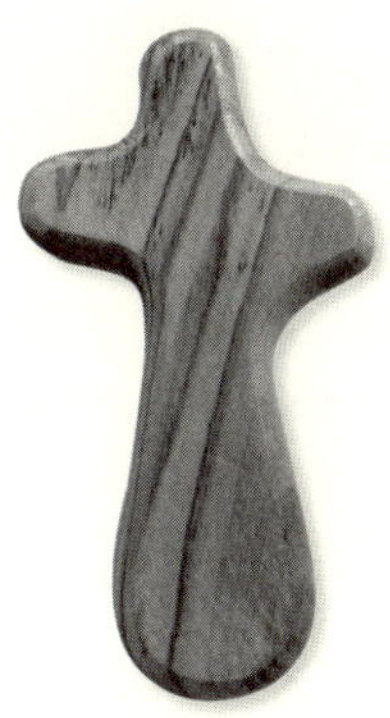

14

WHILE I MIGHT HAVE LOOKED THIRTY IN THE PICTURES, I WAS TURNING A half-century old in September 1996. To help me reflect on a lifetime of adventures, I embarked on a new one—a package tour of the Holy Land, in hopes of finding a semblance of spirituality. To make the most of the trip, I went the long way.

And so my grand birthday adventure actually began at Epcot. My sister Gina had treated me to a trip to Disney World to celebrate my big birthday. I'm so thankful for how close I am with my sister. She knew I loved Tinker Bell, fireworks, and rides—and she took time out of her busy schedule as a doctor to become a kid again with me, just the two of us.

From there, the plan was for me to spend some time in London before continuing on to Athens and then sailing to Israel. My brother's show *One Mo' Time* had enjoyed a run in London's West End in the early 1980s, and Vernel had introduced me to many of the close friends he had made there.

In addition to Vernel's connections, I was fortunate to have the company of one of my old Houston friends, Peter. He was a British boy and sometime West End girl, and it was wonderful wandering around with him and tugging on the different threads of his working-class sexuality. He had short hair, was slightly muscular, and was roughly my height, which I prefer. With his blond hair parted down the middle and his large collection of tank tops, he looked like a Backstreet Boy, and he had an engaging personality of gold. As the saying goes, Peter never met a stranger. He had just purchased a bar in London that played a lot of New Age music, which drove me nuts. It was, after all, the '90s.

The London Tourist Board is more than happy to attract gay and lesbian visitors—no surprise, given the city's wealth and breadth of gay geography. Every time I visit, I immerse myself in the Dickensian world of Christmas decorations and old Gothic buildings, like the ones I'd seen in the movie *Oliver.* Soho's gay history predates the twentieth century, and life centers on the intimate bars and large nightclubs of Old Compton Street as well as the perennially hip old alleys of the West End nearby. I've found pleasure in the city's quiet, cozy bars since my first trips during the 1980s on People Express Airlines from Houston, where you would pay your fare—as low as $99—in cash to an attendant pushing a cart down the aisle. In time, I got to know nightclubs like the cavernous Heaven, roost of Grace Jones herself. The crowds in that bar and in the West End in general have always been a great mix of not only Brits but also Italians, Arabs—everyone. London is truly a cosmopolitan city, and its gay community reflects that international flavor with its pageant of different sexualities and identities.

When my time was up in London, I was ready to proceed with my fiftieth birthday celebration. The next stop was Athens, the cradle of democracy, and point of departure for my cruise to the Holy Land. I've appreciated the gregarious nature of the Greek people since I was quite young, wandering the Decatur Street bars. As the ports of New Orleans and Houston industrialized, I still found bars that catered to Greek sailors where gays were welcome. Now, arriving in Greece for my cruise, I was greeted with the sort of warm weather that reminds me of home, and a welcoming culture of celebration and late-night dinners.

I was lucky to keep Peter's company on this leg of the trip. Civics nerd that I am, I dragged him to one old edifice after another; thankfully, he liked me enough to put up with it! I was truly reawakened to civic duty through this time travel to the beginning of democratic civilization and its foundations in law and philosophy. Greece inspired in me all the deep questions that human beings ask about ourselves. I still have a long reading list of books about the great philosophers, and I hope always to nurture that part of my character that focuses on justice.

As the Athens days grew into nights, we toured the city's many bars—and got lost more than once, thanks to the street signs in an unfamiliar alphabet. With the influence of the church still strong, Greeks don't have the sort of large clubs you find elsewhere in Europe. On our first night, Peter and I found a small, friendly bar that we adored; like others in the Gazi neighborhood, it felt more like a living room than a pub. Set in a large villa that reminded me of a Garden District mansion, our favorite bar was owned by a pair of guys in love who set the tone for patrons with their generous hospitality.

Turning fifty, I was thirsty for a revelation. I had been Catholic my whole life, but it was now time to meditate on my mortality. After a life of working and loving, I wanted to reach a spiritual plane. I imagined the Holy Land would be a place where I could seek guidance not only through Christian but also Jewish and Muslim spirituality. I wanted to find a deeper meaning in life, and I was certain that following in the footsteps of Jesus—especially in Jerusalem, the city where he lived and preached—would let me know him and our Father much better.

I woke up the morning of the cruise's departure in a five-star Piraeus hotel with a big room, sunken bathtub, and TV with American channels—a far cry from the interior cabin where I would spend most of my trip. After bidding goodbye to Peter, I boarded the boat with the other passengers. I immediately noticed that the crew was very attractive, the passengers less so.

Our itinerary included stops in Cyprus, Haifa, and Tel Aviv, with opportunities to disembark and take excursions. When you're on a cruise ship, you get to meet all kinds of people, which is fun at first. But this gets stale after you realize you're stuck with those people. After a lifetime of reading lips and observing body language, I was quick to size people up—who the control freaks were, who the storytellers were—and I noted which passengers were worth getting to know better.

After two days' travel, including the stop in Cyprus, we arrived at the dusty docks of Haifa, where I fell in line beside a woman from New York. Immediately, I picked up on a vibe from the soldiers handling border security. They squinted at me and spoke on their walkie talkies. I felt like I was back in Louisiana—so much so that I predicted, to my fellow passengers, that I was going to get pulled out of line.

"You! Come here!" I heard the familiar order and felt familiar nerves. I knew this Israeli soldier had a full clipboard of bureaucratic nonsense that he couldn't wait to unleash. With a bit of attitude, I dumped my backpack on the table. They rifled through it with haste, even spilling the contents on the floor, all the while asking me about this paper or that paper. While I was being frisked, I caught the eye of the New Yorker and mouthed, "See?"

I wouldn't call myself naive. But my abstract understanding of intergenerational trauma in the Middle East—the persistence of political conflicts over religious identity—now became embodied knowledge, for I presume they thought I was Arab. With this, I realized that my spiritual journey would be entangled with darker themes, and that I should prepare to witness frustration, misunderstanding, and suspicion.

When it came time to head down to the Old City of Jerusalem, I had had enough of my fellow passengers. They were overprivileged and judgmental. And they were tired of each other, too; I heard one lady mumble under her breath that an eighty-four-year-old tour member with a walker was holding everyone up and should have taken another tour. All I could do was glare at the complainer, sending her a wordless admonition about how "Christian" her behavior was.

So I got lost on purpose. I was a seasoned traveler, and I knew we had to meet at Zion Gate at a certain time, but for now it was time to explore. As I set out on my own, I finally felt like I was in the land of the Bible. The tightly clustered buildings seemed to grow out of the same desert stone blocks that composed the pavement, with doors and balconies reflecting centuries of architectural styles. Power lines and satellite dishes grew almost organically from the architecture, like vines and leaves, and there were ample sprouts of umbrellas signifying ice cream shops. With each turn of the alleyway, crosses, Stars of David, and crescents hung above, while below, rapt pilgrims, lost tourists, and unbothered locals mixed in the shade. I was greeted with ancient inscriptions in Latin and with newsstands displaying publications in Arabic and Hebrew. All of these people, all of these emotions, all of this history is packed into a piece of land not much larger than the French Quarter in downtown New Orleans.

Part of my Old City journey was a visit to the Wailing Wall. That was perhaps the closest I came to having a direct line with the Lord. A picture of me standing in front of the Temple Mount still sits in my living room. Here I was, with the glow of the sun in my face and a humble baseball cap on my head, my mouth open as if in the middle of a proclamation. It's a site with a holy hum, with buses coming and going, full of tears and laughter. I meditated on the destruction of the Second Temple and sought clarity for my future path, ideas for achieving gay rights and justice for all. Amen!

Soon, however, the glow would fade. Still in an elevated mood, I heard the beautiful voices of a choir and wandered toward the sound, which came from a shrine on the left side of the Wailing Wall. With my head in the clouds, I was brought back to earth by the bark of an attendant: "No trespassing!" Sensitive to segregation, I had learned through my life's experiences how to get in anywhere. Alas, not this time. I was already

Larry at the Wailing Wall, Jerusalem [1996]
COURTESY OF THE AUTHOR

upset that there were places men could go in Jerusalem that women could not. But those traditions have been around a lot longer than I have, and I was a visitor in this land, so I conceded. Now, however, gazing upon the Dome of the Rock and knowing that—on the orders of men with machine guns—I could not enter, that was a shock.

Having watched Jewish pilgrims go one way and Muslim pilgrims another, I set off to see some of the places drilled into me by catechism. What I discovered wasn't quite the land of camels and robes that I remembered from childhood church pageants. One site I wanted to see was the Mount of Olives, a holy burial ground for Jews and the site of many of Jesus's sermons. Maybe I was hoping to ascend to heaven on the spot, just as Jesus had, but it was hard to see myself as a disciple, with a modern hotel and restaurant across the street advertising air conditioning and a swimming pool! Rather than an oasis for quiet contemplation, I found stalls upon stalls of relics set up for pilgrims like me. True, similar stalls had perhaps stood here even before the time of Jesus, as religion and commerce intertwine in funny ways. I've seen similar phenomena in New Orleans. People of faith are drawn to see our city and experience our culture, yet we still have to eat, so we capitalize on their pilgrimages. In Jerusalem, by the Mount of Olives, everything holy was for sale. Holy water, holy olives, holy crosses, holy souvenirs—you name it. I wasn't immune, as I spent three dollars on a bottle of water sourced from the Jordan River and embellished with a cross, which I took home for my sister.

As the sun drifted high and then started to sink again, the shadows snapped me out of it. I was late! I wasn't just lost on purpose now, I was *lost*-lost. Somehow the local kids noticed the look of panic on my face and approached me with big smiles. They swarmed around, patting me down, searching for my watch and wallet. I consented to letting one of them guide me back to Zion Gate and I was happy, after all that hassle, to tip him $5. Without a blink, he protested, "That is not sufficient!" In New Orleans, we're experts at the small-time hustle, so I turned on my accent and my attitude and said, "You can take this $5 and shove it up . . ."—at which point a police officer overheard and pointed me toward the correct way to leave the old city. My fellow travelers were there, with unfriendly looks. I had already been late to join the group when we were touring the Garden of Gethsemane, and they weren't hesitant about reminding me.

I returned to the boat and, in the mood for solitude, had dinner delivered to my cabin. I didn't know what to expect in Bethlehem the next day. Seeing the Holy Land had been the main goal of my birthday travels—but now that I had arrived, I felt picked on. The Israelis treated me with suspicion, and instead of spirituality, I found a divided society.

Bethlehem is not too far south of Jerusalem; in fact, nothing is very far away from anything else in the Holy Land. We crossed a highway to enter the West Bank, and lo and behold, the atmosphere changed. Just as the Israelis had classified me as an Arab, the Palestinians imagined that I was a Muslim brother. As I wandered around the occupied territory, locals kept greeting me as a friend, inviting me to have tea and hang out in the shops and cafes. I didn't feel hustled; instead, they were just happy to share stories of their inconvenient lives.

Many Palestinians are laborers or service industry workers in Israel who must cross through heavily secured checkpoints every day. Unlike mine, their border crossings aren't simple. They must carry a pass and wait, unpaid, in line each morning to be let in. They would like to live in a functioning country, but their land is practically Swiss cheese, with holes carved out for Israeli settlements. Highways that they're not allowed to ride or to cross keep society segregated. Somehow, knowing that I was Creole made the Palestinians like me even more; our history of segregation made us spiritual brothers.

Encouraged by my warm welcome, I was ready to crouch through the Door of Humilty into the Church of the Nativity to see the gilded birthplace of my Lord and Savior, ready to be touched by an angel. Alas, despite all the new friends I had made in Palestine, I felt the same two-millennia shock that made me dizzy in Jerusalem. See, I was in Manger Square, a holy site for all of Christendom, with its Byzantine grotto and palm trees and other Christmas carol imagery, and right there was . . . Manger Square Liquor! And Bethlehem Laundromat! As beautiful as these old cities were, they were living neighborhoods, filled with the same sorts of characters I see back home. I had a good time in Bethlehem, but it certainly wasn't as spiritual as I'd expected.

That evening, with my ablutions behind me and my small interior cabin on the dark Mediterranean awaiting me, I wanted a night out. We were bound for Tel Aviv the next day, but we had spent every night on the lonely boat, and I was ready for a different kind of pilgrimage, a different kind of spiritual awakening. I wanted to see the gay bars. Having made friends with some of the officers on board, I inquired about Tel Aviv nightlife. I didn't want to miss out on it simply because our schedule only allowed us a daytime tour. They knew of a cabbie who would take me for the evening.

As we zoomed on a modern freeway, halfway from desert to sea, the lights went out! It's pitch black out, but the cabbie keeps whistling along. In perfect English, he explains that they're moving bombs and materiel, and they like to do it in the dark to keep Palestinians and other spies from getting any hints.

Here I was, halfway around the world, in the middle of a divided country, miles away from my boat, intent on finding a gay bar! What I really wanted to see was whether the hateful fictions of the outside world permeated the gay sphere; I hoped to find that gay Israelis and Palestinians got along better. I had the cabbie drop me off a few blocks away from my destination, out of privacy, so that I could wander on my own to the gay bar. I had never done this before, but in fear of being left behind, I took out a $100 bill, tore it in half, and told him that he could collect the rest that evening, when he came back to return me to the ship. Already, I was going crazy.

In comparison to the staid and dusty streets of Jerusalem, Tel Aviv was more Miami than Pharisee. My spirits rose seeing the beautiful beach, the sparkling skyscrapers, and the outdoor cafes filled with young adults enjoying themselves. The city's famous street cats, looked after by Tel Avivians of all colors and creeds, were enjoying the promenade as much as I was.

Gay life in Tel Aviv revolves around Allenby Street by the wide Rothschild Boulevard. The city as a whole has plenty of nightlife, and the drag show I saw that night was pretty good. The best part was meeting the bar's owners, one Palestinian and the other Jewish—who were boyfriends! This was the international and ecumenical spirit that I was looking for, with gays like me from all over Europe, Britain, and the Middle East having a good time. Warm feelings aside, I was jolted halfway through the show when a bomb went off! Despite having only one good ear, I felt the shock wave up and down my body—but when I looked around, no one had flinched. To the bar patrons, it was as if nothing had happened. The show went on. When I asked about it later, they said, "Oh, that? It happens all the time."

So yes, I did find that community I was seeking, that sense of worldwide purpose, belonging, and faith. Here in the gay bar, I didn't see any hate. I saw more love there than I had on any other part of the trip. It was a real spiritual moment. At 2:30 a.m., the driver returned to bring me back to my boat. Safe in my cabin, I slept through the night as the boat cast off from Haifa. I awoke the next morning in Tel Aviv, the city I had so recently departed. Since our tour group was only scheduled to spend one day there, my nighttime escapade was time well spent.

Because gays are oppressed, I've never failed to find togetherness in the gay bars. I'm sympathetic to Palestinians as a gay man because I know what it's like to be segregated and scared. I'm glad to belong to a community where people of all colors and ethnicities can come together in pride and safety. Yet outside my community, plenty of people feel that suffering is God's will. They are comfortable seeing others suffer, if it means that the oppressor's "purity" is preserved. Witnessing the communion of gay

Palestinians and Jews in the Holy Land gave me hope—while the broader struggle for dignity renewed my gratitude for the freedom and acceptance of diversity I've found within the gay communities of New Orleans and Houston.

Our ship departed Tel Aviv after a day of touring—and that night on board sure was bumpy. We had sailed into a storm, and the boat was listing to and fro. I heard that relief could be found by positioning oneself at the ship's center line. So, making my way past an Asian couple clutching barf bags, I found the movie theater, hoping to have it all to myself. Instead, however, I found a friend. He was a cute college kid from the Midwest, traveling with his family. We had made eyes at each other the whole trip, but mothers always know—and his kept following right behind me, her eyes shooting daggers. Hoping to stay out of trouble, I slipped out of the theater and made my way to the deck to watch the sun rise. The storm had passed, and I was lost in wonder: after a half century, I was seeing the world. However, I was not by myself. Across the messy deck chairs stood my friend, smiling.

With the ancient land now receding behind us, I stood on deck and imagined returning to the French Quarter. What would it be like to walk down its streets, after all I had seen on this transformational trip? I felt very blessed to have survived the world so far. But I also felt sobered by my experiences. Again, I hate to sound so naive, but it was heartbreaking watching Jews and Muslims fight over the smallest pieces of Jerusalem. It's not that I didn't know how sensitive people can be about their faith. Growing up Catholic, I've had the Holy Spirit guide me my whole life, and I still go to church on Rampart Street at Our Lady of Guadalupe Church and International Shrine of St. Jude. But I don't let the church control me in terms of who I am as a Black man or as a gay man. I've lived the history of the church's racism and homophobia.

A few years ago, I went to a funeral at St. Louis Cathedral for a friend of mine who ran the nightclub Oz, Tommy Elias. As I watched the priests handling everything, I thought to myself, we've come full circle here—because there are three hundred people from a gay bar sitting in this service. It's not too long ago that I maintained a grim look while doing the Stations of the Cross, attempting to pray the gay away, begging the Holy Spirit to save me from my heart and my desires. Now all these years later I'm at a Catholic gay funeral. Thank the Lord, I've been saved!

CHAPTER FIFTEEN / *Executive Director*

Ray Nagin, Larry, and Annise Parker at the 20th annual INLGO conference, New Orleans [2004]
LARRY BAGNERIS PAPERS, AMISTAD RESEARCH CENTER, NEW ORLEANS, LA

15

THE NEW MILLENNIUM WAS ALMOST HERE. AIDS HAD RECEDED, BILL CLINTON was president, and, like many in the gay community, I dared to hope for a brighter future. On New Year's Eve I wore a shirt that spelled out "Y," "2," "K," and a hearty "Welcome 2000" in battery-powered lights. We would party like it was 1999 until, around the world, the countdown was complete. I watched on TV as the clock struck midnight in each time zone, setting off a fresh round of fireworks. Everyone was ready for a new beginning.

It was around this time that I learned the New Orleans Human Relations Commission was looking for a new executive director. The commission had been founded in 1991 by then-mayor Sidney Barthelemy, who recognized that there was a missing link in the reform process. While activists raised awareness about discrimination in public accommodations, jobs, and housing, the city needed a way to discuss, investigate, and hopefully resolve conflicts. I had been a longtime member of the commission, under director Earl Jackson. Now Earl was retiring, and I really wanted the job.

I thought my odds were good. I was well known around town for my work with the NO/AIDS Task Force—and I was popular with local politicians, having rallied the gay community to throw their support behind a bunch of judges and members of the city council. Even though the directorship of the Human Relations Commission was an appointed rather than an elected office, it was important to me to gather official endorsements, with seals. I wanted council members, judges, and other dignitaries to make it known to Mayor Marc Morial that I was their preferred choice.

The mayor and I already had a relationship. I knew his father, Dutch, himself a former mayor. And I had watched Marc grow up and advance through the same political circles that had nurtured me. Two years out from the next mayoral election, he was already angling for an unprecedented third term in office—which would require changing the two-term limit for mayors in the City Charter.

When I met with Morial in his office, he said, "Ah! Everybody recommends you for this job. What can you do for me for my third term?"

I said, "Well, I've got the support of the gay community, I've got support from the gay businesses, I've got the support of the French Quarter community as well as the Black civil rights activists, is that enough? And I'll have your back, just like I had Earl's back."

Everybody thought Morial chose his staff for purely political reasons, but he really didn't. He was big on partnership and professionalism, and he didn't want to hog the spotlight. Everyone he partnered with worked with him, not for him. My close, collaborative relationship with the current director of the HRC mattered to the mayor. So, thanks to my community endorsements, and particularly to Earl Jackson's backing, Morial appointed me as the next head of the Human Relations Commission during Mardi Gras of 2000.

I formally took over the role on May 7, 2000, New Orleans's official birthday. When I walked into the HRC office that day, I had a clear idea of what I wanted to achieve during the next ten years. I envisioned the difference I could make in people's lives—gay or otherwise—and the opportunity to expand civil rights for all. I started working toward that goal on day one, when a distraught woman called from the convention center. As I headed out the door, my secretary Sidney, who had worked for Earl, asked me what I was doing, and I told her I was going over to the convention center.

Sidney replied that I needed to "send certified letters to the woman and the convention center and wait for an official response and . . . ." She proceeded to rattle off all sorts of protocol, when I interrupted her. I wasn't sending anything! I could only imagine the time previous directors had wasted, following these rules. In the old days, it took a week to even begin an investigation. I was going to the scene of the crime to correct it myself.

I got to the convention center to find a Black security guard at the door, barricading it against a white woman sitting outside with her child, who was hooked up to an oxygen tank. The guard didn't think it was proper for the woman to enter—but no matter how unpleasant the sight of disabled citizens might be for attendees at the current jewelry show, the convention center is a public space.

I knocked and said, "Open that door! I'm Larry Bagneris with the city's Human Relations Commission. You don't let this woman in, I'm gonna have your job and the job of every person who keeps this woman out of this center."

"Ooooooh, Mr. Bagneris," was the answer from the woman who opened the door.

I said, "Don't 'Mr. Bagneris' me—just let this woman and her child get into the cool air." The security guard suddenly pretended to be gracious, but I was still so angry. I didn't have any authority to fire her, but I did take the opportunity to educate her. I explained that they used to do the same thing to us: segregate us from public spaces, because of the color of our skin. And even if it was now a Black lady keeping a white lady outside, the transgression was the same!

I would stay in my job at the HRC for eighteen years, and I would see the same stupidity repeated over and over and over again. When you see it once, and then a second time, you call people on it. You can either be nice about it, so they can cover themselves and apologize, or you can take my preferred approach. I would say that we have an issue here—and you can either work with me to resolve this in-house, or you can have the media do my work instead. Our three TV channels were always hungry for content, and I knew if I were to call they would all show up. No surprise, then, that nearly all discrimination cases were handled quietly through mediation.

My approach worked even better under Mayor Ray Nagin, who was inaugurated in 2002. Nagin was a business-positive mayor, and I communicated that message as a member of his team. I would tell businesses that without their revenue, we wouldn't have a city to run—so let's put our heads together and see what's good for their business and their customers. I started every HRC case on that note, unless I was dealing with the police department or fire department, where a different approach was needed. Cases were typically easy to resolve, once the business owner recognized that our administration preferred to settle matters without getting the media involved.

Ray was a bit of a micromanager, but he was very personable and devoted to the cause of justice. He personally came into the gay community to thank us for our support and wish us happy holidays. Marc Morial acted like a respectful CEO, but Ray Nagin acted like a neighbor and friend.

My office was on the eighth floor of City Hall, overlooking Poydras Street. I was already friendly with many of the workers at City Hall, having gone to school with some of them and worked with others in political campaigns. The eighteen members of the Human Relations Commission had been selected—two by the mayor, one each by the city councilors, and the rest by recommendation of local college presidents—to reflect the city's diversity across lines of race, religion, gender, and sexuality. The HRC was empowered by chapter 86 of the city code to meet once a month. If any New Orleanians felt that they had been discriminated against, they could report this to their local commissioner, who would forward the complaint to my office. Once a month we would take our docket before the full commission; review the actions we had taken; and draft a report for the mayor.

As I look back on my work with the HRC, I'm proud of the many cases I helped to resolve. In one case, a young woman who worked for the mayor's office went to the shopping center across the street from City Hall. Security asked to check her bag, but they didn't seem to be asking the same of white customers, so she called me. I went to the store to observe the employees, and sure enough, I saw the same pattern. No white customers were ever asked to check their bags, but every Black woman was. So after watching these goings-on three afternoons in a row, I went to the store manager to inform her that a discrimination complaint had been filed. She denied the accusation, but I told her I'd personally witnessed Black customers being hassled. I took my usual approach, explaining that we didn't want this to get out of hand, and I invited her to join me and the complainant at the food court. The manager apologized, and I left them sitting there, having a conversation. I always tried to bring the two people together; I'd say my piece, then let them talk. Once they both signaled an understanding, I would wrap the process up.

Later that afternoon I went down to check on the young woman in her office. She was sitting at her desk and said, "Look, I got a $50 gift certificate!"

And I said, "Dahling, this ain't about that. We goin' back over there and give that certificate back."

She said, "What do you mean?!"

I said, "You're putting this Commission in an embarrassing position if you even think about taking that coupon in exchange for your indignity. You're coming with me now!" As we rushed back across the street,

I continued, "This ain't about no $50 coupon. This is about people stepping up to the plate and realizing that they did wrong, and $50 ain't gonna cover it. How many other people were hassled? What's she gonna do, give them all $50 coupons?"

She insisted, "I'm not giving this back!" and I said, "Yeah, you are giving it back!" And I marched her back to the store to make sure she did just that. Our principles are worth much more than a coupon.

During my HRC term, at the urging of Mayor Nagin, I also started cracking down on Southern Decadence. The media had seized upon certain bad behavior on Bourbon Street and they were having a field day. I had worked too hard fighting for Houston Pride and for gay rights elsewhere for people to come down from Atlanta and New York and act disgusting, getting graphic with each other in the middle of Bourbon Street. They wouldn't do that in their own cities, so don't fucking come here and do it. They don't even do that in San Francisco anymore.

"That's what New Orleans is for," they would say.

"I beg your PARDON?" I would respond. I used to argue with people about it, but then I stopped arguing and simply cut to the chase: "Well, you'll be arrested, and that'll keep me employed. The bail goes to my city salary!"

I got nasty letters from people all around the country when I put my foot down for Southern Decadence. I prepared a year in advance, training volunteers to be in the streets with flashlights, and letting people know that if they got unruly they would go to jail. I did an interview with John Quiñones on *Primetime Live*, though it never made the air, stating that we have a right as a community to party, but we also have a responsibility to maintain public standards.

I've had guys at Southern Decadence ask why they can't show their penis, and I say, "Well, how would you like to see women showing their vaginas?" They'll respond that women show their breasts, to which I say, "You can show your breasts too, if you'd like!" But as far as showing your genitals—well, if you start following the route that leads to "That's what New Orleans is for" . . . I'ma put you *under* the jail, not inside the jail.

The bottom line was, we had to send a message. When I received nasty emails and letters, I would type up an angry response—and Page McCranie, my assistant, would then kindly delete it. She was good for me. She allowed me to get these frustrations out of my system, but she made sure they never escaped past the walls of our office. I learned to wait a couple of hours before sending an emotionally charged message. Even today, I take the time to figure out the proper tone, rather than be caught saying something I'll regret.

On New Year's Eve, as 2004 turned into 2005, a college student named Levon Jones was killed in front of Razzoo, a hip-hop bar on Bourbon Street. He was a young patron, and four bouncers took him from inside the bar and sat on him. I was in my apartment in the Quarter when I saw it on the news, and I thought, that's a predominantly Black bar, why would he be killed? So I walked down Bourbon Street myself to see what was going on and calm my mind. I always took my job very personally because I wanted to be on top of everything, whether it was in my own community or anywhere in the city. Levon was Black, and the four bouncers who sat on him were all white. From experience, I knew that you would really have to be acting up to get four people to sit on you. But video footage would later show that all Levon did was get upset that his friend had been denied entrance due to a dress code violation.

I just knew this incident was going to come to the HRC. I was about to leave for a vacation in Brazil, but I was inclined to stay in town to handle the investigation myself. Wise as always, Page convinced me that we needed outside help to conduct a more thorough study of the bars. The Razzoo case touched a nerve and stirred up all the old stories. Mayor Nagin even called me into his office and told me that, according to his son, there were rooms in the Quarter where they lock Black people up. That's a rumor, I told him—but that's how scared Black people were about coming

NO BOTTLES
OR GLASS
ALLOWED
ON STREET
ALL DRINKS
MAY BE
IN PLASTIC
CONTAINERS

Southern Decadence [2013]
COURTESY OF THE AUTHOR

into the Quarter at that time. The mayor told me he didn't want the incident whitewashed. He wanted the truth.

I said, "Me? Whitewash something, when it comes to race?!" I wasn't about to put up with that behavior. I wanted to get to the bottom of it—but we needed a system to get it done.

Our first step was to send "secret shoppers" into the bars to check for discrimination. We selected eighty places around the Quarter and even went to the extra trouble of putting body cameras on some of our agents. Page had recommended that we follow the lead of the Greater New Orleans Fair Housing Action Center (GNOFHAC, now the Louisiana Fair Housing Action Center), whose director, James Perry, was a good friend of mine. They used secret shoppers to test for housing discrimination, and Page knew we could set up a similar system for our complaints—with the added benefit of allowing me to take my vacation while things got underway.

GNOFHAC's report came back, and it wasn't good. In 57 percent of the bars, Black secret shoppers were treated worse than white secret shoppers: they were subject to higher drink charges, made-up minimum drink requirements, and denial of entrance based on dress code. (We made a point of dressing all of our shoppers, regardless of race, basically the same, in the wide-legged jeans and backwards caps popular at the time.) When the report was released, we met at the GNOFHAC office, and reporters from all the local media were there. Sally Forman, the mayor's public relations director, had called the press conference, knowing that the media is always hungry for salacious content.

For my portion, Sally said, "Look, we've prepared a script for you," and I said, "You're not going to tell me what to do. I know how to do this. I suggest you all stand in the back of the room and let me handle this."

I stepped up to the microphone and said, "This is not 1960, and we are not putting up with discrimination! But we have found that this discrimination is not necessarily from hard prejudice but from stupidity. Black people often discriminate against other Black people just as much as white people discriminate against Black people!"

The French Quarter is a hustle. If you go into the bar and you don't tip your server, or you ask an employee if there's a cover charge and don't know that it's free—then yeah, they'll tell you there's a mandatory tip and there's a cover charge. I've done it myself as a joke, standing in front of a bar in an all-black outfit with my shaved head: someone thinks I'm the bouncer and asks me if there's a charge, and I say, "Sure, it's $20," just so I can laugh when they take out their wallet. It's the same thing for the bouncers. They think, hey, I'm not making any money here, so I'll charge that cover. I knew the routine, but I didn't realize it was as bad as the numbers showed. I suggested that we institute a training program and that everybody working in the bars in the Quarter get a certificate from the HRC.

After I returned from an amazing trip to Brazil, we conducted classes for bartenders, which attracted plenty of media attention. Camille Whitworth from WDSU, the local NBC affiliate, showed up. Eighty people had signed up for the class, but 140 showed up. I knew this was less about discrimination and more about habit and stupidity, and I emphasized that the training was a way to prevent future tragedies like the death of Levon Jones.

"If an incident like this happens again, and there's a class action suit, that'll cost the city and the businesses millions of dollars and negative publicity," I explained. We had Synthia Taylor from the US Department of Justice, the Eighth District police captain, a lawyer representing the bars, someone from the ACLU, and me.

It was a high-stakes game, and I was paying close attention to the mood in the room. The service industry people were angry because they weren't getting paid for this, and it was a mandatory two-hour training. Consider, too, that New Orleanians don't often get together—or didn't, back then—in large interracial groups to talk about discrimination. The first three people who spoke were Black.

When it came time for my friend Chris Young, a white lawyer for the bars, to get up and speak, he tried to be sassy: "Notice that everybody who's gotten up here already is Black," he said, as if that wasn't obvious to everyone in the room.

I thought, okay, you want to play that? I went to the microphone and said, "Hey, white boy, the next three people I invited to speak are white as well, so don't come off with 'all Black people.' This is an integrated environment, as you can see out here, so take that back, white boy!" It gave me a chance to show who was in charge as well as make people laugh and show we were friends working together to solve problems. We're all human.

We went through the training, which laid out the legalities involved and the fact that if this shit kept happening, we were going to be facing a lawsuit. Bars needed to post all drink prices and information about cover charges. After we finished the training, Camille from WDSU wanted to interview me live. She started with, "Those people were very hostile." I said, "You'd be hostile too, if they weren't paying you, and you had to have a certificate to go back to work to make sure you weren't hustling people." I was very me on the television, and I put on the whole bit. I used the force of my personality to tell truths about the ancient hustle of Bourbon Street. Even if race wasn't a direct factor in the money grab, I observed, minorities were affected the most.

We ended up holding a total of four training sessions. At the last training we hosted six or seven major bars, three of which were owned by the same white woman. She asked, "Why do these patrons gotta walk around with all them hip-hop clothes on?"

I thought, but didn't say out loud, "All right, all right, ALL RIGHT!! I get that you are really out of place, and I personally wouldn't go there." It wasn't my desire to explain fashion and discrimination to an older white lady, and show her up in public—considering that her outfit wasn't going to win any prizes, either. Later we had a private discussion about why we could not discriminate against those wearing hip-hop clothes, and by the end we were laughing with one another.

We trained 1,400 bar representatives through that program. I also built a relationship with Synthia, which was helpful when the Essence Festival—a major Black entertainment and empowerment event—came to town in

July. We were walking around Bourbon Street during the festival, letting visitors know the HRC was available to help with any problems they might encounter.

A Black woman came running out of a bar and said, "They are discriminating against me! SEE, that sign says they are!" The sign said the drink was $4, and the register rang her up for $5.

I took her back inside and told the bartender, "For God's sake, give this woman her dollar back, and get your register corrected before we have an international incident on our hands." For a DOLLAR. He said, "I gotcha," and took care of it.

When the first of the four bouncers who killed Levon Jones went to court, the trial was moved to Lake Charles, two hundred miles west of New Orleans. It was 2008, a few years after Katrina, but the reason for the move, or so they argued, wasn't storm damage—it was the possibly prejudicial effects of all the media coverage.

"They're all going to get off," I thought, when I heard about the change of venue. And sure enough, a jury of eleven whites and one Black found that first bouncer not guilty. A Baton Rouge jury acquitted the second defendant, and then the prosecution dropped charges against the last two. So that kid died, and not a soul was found guilty.

CHAPTER SIXTEEN / *Katrina*

NOAA/NASA satellite image of Hurricane Katrina [2005]
COURTESY GOES PROJECT SCIENCE OFFICE

16

WHEN HURRICANE KATRINA HIT NEW ORLEANS IN LATE AUGUST 2005, I WAS working for the Nagin administration. As the storm crossed the southern tip of Florida into the Gulf of Mexico, I didn't think too hard about the danger and chose to stick with my usual hurricane routine, which is to secure a po'boy sandwich, dressed, and a cup of gumbo for safekeeping in the refrigerator. The French Quarter never loses power. And after a lifetime of potential evacuations, this time, as always, I thought, "I'ma sit this one out." In the years before we were aware of climate change, before routine 160 mph winds, it was easy to simply close my apartment's shutters and wait out the storm at a bar. I'd been through two or three serious hurricanes, when Jimmy and I would go to the bar, hang out until the wind escalated, and then head home. Even then, Jimmy and I would roll up our pants and wade through knee-deep water when we needed to refresh our cocktails.

It took a long time for everyone to truly understand the gravity of the situation. We had lived through so many tropical depressions, tropical storms, hurricane watches, and hurricane warnings that I didn't expect Katrina to be any worse than usual. So I decided to go to the bar. Then I turned on the news and was struck.

For the first time, I saw lines of people with suitcases and sacks of belongings waiting to enter the Superdome. They could only pack what they could carry, even if they needed extra food or medication or toiletries. Some were so disconnected from the news that they only realized that the storm was coming as the first sprinkles and warm gusts of tropical air arrived. I immediately thought to help. It was easy for me to take my city car, which bore the city's seal on the doors and "Mayor" on the bumper, to park on Poydras Street and volunteer at the stadium. I wore my city shirt and carried my city ID, but I only recognized a few other volunteers. I helped people check in, gave them directions to various parts of the Dome, and most importantly, pointed out the bathrooms. After about forty-five minutes, Clarice Kirkland, with the mayor's office of community affairs, came around and informed volunteers that anyone with a city car was ordered to drive it out of the city.

I was happy to see that preparations seemed to be orderly, and I wasn't too concerned about my car because the Quarter never flooded. Soon, word reached us that Mayor Nagin was making his rounds to inspect operations and thank everyone. Dressed in a pair of jeans, he was clear-headed and in charge, and many essential city personnel were staying just across the street at the Hyatt Regency.

The mayor reiterated his order that anybody with a city car should leave to protect the vehicles from any potential flooding. I said, "Well, I don't have to go because I have off-street parking."

Ray said, "Handle it the way you see fit, but if you can get out of here, get out of here." By then, it was close to ten on Saturday night, so I left for home, stopping in the French Quarter bars to check on my community before heading to bed early.

I happened to wake up at seven o'clock the next morning—Sunday, August 28—which was unusual, as I usually wake up at noon on weekends. I turned on the TV in the bedroom and saw the size of the hurricane that was approaching. To me, it seemed like Katrina's clouds stretched the entire length and width of the Gulf. I thought to myself, "I gotta get out of here."

By then I was getting calls from everybody—a first for my new cell phone—urging me to evacuate. My sister Gina had called. My brother had called from New York. Ramon and David had called, and everyone was saying "you gotta get outta there, this is a really big thing." I only needed to worry about evacuating myself, as my dad had passed away in 1999 and my mother had passed in 2003. As I was packing, I was thinking I'd be back in two or three days. Even after seeing the size of Katrina on TV, and even after the first, light effects of the storm arrived Saturday night, Sunday had dawned as bright as any summer's day, with only a few high-altitude clouds whirling past. I took the sandwich, put it in a cooler, got some cold drinks, and started on my way. Sixteen hours later, after traveling bumper to bumper on I-10, I was at Ramon and David's house in Houston.

Ramon and David are my best friends, and they were truly like family throughout the entire Katrina period. I was so tired after arriving in Houston Sunday night, I had slept all the way into Monday morning. Unbeknownst to me, Katrina made landfall east of New Orleans around sunrise that morning. Then, one at a time, the levees started to break. The worst of the storm had passed, but the worst of the tragedy had just begun.

That first night in Houston my sister Gina came over with her dog; she was staying with a girlfriend of mine, Natasha Gomez. We cooked gumbo at the house and had margaritas, and we couldn't help thinking everything was going to be okay. We were just hanging around, hanging out the way you do when you're with close friends and family. Then we woke up on Tuesday and saw on TV that everything was flooded. And I thought, "All right, I'm going to be here in Texas for a while."

For years, in my office at the HRC, I had kept a "For Colored Patrons Only" sign from a New Orleans streetcar, just to inspire me and remind me why the job mattered. At some point I had given it to Ramon and David—and now they pulled it out and set me up with a little desk in their kitchen to be silly. Before that, I'd been sitting around, with real tears and puffy eyes, feeling sorry for myself. But Ramon and David knew exactly how to straighten me out, to remind me of the racism all of us had faced growing up as Mexicans in Texas and Creoles in Louisiana.

Ramon said, "Get your stuff, come on." They took me to the Astrodome, where refugees were being warehoused, and they said, "You've got your own room, your own bathroom, and air-conditioning, and you wanna CRY?! You better get your shit together." Their message was clear: either you get your reality together, or we can dump you off here. And it was a good slap in the face for me.

Everybody displaced by the storm had to get identification cards and deal with a whole bunch of other government paperwork. By Wednesday, August 31, Houston City Hall had set up a major satellite office in East Houston to issue "Katrina Victim" cards—and every day thereafter, on my phone, something or somebody would tell me what to do—go file for the food card, do this, do that. And every time, I wondered, "Who is sending me this?" To this day, I don't know where those messages came from—they were just texts, with no number connected to them. Remember, this was 2005, and it was a hassle to juggle messages on a flip phone.

I also reconnected with my contacts at the Houston Pride Committee to set up relief for gays in our community who were stranded after evacuation. I contacted several bars to see if they would be willing to do fundraisers—and I got in touch with the Montrose Counseling Center to see if they could handle any accounting related to cash flow from donors to evacuees. The community response was overwhelming. Many Houston residents provided clothing, food, and gas vouchers, and even offered to open their homes to provide spare rooms and beds.

By the first week of September, I had joined the YMCA gym and collected my food stamps. I had also inspected the donated clothes I'd received and realized I needed to return home for a day and retrieve my essentials.

So on Saturday, September 10, Ramon, David, and I snuck back into New Orleans in my city car with the city insignia. We came in along River Road on the West Bank, up across the Crescent City Connection bridge, and into the Quarter. It was dead and derelict. We saw how much damage had been done to the city, but fortunately, my building was mostly okay. The power was out, my plant had died, and the fridge stunk of rotten food. A brick wall had caved into the condo's pool, tearing out supports for balconies on the back end of the complex, and a tree had fallen onto an exterior air conditioning system.

By Sunday, I had returned to Houston to check on my friend Aletha Bryant. She was my favorite bartender in New Orleans, a straight Black woman who worked at the gay bars and had earned a loyal clientele through her nurturing energy. Aletha had evacuated to Houston with her family and called me in need of a job. In short order, I had her working at JR's. On the night of the 11th, I walked in, and the place was packed with New Orleanians. We have a decades-old tradition on Sundays, where we toss napkins to the song "Love Is in the Air." The song was playing as I walked in the door.

The manager, new to this tradition, came to me with eyes popping out of his head, saying, "This can't be tolerated! You don't just throw stacks of napkins all over my floor." Aletha was behind the whole ritual, and the manager, exasperated, yelped, "I can't keep her on." This was only her second shift, and already, everybody knew Aletha. But in the manager's eyes, the napkin tossing was "a little bit too much for this bar." Aletha was quick to respond, "I don't want to work the fuck here anyway." She took it in stride. She had evacuated with her family—and spending time with them was more important than putting up with nonsense at work.

By Monday, September 12, I was invited to speak on the local Pacifica station about the Houston gay community's plans to support gay evacuees, and by Wednesday, September 14, New Orleans city workers were called to Houston City Hall to set up a government in exile. September 15 was my fifty-ninth birthday, and I celebrated with chicken and mole.

In the weeks that followed, I continued to build bridges between the gay communities of Houston and New Orleans. The relief efforts I had started in Houston—getting all the bars together to solicit donations and host fundraising events, including drag shows—were a big hit in the local leather community. And the broader gay community was extremely responsive, both in Texas and beyond. The Metropolitan Community Church of Dallas made a $10,000 donation on behalf of the Lesbian and Gay Community Center of New Orleans. The International Network of Lesbian and Gay Officials, or INLGO (now known as the LGBTQ+ Victory Fund) had hosted a big conference in New Orleans the previous year, so sympathies ran strong and sparked generous giving. In Houston, the Montrose Counseling Center was a hotbed of activity, our dropoff spot for clothes, water, and gift cards for people who had evacuated to Texas. I stopped by the community center on a daily basis, asking if anybody needed money or assistance to carry on. Fortunately, all these supports were in place when Hurricane Rita, another powerful storm, hit near the Texas-Louisiana border early on September 24.

On September 29, one month after Katrina, the city finally emailed all of us employees and told us to return to work in New Orleans on Monday, October 3. We were to report to City Hall, at 1300 Perdido Street—but since so many people had lost their homes, the city had docked a pair of cruise ships for us to use as lodging, beginning on Saturday, October 1.

I spent Friday night with my sister Gina. She had received a call to return to work as an emergency room doctor and was assigned to Lafayette. The next day, I crossed the river at Baton Rouge and was speeding along the Bonnet Carré Spillway when my radio finally found WWOZ on the dial. After everything I had been through, that long month, it didn't take long for the tears to stream down my face when I heard Fats Domino's "Walking to New Orleans" followed by Louis Armstrong's "Do You Know What It Means to Miss New Orleans."

My brother, Vernel, had been in New York during this whole time. The storm had hit just as he closed on the sale of his New York condo. Luckily, the purchasers allowed him to stay in his old place as long as he needed, while New Orleans recovered. My sister Joanne had flown up to stay with Vernel in New York. Her husband and one of her sons had been in their house in Gentilly, behind Dillard University, as the water rose. They had frantically texted as many people as they could to turn on the pumps. Now, weeks later, they were working on their house as the water receded, and I got them a room at the French Quarter Courtyard Hotel and Suites on Rampart. I was trying to take care of the family, but I also felt a responsibility to the city.

By this time most of the water had drained out of New Orleans, but almost nobody was back yet. It was terrible. I was so homesick, however, that my return home was a joy. I was blessed that the city was surviving and that I was in a position to help.

As staff members in the mayor's office, my secretary Page and I were deemed essential employees. This meant that the city provided us with rooms on one of those cruise ships on the Mississippi River—and it was awful. When I arrived on the boat I found it crowded with people, all of whom had horrible hurricane stories. I had been assigned a roommate. I didn't know this guy, but I quickly pegged him as a slob because the room was a mess—old pizza everywhere—and I thought, "Oh, NO." So I put the "do not disturb" sign on my luggage, set it in the cabinet, and went down to the front desk.

The Scandinavians running the ship wouldn't give me a room by myself, so I called Page to see if she could come and pretend to be my wife. She was staying in her own house in Metairie because it hadn't been touched by the storm—and she couldn't make it downtown that first night because of the citywide six o'clock curfew. Rather than spend a miserable night with my mystery roommate, I decided to get off the ship and go get drunk. There was only one gay bar open—Lafitte's—and I just hung out in the bar and drank all night long. It was packed with day laborers, FEMA workers, and some gays who had returned now that the city was reopened. And wouldn't you know, Aletha Bryant was back from Houston!

Page made it out to the ship the next day, and we signed up as husband and wife, so I got my own room. My new living arrangement lasted a while, but even without a roommate I didn't like it. I thought I was going to get fat on that boat because they were feeding us so many carbs, I was constantly eating ice cream from the stress of hearing everyone's depressing stories, and there was no fresh food. Somebody on the boat had said that a Popeye's had opened up across the river, and I was dying for some Popeye's chicken. I drove over the bridge right before curfew, just as they were closing for the night.

The guy said, "All we've got left is an eight-piece box."

I said, "Gimme that—here's twenty bucks." I took the chicken and went home to my condo. I was sitting on the floor, sweating my ass off, and I said to myself, "Tomorrow, I'm getting an air conditioner and some water, and I'm going to move back into my home."

The next day I drove to Baton Rouge, bought that air conditioner, put it in the wall in my apartment, moved everything into one room, covered the door to minimize air leaks, and waited for the water to come back on. My plan was to keep the room on the cruise ship to shower and to keep food cold in the fridge. But after a week they caught on to the fact I wasn't sleeping there and informed me that they'd confiscate all my clothes if I didn't check out in twenty-four hours.

So I moved back to my apartment full time—even though the city water wasn't safe for drinking or bathing. I showered with bottled water. None of us city employees were looking our best, during those early days of the recovery! People would show up to meetings, in the ballroom of the Hyatt

Regency, without having shaved or ironed their clothes. You might think that life on a cruise ship sounds luxurious, but that was far from the truth. There were so many people living on those ships—the police, fire department, all the city employees—and the crowded conditions were draining. The whole scene was chaotic: people parked wherever they wanted in the lot by the cruise terminal and didn't care whether or not they were blocking other cars. Forget about using your car if you needed to run errands, buy toiletries, or travel out of town for groceries and other essentials. I was glad I'd decided to escape that nightmare and make do in my own apartment, despite the lack of city services.

New Orleans reopened slowly, one neighborhood at a time. Even when an area was cleared for residents to return, businesses were still closed. Around Halloween, I noticed that more and more service industry folks were returning to town—but they didn't have jobs to go to.

I made it my mission to work with the administration to get more bars open. Aletha was of great help, as she worked for the group that owned Lafitte's in Exile, Good Friends, and the Rawhide—and she knew Tommy Elias at Oz, the big gay club, very well. At the time, only three bars were serving drinks (and employing workers) in the French Quarter. Johnny White's had remained open through the storm and was still doing business 24/7, while among gay bars only Lafitte's and the Bourbon Pub and Parade had reopened. The police enforced the midnight curfew upon our establishments with much more enthusiasm than elsewhere.

The heart of our community beats through our service industry workers, and I knew they needed to get their livelihoods on track as fast as possible. So on Wednesday, October 26, I went to the mayor and said, "Look, Halloween is coming, and we need to get the bars open again, particularly the gay bars." I played up the economic angle: Halloween was the first big holiday after Katrina, and there was money to be made by local businesses.

The mayor wasn't convinced: "Have you been down there? That's a formula for disaster—it's FEMA people, day laborers that don't speak English, and people from the Wild West." But he gave me license to approach the police and see what I could come up with.

Sure enough, I managed to cut a deal with the Eighth District police. The Pub and Lafitte's would keep their doors open until midnight—and then everyone who was already inside could stay, but with the doors shut until six in the morning. Everyone would behave themselves, and we'd be fine. With this compromise, the bars wouldn't lose so much money, and neither would the kids who were the bartenders. Once everyone saw how much money people were willing to spend for the holidays, it was easier to convince the city to keep loosening up its restrictions. The other neighborhood bars still needed repairs and had to miss Halloween, but they were able to open not too long after. It was the beginning of the end of all the shit we had been through.

Katrina was a devastating blow to my city, and to so many people. I didn't want all of it to overwhelm me mentally, so I kept an emotional distance. I kept saying to myself, "Pick and choose your battles, and don't get too deep into your misery." Volunteering and community organizing allowed me to contribute to New Orleans's recovery without breaking myself emotionally. I was lucky that my apartment hadn't been damaged as badly as other residences in town; everything inside was more or less intact. For comparison, I only had to consider my sister Joanne's place, in Gentilly. She had taken ten feet of water.

In the middle of everything, a friend of mine came over to my place and said, "You see all the bricks that fell in that pool? You could hire some day laborers to get those bricks out, and you could make a lot of money selling off the materials." His mind always went to disaster capitalism. But for me it was about quality of life, and I didn't need that responsibility—or any more stress. That was one hustle I could ignore. Years later, when legitimate contractors were restructuring the pool, I told them that story, and they said, "Thank God you didn't do that because this pool would have collapsed!"

Thankfully, I had somewhere to put my pent-up emotional energy. The week before Thanksgiving, I had a meeting in Seattle with INLGO, the group that had given so much money, time, and energy to assist with Katrina recovery. I gave a report, which was well received, as every cent was accounted for—and they were happy to know their resources had done some good. While I was out west, I invited an aide to Seattle's mayor and two other friends from Washington State to join me in December for our Christmas Eve celebrations. We ended up having a great time, with twelve of us taking a limo out to the River Parishes for the famous bonfires. They were as magical as they have always been.

CHAPTER SEVENTEEN / *Recovery*

Monument to Latin American workers who helped rebuild New Orleans after Hurricane Katrina [2024]
PHOTOGRAPH BY KEELY MERRITT, HNOC

17

BACK AT THE HUMAN RELATIONS COMMISSION, ONLY A FEW DISCRIMINATION cases were landing on my desk. Everyone was distracted by hurricane recovery and the demands of rebuilding. However, the large influx of Latin American day laborers and construction workers was beginning to create a fresh source of friction. New Orleans would need to adjust to its new demographics.

The HRC received word that day laborers were being ripped off, exploited by the many slapdash contractors who had lived in the city for decades as well as the fly-by-nighters who came swarming in. In addition, restaurants were complaining about the proliferation of taco trucks and food stands that they swore were threatening their business. Always sympathetic to my construction-working brothers, I needed to find the words to keep everyone calm before getting down to the task of protecting the laborers. I told the city council that the food trucks represented no true threat to the restaurants. When these workers, all sweaty and covered with sawdust, went in search of lunch, they understood other patrons would be upset if they entered a traditional restaurant, so they preferred to patronize the mobile vendors. The gambit worked—and that gave me the space and confidence to recruit Eva Hurst to translate in Spanish and get to the bottom of the discrimination complaints.

At the time, Eva was working with Catholic Charities on outreach services to the Hispanic community. Since my role was to stamp out discrimination in New Orleans, I was introduced to Eva through her boss Martin Gutierrez, who was a member of the HRC. Before long, Eva and I had developed a close friendship. We went into the field—visiting points on Claiborne Avenue and Martin Luther King Jr. Boulevard as well as all the Lowe's and Home Depot stores—to let day workers know the HRC was open to hearing any complaints they had about how they were treated. What we found was that they were working hard, but not getting paid! Since many of them weren't documented, it was easy for people to shoo them away after their construction work was complete, without paying them.

Eva volunteered her time endlessly. She made arrangements with Luz Molina of Loyola Law School, and soon law students were set up at a church in Mid-City, screening complaints from day laborers. In addition, Eva and I personally took on fifteen cases, visiting contractors directly to encourage them to pay their laborers. They all refused, and some were quite tough.

Thankfully, Professor Molina provided some legal muscle by documenting the workers' claims of abuse and preparing the cases for court. Her project, aptly named Workplace Justice, quickly established itself as an invaluable resource for workers reconstructing New Orleans, most of whom earned very low wages. By 2007, Professor Molina's former student Vanessa Spinazola, by then a licensed attorney, joined the effort through her work with the New Orleans Pro Bono Project and hosted a Thursday-night wage-claim clinic. We thought we were providing a legal service of limited duration, but it turned out to be a long-term struggle.

On my end, I contacted Marc Morial's sister Monique, an attorney working in the First City Court Clerk's Office, to see if the courts would set aside one day a week to hear cases in Spanish, with interpretation provided by Loyola Law students. Monique and her colleagues enthusiastically agreed. Now, when the contractors received subpoenas from the court, they realized that the HRC, the Pro Bono Project, Loyola Law School, and the day laborers meant business.

The Workplace Justice Project, in operation since Katrina, has represented over 1,600 individuals from a broad demographic of low-wage workers, and has recovered more than $600,000 in unpaid wages. I'm proud to have collaborated with the WJP and the Pro Bono Project on behalf of day laborers. Through these efforts, I was blessed to get to know my friend Eva, who ultimately joined me in City Hall to serve as coordinator for the city's Americans with Disabilities Act obligations.

Full meetings of the HRC had resumed in January 2006. It was a tense time in the community; we had all been through hell, and finger-pointing had begun. Rumors were spreading and trust was a scarce commodity, particularly between the day laborers and the native Black community. So the HRC decided to hold regular meetings in the grand old Basin Street Station to hear more from the different communities that comprised New Orleans.

We identified ten demographic groups from around town, including African Americans, public housing residents, LGBTQ+ people, Jewish and other minority religious groups, communities of Vietnamese-, French-, and Spanish-speakers, and more. Working in pairs, members of the commission approached these different communities and recruited representatives to testify before the HRC. And then, meeting with one group at a time, we convened beneath a large map of New Orleans, with pins representing each comment or complaint that had been sent to the commission. Sometimes the press was there to take notes and pictures. We asked each witness three simple questions:

What is your history here in New Orleans?

How do you feel discriminated against?

What can we do to help?

That year of testimony was revealing. For all the talk of blame in the media, all the alarm over who was invading and who was being invaded, the public meetings were much calmer than we'd imagined they would be. No one really hated anybody else—and everyone loved the city and wanted it to rebound. Most everyone agreed that we wanted the day laborers to integrate, so the commission's final eighteen-point report included abundant recommendations for ways to help Latino immigrants and protect the economically precarious in their fight for fair wages. These recommendations were systematic and required involvement from every sector of the city.

I was proud of the way the HRC had risen to the challenge at hand, developing new measures to protect residents—new and old—from discrimination. And our work drew the attention of national policymakers. Over a two-year span, beginning in 2006, I was invited to participate in a series of workshops at Harvard's Kennedy School of Government. Police chiefs and representatives of antidiscrimination commissions from all over the country gathered quarterly to share strategies to reduce tensions in our communities. I was partnered with Atlanta's police chief, Richard Pennington, who had been chief of police in New Orleans under Marc Morial. It was wonderful to see the chief again, on his new home turf, when several of our workshop participants attended an NAACP meeting in Atlanta. When I arrived, he picked me up personally in a police cruiser and took me to see his wife and family, with whom I had become good friends when they served the people of New Orleans. What impressed me the most was that, after lunch at his place, on the way back to the hotel, the chief went out of his way to give me a tour of Atlanta's gay community. We drove right through the heart of the neighborhood, while he explained which crowd frequented which bars. He made me feel welcome and completely at home.

Looking back now, some twenty years after Katrina, I can't help mourning the fate of Ray Nagin. Born in Charity Hospital, Ray grew up on my side of town, in the Seventh Ward, before pursuing an education and career outside New Orleans. Just as I had left for Houston, Ray had left for Tuskegee, where he studied accounting, eventually traveling around the country working for General Motors, Cox Communications, and other companies.

Ray and I returned to New Orleans around the same time, in the mid-1980s, and as his stature grew I came to really adore him. Not only did he have professional experience, he was down to earth and entertaining. As he joined various for-profit and nonprofit boards and became president of the Brass—a short-lived minor-league hockey team—it was only a matter of time before he ran for office.

Having been in business for a long time, Ray understood the value of having friends on both sides of the aisle, and he contributed to both Democratic and Republican campaigns. When it came time for his first mayoral race, in 2002, he defeated veteran politicos like my good friends Richard Pennington and Councilman Troy Carter. A surprising portion of his support came from the white business establishment. With a runoff victory over Chief Pennington, Clarence Raymond Nagin Jr. became mayor of New Orleans, succeeding my great supporter Marc Morial.

For the first few years, Ray fulfilled his promises to make New Orleans more business friendly. The convention industry was booming, and tourists were filling the city's coffers. Unfortunately, storm clouds ultimately burst the shoddy concrete of seawalls, leaving the infamous image of an overwhelmed and desperate mayor outside the Superdome, wearing a t-shirt and standing knee deep in water, begging for help. The mayor's fortunes had flipped, along with the city's.

And so, in the messy aftermath of Hurricane Katrina, the city was holding its breath for the mayoral election scheduled for April 2006. Mayor Nagin's support was shaky. He had lost ground to Mitch Landrieu, a politician with a famous family and a statewide profile—and there would soon be many more candidates. Nonetheless, the gears of city government began to grind once again, and I was tasked with putting on a function to thank the world for the aid we had received to help get us back on track. Even small African towns and the Mexican military had offered some measure of aid, and we were humbled and grateful for it.

The event was scheduled for January 16, Martin Luther King Jr. Day, in front of City Hall, with Mayor Nagin as the featured speaker. We put together a beautiful program replete with Buddhist drummers and school choirs; I wanted to focus on a theme of unity and togetherness. Planning functions is my forte, and I always design my ceremonies carefully.

You have to remember, in the months after Katrina, many people had questioned whether New Orleans was worth saving. Developers, insurers, and members of Congress were asking whether low-lying swaths of town were worth rebuilding. A large percentage of the city's population was still displaced, scattered across the fifty states. Many of the refugees were waiting on insurance checks and still saving up the resources to return. These facts weren't lost on the mayor. He had just spoken with Congresswoman Maxine Waters of California, who warned him that developers were interested in taking advantage of the low real estate prices.

Right before the ceremony got underway, Kenya Smith, Ray's deputy mayor of intergovernmental relations, informed me the mayor was ready to review the program—but warned me that he was in an awful mood. I gave Ray a breakdown of each step in the program, as I had done many times before. I could tell he was agitated but chose to leave him be. I needed to put on my own game face as emcee for the large crowd that had gathered. With that, I presented my glowing introduction, and the mayor stepped into a steaming pile of history.

Ray was evidently moved by the spirit of Martin Luther King and, in his exhaustion and fervor, claimed to have spoken with him that morning. The speech began low and slow, with Ray preaching on the virtues of the city and how we would survive thanks to our spirit and despite insufficient help from the federal government. But as the fire descended upon him, he spoke louder and louder, testifying, in his mind, on behalf of the Black people of New Orleans—the many, many refugees still worried about whether they had a city to return to. It was time to rebuild New Orleans, he said, to rebuild a "chocolate New Orleans." He didn't care about what they were saying "Uptown, or wherever." At the end of the day the city (with apologies to Washington, DC) was to be a chocolate city!

Furthermore, the mayor explained, he wasn't merely channeling the great MLK, who surely would have cried at the response to our natural disaster. It was God himself who was expressing his displeasure at the modern dysfunctions of Black America. It was God's wish, then, that we restore a shining Black Jerusalem.

I felt so bad when it all hit the fan. I understood where Ray was coming from. Those early days and nights on the cruise ship, with staff, couldn't have been easy to endure. And while I had been lucky with my own apartment, many city employees had been dealing with insurance adjusters and contractors while trying to run the city.

Ray was pilloried in the media. But no mayor had lost reelection in New Orleans since the 1940s. Even in the chaos after Hurricane Betsy in 1965, Mayor Vic Schiro had retained his office. Many city council members lost their seats in the 2006 election cycle. But despite all the polls' predictions, Nagin squeaked ahead of Landrieu and won!

What was surprising was the overwhelming support of the Black vote in Gentilly and the East. Remember, this was a complete reversal of the previous election, when Ray received most of his votes from Uptown. During the 2006 primary season, no other Black consensus candidate really emerged. Mitch Landrieu split his vote with Ron Forman, the affluent leader of the Audubon Institute and Zoo. To his credit, Mitch's policies were similar to Ray's, and his attacks were mild. Meanwhile, in an unusual twist, business-friendly Republicans were quietly supporting the incumbent. In the end, both Ray and Mitch garnered significant cross-racial support.

As Ray settled into his second term, I was honored that he asked me to remain as HRC director. I accepted enthusiastically, inspired by the ongoing challenge of fighting for justice in the city.

The first post-Katrina Mardi Gras fell on February 28, 2006. What might surprise you is that, at first, a lot of people were screaming that they didn't want to celebrate. The tragedy was too fresh; too many people had lost everything in the storm. Tempers flared at the public meetings called by the mayor to gauge everyone's attitudes. The police had to remove some attendees for interrupting loudly and showing disrespect for the mayor and each other. However, with Carnival season approaching, public sentiment eventually coalesced around celebration rather than cancellation. The Mardi Gras krewes were determined to go ahead with the holiday, to show the world that New Orleans was still alive—and the mayor gave the go-ahead. Zulu, the oldest Black krewe, returned in triumph despite flood damage to its Broad Street headquarters. Members of Rex, among other old-line white krewes, were generous in their charitable efforts. And although news coverage of water in Canal Street's neutral ground remained fresh in the minds of potential visitors, the reality was that most of the downtown hotel area had avoided serious flooding.

The parades that February gave people hope that we would survive. And survive we did. It was a wonderful Carnival, one we would remember forever. And in 2010, when the Saints won the Super Bowl, and the grand championship parade drew over one million people—even then, with the entire football team on floats, pitching Saints beads and celebrating our Saints miracle, many of us were still savoring memories of that first patched-together Mardi Gras after Katrina.

First Mardi Gras after Hurricane Katrina [2006]

PHOTOGRAPH BY CAROL M. HIGHSMITH; LIBRARY OF CONGRESS, PRINTS & PHOTOGRAPHS DIVISION, LC-DIG-HIGHSM-04019

CHAPTER EIGHTEEN / *Cuba*

Troy Perry, Mariela Castro, and Larry in Cuba [2017]
COURTESY OF THE AUTHOR

18

A CERTAIN GYRE IN THE GULF OF MEXICO HAS ALWAYS TIED NEW ORLEANS TO Havana. In the era of sailing ships, rather than fight for passage across the Straits of Florida, it was easier to drift just a touch west toward the Yucatán Channel and catch a lift from the Loop Current to reach the north-central Gulf Coast. That same current made the return trip just as easy. These days, of course, we can simply fly, and in May 2017 I was lucky enough to make the quick hop from Miami down to Cuba as a guest of the Reverend Troy Perry and the Metropolitan Community Church.

New Orleans is famous for being unlike anyplace else stateside; our city is treasured by Americans as a rare and singular Gallic gem. What most people don't know is that the French Quarter doesn't look very French at all, because the architecture carries mostly Spanish influence. For forty years, from 1762 to 1802, the province of Luisiana was part of New Spain, with its administrative seat in Havana. At first, French-speaking New

Orleans wasn't terribly impressed or obedient, but when fires decimated the wooden structures of the Vieux Carré in 1788 and 1794, the Spanish rebuilt New Orleans in their own image. Stringent fire codes were put in place, and the city was rebuilt wall to wall in Spanish Colonial style, with brick, plaster, wrought iron balconies, and bright colors. This style persisted even after the Spanish left, so much so that the French Quarter should more accurately be called Villa Hispañola or even Villa Cubana! The streets of Havana are the closest I've ever seen to my favorite cozy corners of New Orleans.

Havana is our big sister, by two hundred years, and for centuries it was our close trading partner. Mountains of sugar, destined for Louisiana, were borne on the swift currents of the Gulf. Those same cargo ships were quickly loaded with midwestern grain and corn and rushed back to Cuba. A monument on Poydras Street recalls New Orleans's role in nurturing an early band of revolutionaries who fought for Cuban independence from Spain in the 1850s. Cultural exchange has flourished alongside the commercial and political connections. What Jelly Roll Morton called the "Spanish tinge" put its mark on New Orleans music, and in trade, we returned American jazz and blues.

This is nearly all forgotten today. It was with frightening speed that an embargo was enacted after the Cuban Revolution of the 1950s, and we were cut off from our sister city and trade partner. This happened when I was a child, and thanks to the Cold War, I was raised to be thankful I was on this side of the wall—and to think little of who might live on the other side.

Troy Perry Jr. grew up in North Florida and was struck by the gospel to preach at a young age. Still a teenager in the late 1950s, he married a preacher's daughter and planned for Bible college. Despite his prayers, it was only inevitable that his family and church found out about his sexuality. He was ordered to denounce himself in public, from the pulpit, and leave the church.

Now divorced, he wandered aimlessly, working and spending time in the army. The gay world around him, with its police raids, offered little comfort. Right when his life had descended into despair, his prayers were finally answered, and his old passion to serve the Lord was reignited. He felt called to start a new gay church.

So in 1968, from his condo in West Hollywood, Troy took out an ad in the local gay newspaper, which attracted a handful of sheep to his flock. A group composed mostly of his personal friends, and eventually his mother, started gathering for a prayer circle in his living room. But this spark soon started a fire—and within a few years, hundreds of Christians were gathering in cities across the country to worship in a space that affirmed that God loved, accepted, and created his own gay, lesbian, bisexual, transgender, queer, and even straight children.

This was in direct conflict with nearly every traditional religious strain, Christian or otherwise. Yet over the years, the Metropolitan Community Church continued to grow, despite threats and violence. There were schisms and triumphs, and still the MCC grew. The first extralegal same-sex marriages were affirmed, and of course, the MCC grew even more.

It was inevitable that Troy and I would become the best of friends, as he had been a regular presence at landmark organizing events, rallies, parties, and conventions for the LGBTQ+ community. We hit it off, and soon he was staying at my place at 2001 Branard whenever he was in Houston.

At the time, I was quite corporate and buttoned up—and, like Troy, I knew a thing or two about keeping my appearance together for the sake of the flock. But it was important for the "Gay Pope" to understand the fullness of gay life, and so it was a joy bringing him out to Houston's clubs and social events. By showing his face on Saturday night, it was easy for him to find a receptive audience to fill out the pews on Sunday morning.

In 1980, a few years into our friendship, he invited me to the MCC National Convention in Houston. While the denomination's core mission is self-evident and firm—and while inclusive language and interpretation ensures the security of the Lord's queer flock—each congregation is by and large free to follow its own path, ritually and theologically. As difficult as my own upbringing and relationship to Catholic dogma had been, it was still quite a shock to attend a proper Protestant service. The services were just so . . . Baptist! True to Troy's North Florida roots, the MCC nationwide had plenty of clapping, joyful noise, and yelps of hallelujahs. Ever since, we've joked about the jolt the MCC gave this Catholic altar boy. Initial culture shock aside, I learned so much from witnessing queer Christian faith, as I've learned from all experiences of faith. The MCC service was another brick in the construction of a remarkable edifice: a full and equal life for my brothers and sisters. I was blessed!

In 2017, in recognition of Troy's lifetime achievement, a ceremony was planned by Cuba's National Center for Sex Education, or CENESEX. When Troy invited me to join him and a few other close friends for the "Journey Against Homophobia" in La Habana, Cuba, how could I say no?

The Cuban Republic holds over eleven million people, some two million of whom live in Havana. After landing at the airport, it was a quick ride into the more touristy parts of Old Havana, where I had my Airbnb. The city spreads from the eastern lobe of the western shore of a deep port. The sight of ships coming and going reminded me of New Orleans's riverfront—even though Havana is genuinely seaside, whereas we're far from the Gulf. My small room was in an old family-run building, with short-term rentals mixed in with apartments occupied by Cuban locals. It featured a simple room attached to a bathroom and had excellent air conditioning. It was right across from their old capitol building, built to resemble the US Capitol, its dome just a bit taller and wider than our own.

Just as in the postcards, fleets of classic cars took their turns round and round the Paseo del Prado to the delight of tourists. The brightly colored Bel Airs and Plymouths reminded me of my own first series of cars back in the 1960s, and it was amazing to see them run once more, even if at this point they use shampoo for brake fluid.

Today, most Cuban Americans live in the Miami area, and the strong bond between New Orleans and Havana is largely a thing of the past. Fortunately, however, a great friend of mine from the public engagement office at City Hall, Lisbeth Pedroso, was herself Cuban, and she was excited to learn of my trip. Her family, many of them beauticians, still remained in Cuba, and she gave me a whole box of supplies and hair extensions to hand out when I arrived. She didn't forget the ballpoint pens and USB drives that serve as coveted prizes for modern Cuban life, either. She also helped me arrange my accommodations.

Old Havana, and the city as a whole, reminds me of the French Quarter of my youth, when it was a charming slum. The doors and brackets, the stucco and building dimensions were all familiar—though unlike in New Orleans, each wall, door, and window seems stitched together with vines of extension cords. As night fell, the breezes would pick up, and neighbors would casually gather by the doorways and windowsills to catch up, guitars and bongos in tow. Beautiful as this was, it turned out the main action was on the other side of town.

Cuba has been opening up to both private bars and the gay community since the early 2010s, but gays have always found ways to meet despite a lack of open spaces. Today's informal gay neighborhood is between the Malecón, the famous seaside promenade, and Avenida 23. Especially on the weekends, it's not hard to find gaggles of young gay boys with flashy haircuts and fashionable gear. All by myself, I drifted in and out of bars and admired the vast expanse of the sea. The Malecón itself was a beautiful rampart, a spot to watch young couples, gay and straight, flirt, kiss, and waste time. Soon enough, it was time for dinner, and I headed to the main landmark in the neighborhood, El Presidente hotel. Having switched from vodka to rum, I was already quite buzzed, and I just presumed that Troy would be staying at that very historic landmark.

Thanks to a few words of broken Spanish, I inquired of the friendly staff if they would ring Troy. And lo and behold, he appeared to greet me in the lobby. I had called it right: El Presidente was just his taste.

Troy's room in El Presidente was commensurate with his status as a guest of Mariela Castro herself, with a wide view of both the city and sea. I swore I could even see Key West, although I'd been told, repeatedly, that it was impossible! In the palatial suite, I caught up with Troy's husband, Phillip, and with the editor of the *Washington Blade*, and we confirmed our plans for the weekend ahead. We were all thrilled to be in Cuba and took our presence there as a sincere and humble grace.

Troy characteristically gave out a big yawn and retired to bed. This was as good an excuse as any to tuck him in and revisit the bars I had discovered earlier.

With the lights flashing and music throbbing, it was time to find dates! With my limited Spanish, however, it was a bit of a challenge—so it should be no surprise that I ended up spending time with another American, a minister! This American was somewhat my type: of Mexican ancestry, and sporting a Texan buzz cut. He was in town for the same reason as I was, to celebrate the MCC's arrival in Cuba. We made fast friends and faster wingmen as we popped in and out of the dozen gay bars in the neighborhood. The whole neighborhood was dressed to the nines that weekend, both streets and sidewalks packed with fairies and tough guys, rainbow flags fluttering alongside the Cuban tricolors. It was a wondrous, tropical night.

With a flash of lights, a large bang marked the start of the CENESEX gala the following evening at the Karl Marx Theater. Dancers of all shapes and sizes appeared, writhing and contorting to techno music, all under the auspices of Mariela Castro.

For visitors like me, it was just a grand party. But for members of Cuba's gay community, familiar with their country's history, the scene must have seemed almost surreal. With its reputation as a haven from Prohibition, prerevolutionary Cuba was a magnet for the American party set—and Havana had legendary gay bars before and after World War II, around the time New Orleans was developing its own nascent gay scene. Yet as a Latin country, Cuba didn't particularly welcome homosexuality: machismo and Catholicism were inhospitable to a healthy gay life. Instead, as is often the pattern, gay men were best hidden away, shameful fodder for the appetites of married straight men. It was no help that the throng of American tourists and servicemen made prostitution an easy hustle, and gayness was twinned closely with hustling, gambling, and crime.

The Cuban Revolution could have served as society's purification from traditional rural perspectives on gay life. Instead, effeminacy was branded a state enemy: not only unnatural but, worse, a product of the appetites of Western capitalism! Now associated with Batista-era decadence, many gays were rounded up and sent to labor and reeducation camps. Lucky gays and lesbians fled to Florida through the Mariel boatlift in 1980, while those that remained had to reckon not only with Cuba's but also with the Soviet Union's unwelcoming attitude toward sexual minorities.

Seeds of change, however, sprouted through the late 1970s and 1980s as a few courageous artists maintained that gayness was nothing unnatural. While the population at large still held antipathy for queers, court cases paved the way for change, allowing homosexuality to be redefined as an orientation rather than a disorder. Just as in the United States, by the 1990s—despite the ravages of AIDS and the continual prospect of police raids—gays in Cuba had glimmers of hope.

It finally took a member of Cuba's own royal family, Mariela Castro, to make the hardest push for popular gay acceptance. The daughter of Raúl Castro and a niece of Fidel, she spent her early life as a dancer, a product of Soviet Bloc excellence. As any theater kid knows, it's not hard to form deep and enduring friendships with gays in the dance world. When her best friend, a gay boy, committed suicide in high school, Mariela made it her crusade to extend the protection of the Cuban state toward the republic's gay children.

In 2000 she became director of CENESEX, and by 2010 her uncle Fidel had begun to apologize for the suffering of gays early in the revolution. When Troy Perry was recognized in 2017 as a leader in the fight

Larry on the Malecón, Havana [2017]
COURTESY OF THE AUTHOR

#NOLALOVE

for gay rights, he became the first American so honored by Mariela and CENESEX. The celebration coincided with the International Day Against Homophobia, Biphobia, and Transphobia—an official gay holiday in Cuba and many other nations, celebrated in mid-May.

Part reunion, part junket—my Cuban adventure was a whirlwind. On Sunday, an impressive parade snaked down Avenida 23, with Troy and his husband perched like beauty queens atop a beautiful old Impala. Famously, I'm a connoisseur of parades, and the Cubans did a good job, infusing familiar elements (costumes, dance troupes) with the ceaseless rhythms of son cubano and rumba, all under the auspices of a huge Cuban flag. As with all gay festivals, boys on the street were dressed to impress—and in a world without apps, the games of eye contact were further refined. It was there, on the parade route, with a new group of Cuban pals, that I met mop-headed Marty, who made my entire trip truly special.

Marty wasn't quite who I expected to meet in Cuba. Young and blond, he proved to be a great companion, tour guide, and interpreter, and he provided a vibrant introduction to Cuba filled with great passion. We were introduced by members of the MCC delegation, who had picked up on the characteristics that appeal to me in a date. Delicate and soft spoken, neither too big nor too small, Marty was special—and the more I got to know him, the more I liked him. Fortunately, my poor Spanish was no obstacle, as he delighted me with his strong English.

His story struck me as a sign of progress within Cuban society. He came from a small town on the outskirts of Havana, raised in a family that encouraged his individuality. Marty had landed comfortably within the gay community due to his long-standing participation in his local MCC congregation, la Iglesia de la Comunidad Metropolitana. By this point, his family was very supportive and were themselves great fans of Troy Perry, and they were excited Troy was coming to Cuba.

Without Marty, I would've been lazy and just stayed in the gay neighborhood of the Vedado. Instead, in the company of Marty and a handful of other companions, I walked all over Havana, discovering small bars and tolerant corners of the city where gays were as welcome as everyone else. Despite years of embargo and isolation, Cuba was still home to a fraternity of good-looking men with time and money to hit the gym, shop, and use moisturizers. There's a familiar spirit of queens that can't be contained, and it was easy to spot family against the backdrop of working-class Cubans.

Many of the bars we visited reminded me of the gay bars I had seen the world over. Some were old cruisy dives, and some were a bit larger, with lights and DJs. A popular cabaret, owned by the government, had regular drag shows. And all along the Malecón, flocks of gay boys and men hung together in cliques stratified by age and attitude. Against the wide expanse of aging concrete, waves would crash, providing a romantic, northern-facing backdrop for lovers of all genders. The widespread tolerance filled my heart.

I'm so grateful to the Cuban congregations of the MCC for helping us feel at home on our trip. You could tell that they were quite interested in the world beyond, and that they appreciated the opportunity to share their culture, practice their English, and make trivial exchanges. I was told later that Marty and all his friends had been saving up in anticipation of the weekend. For this, and for their generosity, I give them my thanks.

Troy's circle of friends was greeted as an official delegation, and by day, officials would take us to the Cuban state's premier museums and monuments. We visited Plaza de la Revolución, or Revolution Square, which urged us to reexamine our own relationship with Cuba. Wherever we went, we sensed the immense national pride that the populace feels for their island, a place of such great natural beauty.

Aspects of Cuba's story were familiar to me, having grown up in Louisiana. Cuba was once a land of large haciendas, or plantations, run by American individuals and corporations with the blessing of former Cuban governments. It was routine in swinging, prerevolutionary Havana to have segregated hotels where native Cubans were only welcome to appear if they were maids and cleaners.

In my interpretation, the embargo imposed in the 1950s was only successful in encouraging Cubans to rely on the Soviet Union for help. Recent US policy hasn't been much better. Everyday people have been made to suffer needlessly by the American reaction to the Cuban regime—and our actions may have allowed the regime to hold on longer than natural. The nation's poverty is indeed a shame. Cuban food is much better in Miami, and the grocery stores during my visit contended with a shortage of milk.

Certainly, my outlook was shaped by my standing as a guest on an official state visit. The reality, of course, is much grittier. Indeed, the Cuban government had a history of treating the gay community harshly, and in a single-party state, there's no recourse for a persecuted minority confronted by persistent ignorance, violence, and existential threats. Mariela Castro has been a great inspiration, elevating the needs of the LGBTQ+ community, but always within the structure of the party and state.

Mariela had gone to all the little cities in Cuba and, together with her husband, encouraged gay and trans people and their parents to come out as part of a stop-the-bullying campaign. Thanks to her, the Cuban government has sponsored gay community centers. It's a welcome thing that gender confirmation surgeries are now provided at no cost—but before the transition can begin, the patient must take an oath of loyalty to the Cuban state. Given Cuba's robust, state-sponsored healthcare system, one might expect the HIV and AIDS rates to be very low—but I've learned, since my return to the US, that it's not difficult for the government to fudge away any inconvenient truths.

Gay life has always been transgressive, and I hope that never changes. It would be a mediocre thing if queerness was suddenly normal. Therefore, I'm left wondering what it's like for gay activists who aren't so enamored of the Cuban revolution. There's nowhere for dissidents to turn—and despite the official line, it's still not uncommon for the police to raid certain bars and to round up trans people and sex workers needlessly.

No system is perfect. As an activist, I'm glad that gayness is no longer given an automatic stamp of disapproval, thanks to Mariela Castro's efforts. I hope that freedom for sexual minorities can extend further in the future, and I have great hope that a better relationship between the US and Cuba can help all of us. I'm not naive about the pressure exerted by many affluent, anticommunist Cubans in Florida and elsewhere, pressure that works against any rapprochement. My only message is that I found the Cuban people to be very warm, accepting, and, at least officially, tolerant of Love.

I felt at home in Havana, comforted by the architectural and cultural reminders of New Orleans. Havana is more visibly Spanish than New Orleans, with the added benefit of the ocean and the palm trees that are just a bit out of reach in Gentilly. And the heat! It's hotter in May in Cuba than it is in Louisiana. By two in the afternoon, business has to stop, resuming only when the sun gets low around 5:30. But as a native New Orleanian, taught always to believe that we were one-of-a-kind and special, it was quite the homecoming to find myself in Havana—a city that made me feel much less unique in the world, in the warmest of ways.

CHAPTER NINETEEN / *New York, New York*

Larry and friends at the Continental Baths, New York [1971]
COURTESY OF THE AUTHOR

19

NEW YORK CITY, THE CROSSROADS OF THE WORLD—WHERE PEOPLE OF every shape, size, age, origin, and creed come together to hustle up one dollar or a billion—will always remain my second home. I even considered retiring there, but I knew I'd have too much fun among the towers and brownstones. I'm content to spend weeks and weeks there, revisiting old haunts and making new memories. It is the worldwide capital of gay life, a city we all pray toward and make pilgrimage to. Some people thrive in the ocean of possibilities, dreaming of catching whales, while others find the surf too rough and prefer to stay ashore. In New York, I see a community that matches the vision and ambition I continue to feed within myself, and in New York, I enjoy a garden where each of my appetites is satisfied.

When my college mentor, Professor James Schaffer, brought me up for the first time in 1969, I began to see the docks, baths, bars, halls, and working boys in the same fashion that Walt Whitman did 120 years earlier when he wrote of the "frequent and swift flash of eyes offering me love." I will forever marvel at how ordinary it seemed to survive a raid at Stonewall—and how, a month later, the same kind of raid would march us all into history. As the city changes decade after decade, I continue to return to my childhood at the sight of the large balloons of Macy's Thanksgiving Day Parade, or the boisterous St. Patrick's or National Puerto Rican Day parades. The city finds endless ways to inspire awe—indeed, New York was where I saw my first snowstorm—and its magic extends to the outer boroughs, where I've reveled in Brooklyn and Queens Pride. I love New York because, after all these years, I've only begun to experience it, and there is always more to see.

Twenty-five years after my first visit to New York, I sat on board the D subway train headed to the Bronx. I was no longer in my early twenties, shy and naive in a new city. Instead, I was surrounded by gays and lesbians just like me. We were survivors of the continuing AIDS crisis and had elected a president who wasn't going to ignore us—and now, to celebrate Stonewall's silver jubilee, the whole city was putting on events. On Saturday, June 25, 1994, our entire community was on its way to Yankee Stadium to celebrate the closing ceremonies of Gay Games IV with a big tribute to our triumphs. The trip had gotten off to a bit of a bumpy start, despite my high hopes. Ramon, David, and I had formed a squad to attend the reunion together, and I had found lodging in Greenwich Village with Doug Weiss, my NO/AIDS codirector. But I promptly made the mistake of getting food poisoning, confining me to my room for the first few days. Ramon and David knew to leave me alone while I was sick, but by the time of the Yankee Stadium event I was ready to see all my old friends from both Houston and New Orleans. Everybody was wasted, and there was electricity in the air.

Over the course of a magical two weeks, not only had more athletes competed in Gay Games IV than in the previous Olympics, but the city pulsed with rich cultural programming celebrating gay art, gay cinema, gay dance, gay theater, and gay activism. Sir Ian McKellen brought his one-man show to the New York stage, just a few years after coming out, and the world of Broadway was showcased at a benefit that featured Liza Minnelli, Eartha Kitt, André De Shields, Julie Halston, Billy Stritch, and more. Prominent lesbians including Janis Ian, k. d. lang, and Melissa Etheridge came together to raise money for the continued fight against AIDS. A choir of gay choruses, numbering over four hundred voices, convened for many performances. For so long, so much of the world's greatest art has been made by, for, and about LGBTQ+ people, who often had to hide in the closet, navigate open secrets, or find their messages, identities, and contributions erased.

That's why that night at Yankee Stadium felt historic. It felt like the first time in all the epochs that gay artists, athletes, and activists could celebrate our achievements openly and take full credit for our rich contributions to world culture. Allies including Aretha Franklin, Cyndi Lauper, Taylor Dayne, and Diana Reeves sang to the tens of thousands of us assembled at the stadium. Sir Ian McKellen and the gay chorus provided rousing inspiration. And the highlight of the whole affair was Patti LaBelle, who kicked off her high heels and led the crowd as we rocked the House that Ruth Built. To this day, I tear up whenever I hear any version of "Somewhere Over the Rainbow," as it transports me back to the celebration's conclusion, with fireworks in the air and voices singing so loud we were all out of breath.

The next day—Sunday, June 26—found me heading up Fifth Avenue into Central Park as part of the International March on the United Nations to Affirm the Human Rights of Lesbian and Gay People. I was already feeling nostalgic about the previous night's ceremony. This memorable occasion sums up my passion for New York, where high art, low commerce, and wide diversity are forged in the world's loudest and brightest cauldron, resulting in a family as strong as steel.

Out on Long Island, gay life coalesces on the barrier island villages of Cherry Grove and the Fire Island Pines, which are linked together by a path. Cherry Grove is older, originally a retreat built by and for eccentric elites. Today, it is popular with women. As Robert Moses clawed the channels and islets around Long Island away from mistrustful fishermen in the postwar era, it became easier for even more eccentric elites to establish colonies for gays on Fire Island. To this day, a spectrum of loud and quiet neighborhoods exists on the island, among docile deer and active bears.

I enjoy Fire Island, but I feel most at home in Greenwich Village. Its history and location naturally attract a diversity of working people. When Greenwich Village was first platted by the Dutch, it was already in use by Native Americans, and it remained at the edge of town for many years, a patch of woods and fields that separated traders from the wilderness. It even contained parcels settled by free Blacks who sued successfully for farmland. These village origins result in streets that break the regularity of the New York City grid. Bleecker, Christopher, and Greenwich Streets meet at odd angles to create quiet blocks, hidden alleys, and irregular shapes conducive to human interaction.

As financial activity coalesced in Lower Manhattan, the Village attracted a different sort of industry: the newspapers, galleries, theaters, and inns that made the neighborhood an intellectual and bohemian enclave as the city continued to grow around it. One such inn was the Stonewall, built in the 1930s and raided repeatedly for breaking Prohibition.

Other neighborhoods, too, have become special to me. For my first Pride march in New York, in late August 1971, I didn't stay in the Village but at the YMCA near Columbus Circle. It was there I had my first startling sightings of drag queens. Started as missionary outreach, offering counseling services and sports, the YMCA has long filled a gap between youth hostels and hotels. The famous shared bathrooms, skinny-dipping, and private rooms at this location certainly added to the popular appeal.

As I gained my swing, the YMCA was convenient to many Midtown and Upper West Side clubs and bathhouses like the Continental Baths. Located on Broadway in the basement of the Ansonia, the Continental had pools, bunk beds, rooms, saunas, hot tubs, an alarm system in case the police were nearby, and even a stage. During that visit in 1971, even as Tropical Storm Doria was creeping closer to the city, the Continental Baths were packed. This was at the peak of Bette Midler and Barry Manilow's residency as performers at the baths. These campy shows would ring in each new day at midnight with milk and cake. The space had room for up to one thousand people, though straights started coming in droves to see the concerts and eventually killed the vibe.

While Studio 54 is famous today, I only went once and hated it. It struck me as a way for the bridge-and-tunnel crowd to earn status points. Once inside, I found little color and the air thick with privilege. Drugs were popular there, but I was no fan, so it was easy for me to get bored with all the straights. I didn't know who Andy Warhol was. Today, people recall legendary crazy surprises and hot music, but I preferred the Mineshaft, two warehouses combined into one with bars on different levels hosting thousands of men, in the Meatpacking District.

Toward the Village, there was an abundance of bars for leather, like the Eagle; for dancing, like the Monster; and for cowboys, like Boots and Saddle. Many of these survived for decades, and some remain open even today. One favorite of the Black crowd was the Hangar—and in those days, bars would also line the river by the cruisy docks, at the end of Christopher Street's downward slope. Fortunately, I've never personally found a use for sex on sale. As laborers, sex workers should be protected and their trade regulated. But sex for me has always been the thrill of personality and connection, too holy for cash. I credit my New Orleans upbringing, to this day, for the street smarts that saved me from an uncontrollable spiral of partying and drugs.

Further uptown, toward Harlem, the gay ballroom scene thrived in the 1980s, when old theaters and warehouses were cheap. This tradition was a reaction to the primarily white drag beauty pageants put on closer to the Village and Midtown, which started as early as the 1940s and often parodied silly straight rituals. Today, as gay culture grows to celebrate the scrappiness and sequins of the genderbending queers of color, I feel lucky I was twice able to attend a true Harlem ball. Even though I was born and raised in New Orleans, I don't wear costumes, but I honor the talents of those performers. Fortunately, the ballroom scene survives to this day.

I can appreciate pageantry, but in my twenties and thirties I preferred the boyish crowd at the few gay Puerto Rican bars that dotted the Village. By the time cocaine arrived in the 1980s, many of the bars started hosting more commercial go-go dancers. Through the 1990s, drag shows made a revival—and as the internet spanned the world in the decades that followed, niches and fetish communities would add to the numbers of scenes and performers. Soon, that same internet would fit in the palm of one's hand, and the old bars would be plagued by smartphones and the illusion of convenience provided by dating apps. Technology has changed the vibe of the bathhouses, too, continuing a transformation set in motion by the AIDS crisis. In New York, they've replaced steam rooms and saunas with lonely snack machines, while shoebox cubbies share space with a TV tuned to CNN. I've seen it all. I've returned to these same gay blocks again and again, around the world, to watch our community mix, mingle, and grow. I hope anyone visiting these spaces today will be smart enough to put their phone down, and lucky enough to make the same personal connections I did.

Fortunately, when returning to New York since the 1990s, I've no longer needed to stay at the Y, whose branches rarely keep rooms for rent today. Instead I've stayed at the Savoy on Seventh Avenue, the Hotel Edison, and even the Holiday Inn, where three stars are more than comfortable. I'll keep to myself the precise way to find my favorite places to stay, and share those secrets carefully.

Like many of my close friends, Randy Flood entered my world as a friend of my brother, Vernel, from his days on Broadway. Randy is a gay Black man from Michigan, born in the 1950s, who arrived as a young dancer on Broadway and was featured in productions like *The Wiz*. To this day, he has broad, thick shoulders honed by many years of dance; freckles; and long braids that make him appear like a pharaoh.

In time, Randy left the stage, and like many other New Yorkers he had to develop different hustles to thrive in such an expensive city. He was very lucky to have a rent-controlled apartment in a prime location, the West Village. Today, his neighborhood reflects a mix of gentrification and tradition. Old tenement homes march, updated and well appointed, into the new century. Just a few blocks away, familiar bodegas, florists, and pizza parlors line the streets near Jackson Square, one of New York's oldest parks.

Randy's status as Big Chief of the neighborhood owes a lot to the magic of the West Village's urban geography. When the Europeans arrived, two large footpaths met in the area that today features a smattering of playgrounds and the triangular shapes of Jackson, Abingdon, and St. Vincent's "squares"—valleys in canyons of large, wide buildings. Those two footpaths are now Greenwich and Eighth Avenues, which converge just off Fourteenth Street, the easiest path for cars moving around the Village. Add in a subway stop on the A-C-E train, and you've got a feel for the whirl of people, cars, goods, and gossip that flavors the West Village. Randy rests in his quiet perch, a paragon of serenity between the Village, the Meatpacking District, and Chelsea.

As a Broadway dancer, it was easy for Randy to meet all manner of artists and patrons, and as a Black man, it was easy to make friends uptown in Harlem as well. His apartment became a palatial crossroads for an array of thinkers and troublemakers. For me, it has become a second home—and a perfect place to get ready for a night out in the vicinity of Christopher Street and Seventh Avenue, the historic citadel of gay life. For both of our sanities and schedules, I like to stay at my own place rather than bunk

Vernel Bagneris, Orange Kellin, and Randy Flood [2015]
COURTESY OF THE AUTHOR

with friends when I travel. Thus, I like to get ready at my hotel and then meet Randy before setting off on our adventures.

Entrance to his world requires the pull of a bell to announce one's arrival. His artistic salon sits at the apex of a steep staircase, from which one enters his kitchen. His studio apartment is long and painted green, and appointed with carpets and ottomans; a tall, shiny black sound system; and many generations of jazz and African artifacts. Past the Murphy bed is a cozy living room, with a couch close enough to the street that you can hear the conversations of anyone passing by, and enough foot traffic outside to suggest a bit of Bourbon Street.

No one ever refuses an invitation to one of Randy's legendary dinner parties, lest they miss out on the meeting of the courts. Whether the other guests are Russian playwrights or Brooklyn breakdancers, Randy always treats his friends like royalty. He has mastered the highest art of hosting, where everyone is invited to kick off their shoes and stay late—a style that reminds me of New Orleans, a city that does its best to lubricate the masses and banish awkwardness. Guests of Randy's have their questions answered before they even ask them. With an ample mix of vulgarity and refinement, everyone is quickly introduced to one another, and instructed where to find the bathroom and how to top off their drinks. In this way, new ideas ignite before everyone's eyes, as people who would never otherwise meet start to trade intimate experiences, like show-off chefs in a well-stocked kitchen.

Since he liked to cook and had theater connections, Randy became a caterer and now manages a staff of twenty people, whom he ensures are dressed to the nines in tuxedos. He can feed hundreds of people with the food he cooks; he crafts centerpieces in his apartment, rents chairs and silverware if needed, and manages the entire affair like a military logistician.

Randy is also my guide to the wider city. He introduced me to Brooklyn and its house music and taught me to appreciate the slower pace of the borough across the river. It only took a few gay bars for me to shed my tough exterior and learn how easy it was to make friends in Williamsburg or Bed-Stuy. It has been a joy to follow Randy's lead and discover the friendly, diverse array of folks who call Brooklyn home.

Indeed, despite what many Southerners may have heard, New Yorkers, while direct, are extremely friendly and accepting of everyone. As in New Orleans, the atmosphere is pregnant with possibility. With Randy's help, I've come to consider New York an instrument—like a piano—with which I can engage the world, playing different notes to explore different expressions and sexualities. Every neighborhood in New York attracts its own unique species: on the Upper East Side, you'll find Asian and white gays, until you run into Spanish Harlem with its Hispanic men.

Just as Randy loves to show me New York, Vernel and I love showing off New Orleans—and Randy has taken to our city like Peter Pan finding his shadow. His soul resides here, and my brother and I are pleased that he visits as often as he can.

For his sixtieth birthday, in 2014, Randy invited more than ten dozen friends and family—including his mom—down to New Orleans for the weekend, with many flying in from across the country for the occasion. We helped him burn personal mixtape CDs to hand out as party favors; needless to say, he made all the food. We used our local connections to reserve a block of rooms at the Maison Dupuy and timed the weekend just right to begin with Jazz in the Park on Thursday in Armstrong Park. On Friday, we had an elaborate happy hour at the Westin Hotel, thirteen stories above the French Quarter. Finally, we met at Basin Street Station on Saturday for the big dinner, where I read from a touching proclamation from New Orleans Mayor Mitch Landrieu: Randy was now an honorary citizen of New Orleans. That was my present. Vernel, after a proper explanation, invited the Mardi Gras Indians to come and bless Randy as everyone sang "Iko Iko" and tossed Mardi Gras beads.

As thanks for the effort we put into his birthday party, Randy invited me to join him in Mexico the following year, 2015. We took a tour of Playa del Carmen, where all the gay resorts happen to be. This was our first time "living" together, renting out two-bedroom apartments wherever we went, and boy, was I spoiled. He'd wake up every morning and make breakfast and treat the hell out of me. At night, he would find new and old friends and make them dinner at the apartment.

That's just the kind of guy Randy is. His home may be in New York, but he has opened up the world for me. Thanks to Randy, I have enjoyed cultural performances and exhibits in Mexico, obtained a visa to visit China, and explored the Brazilian northeast. Randy collects friends and then maintains those friendships well. To me, he exemplifies Village life—a life where minding one's friends and intimate relations enables one to feed and be fed by life. It is this practice that keeps us forever young.

Exactly twenty-five years after the first Yankee Stadium reunion, I returned to New York to celebrate World Pride, commemorating fifty years since Stonewall. This time, I took a markedly different approach. My friend and neighbor Frank Perez, a New Orleans historian, explained to me that the traditional Pride parade had been quite corporate for years, and he told me about events sponsored by a more woke community led by today's more political and activist queer youth.

Ahead of the march, I was honored to attend some planning meetings in a fluorescent-lit, walk-up Midtown Manhattan meeting room with chalkboards and bookcases. The meetings were organized by youngsters who wanted to remind the world that Stonewall started as a riot—and that Pride was more than banks and big businesses showering the crowd with rainbow trinkets. They had their own democratic process, and I was happy not to say a word. To signal affirmation, they would snap their fingers—and to organize motions, they would collect talking points in a "stack" and prioritize underheard voices when choosing speakers to argue positions, a practice designed to be inclusive for everyone. I thought back to the past and soaked up an old message spoken with a new language. The attendees comprised all ages, colors, genders, and nationalities, all ready to "Reclaim Pride" on June 30, 2019. The flame in New York City still burns brightly.

New York is so large that no one expression of pride can cover it all. The streets by Washington Square aren't the only blocks painted with rainbows. My tip for anyone planning to visit New York in June is to go before the big Pride weekend and instead catch Brooklyn Pride, Queens Pride, and Leather Pride throughout the month.

For Stonewall's fiftieth anniversary, in 2019, I had already seen my share of street-painting ceremonies—and so I chose instead to march with the grassroots organizations. When their parade was over, the traditional parade was still going on; I was only a little tempted to join back in and find something else to fall in love with. Instead, I decided to hang out with Randy. Together we had cocktails with Harlem friends and sat on the curb to people-watch. When the time came, I wandered back to my hotel, only to find it behind police barriers. Fortunately, thanks to Randy, I knew how to talk the police into letting me return to my home away from home—those same NYPD I first met, knocking heads at Stonewall, in that same precinct a long time before.

Larry at the 50th anniversary commemoration of the Stonewall uprising, New York [2019]
COURTESY OF THE AUTHOR

CHAPTER TWENTY / *A Far Eastern Future*

Larry in Chinese costume made by his mother [1957]
COURTESY OF THE AUTHOR

20

IN MAY 2018, AFTER GOING A MILLION MILES A MINUTE WORKING AT CITY HALL for eighteen years, I was now planning to retire. Even so, I did not expect to drift off into a sleepy life fishing on the bayou. I always need to keep moving and make plans. I had recently visited Brazil to get a deeper sense of the past and explore Africa's influence on the Western Hemisphere. My appreciation of the long history of my ancestors and the legacy of slavery grew. Now I wanted to explore the future. To expose myself to something completely different, I decided to head to China, where I had never been, to get those glimpses. Much has been said of the coming "Asian century," and I wanted to see it for myself. I wanted to see China—an economy and culture on the rise. I wanted to see a country that plans ahead on long timescales in a way that the United States has never mastered. Plus, I'll never tire of falling in love with someone tender in a new landscape and holding on to that friendship for a lifetime.

When I was growing up, most children in working-class New Orleans knew virtually nothing about Asia or Asian people, even though there had been a Chinese presence in the city since the late 1800s. New Orleans has pockets of Chinese history. For instance, if one looks carefully, one can see the scripted characters of old Chinese trading shops above the doorways of some Bourbon Street tourist attractions. The Carnival celebration was always a highlight of my grammar school years, and for one occasion, my mother—whose skills were the envy of the neighborhood—put together an intricate "Chinese" outfit, with a cone-shaped straw hat and silks decorated with intricate beadwork and embroidery. My brother was "Irish," with a green suit, top hat, and corncob pipe, while my sister was dressed as the Queen of Mardi Gras.

It was only through my travels that I first started learning about Asian people and noticing in some of their faces a resemblance to my own almond eyes and golden skin. My first explorations of New York City and San Francisco included the discovery of their Chinatowns, each of which have been part of the American landscape for centuries. I learned more through Randy, who has made it his mission as a chef to master Chinese recipes. On my visits to New York, we would wander together past Little Italy and into Chinatown, hopping between groceries to collect prized culinary flavors. Each shop was festooned in red with bright dashes of brush-stroked calligraphy—and filled with strange vegetables, noodles, and powders. I've never been a foodie because I was born without a sense of smell. In fact, I didn't know until I was a teenager that I was missing out on this fifth sense. So it was hard to get a real understanding of the local cuisine. Chinese flavors are so complex and subtle that I usually just reach for fortune cookies.

The idea of visiting China after my retirement was first suggested to me by Charles Sydnor, who—along with Ramon, David, Pablo Escamilla, and Annise Parker—completes my cabinet of Houston friends. Charles was born in the 1980s and is a Houston native with a healthy career working in the clinics I lobbied for, clinics that fight against stigma and STDs and promote health in our unique community. Pablo introduced the two of us, and we bonded easily over our mixed Black and white heritage. Charles is married to his fun-loving midwestern boyfriend, Ryan Rydman, once baby-faced but now growing into his new mustache. We all click together over our shared love of travel. Charles had visited Thailand, and Ryan was just back from Dubai, so China was next on their list, and I just had to tag along.

I like making plans, lists, and phone calls. Keeping an ordered address book served me well in City Hall, and when that chapter ended, I paced up, down, and around the apartment, looking for new tasks to complete. Collecting an official visa from the People's Republic of China was the perfect challenge—and a great excuse to spend more time in New York. I followed Forty-Second Street to its western end to try my charm at the Chinese consulate. As a City Hall veteran, I'm no stranger to red tape. Heading into my first encounter with Chinese bureaucracy, I planned ahead and allowed myself cushions of time to fill out form after form and compile a list of hotel rooms, with support from the helpful tour company that Charles and Ryan had picked. It still took days of waiting to see whether I was deemed safe enough to be allowed into the country. I'm sure they have a whole file cabinet on my browser history alone!

Happily, I wasn't on any Communist Party no-fly lists—and all of the hassles of application were forgotten once I arrived in Shanghai after crossing oceans and time zones. The privilege of visiting China makes the whole process worthwhile. Looking out the plane window as we approached Hongqiao International Airport, I could see plots of land that had been tilled for centuries alongside neighborhoods that had sprung up overnight. We would see these streets, inch by inch, as our hired car carried us deep into the center of this galaxy of twenty-five million people. These weren't the dusty and potholed streets I know from Texas and Louisiana but freshly paved roads and clean avenues. I was struck immediately by the amount of effort the government puts into maintaining its image. In a land of a billion people—where labor is abundant and relatively cheap—it is nonetheless a Herculean task to keep everything shiny, glittering, and pristine. I really felt I had arrived in the future.

The space-age feel was reinforced when Charles, Ryan, and I opened our hotel room windows. Our view overlooked Pudong, the portion of the city on the east bank of the Huangpu River. The skyline puts even New York City to shame, with skyscrapers that are newer, taller, more daring, and more densely situated. With a muggy climate, Shanghai felt like home. The latitude is nearly identical to New Orleans's, so the sun rose and set when I expected it to—and the city is built on the same silty soil as ours was. A port city upriver from the ocean, Shanghai even has its own French quarter.

China today is still very sensitive about its "century of humiliation." Having been forced into a series of unequal treaties with foreign powers from the mid-nineteenth through the mid-twentieth century, a wish to assert itself as central to the world drives its foreign policy. Shanghai, however, has long hosted foreigners—including the French, who used the neighborhood where my hotel was situated, the French Concession, as an entry to trade with vast China. This part of town boasts beautiful buildings, far more French than our own Spanish-inspired ones, its colonial architecture embellished with Beaux Arts columns and its cafes shaded by leafy plane trees. The beauty and attitude of the French Concession is a magnet for gays, just as the French Quarter is in New Orleans.

In spite of China's tremendous technological advances, their society remains profoundly different from ours. Long after the Communist revolution, Confucianism still exerts a strong influence: the basic unit is the family, and ideally, everyone in society would fit into a harmonious hierarchy. This philosophy affords leaders the widest freedom and prioritizes the good of the community rather than the desires of the individual. Young people are expected to get married and to continue their family's bloodline.

Thousands of years of Chinese history have produced plenty of poems and tales of emperors exercising their power and freedom by cavorting with young male commoners or other noblemen. Familiar is the story of the concubine, the good-looking boy who lives a charmed but kept life. An old expression for homosexuality in China is "the passion of the cut sleeve," because legend has it that one emperor was so in love with a young imperial secretary that he chose to cut off the sleeve of his silk robe rather than disturb the lover who rested upon it. As in the West, however, the pendulum of acceptance swung back and forth, and prohibitions on homosexuality became entrenched in the second half of the nineteenth century, when China's Self-Strengthening Movement encouraged the adoption of Western mores.

Today, young people in China are taught next to nothing about sex, and much of the country still lives in a "don't ask, don't tell" world. Actual figures are impossible to know, but if even one percent of the population were LGBTQ+, that would amount to more than 14 million people. As is true everywhere, the queer experience in China varies by class, location, and circumstance, with very little visibility existing outside the communities that have formed in the cities. Furthermore, our guides explained that sex that doesn't involve a man isn't considered sex at all, so lesbians, bisexuals, and transgender people are spared a degree of unwelcome attention but suffer corresponding invisibility.

While I was in Shanghai I was quite surprised at how open gay life was there—I found an abundance of Chinese men to drool over. I was in Shangri-La just walking through the neighborhood. Of course, Shanghai is the nation's most cosmopolitan city; gay youth elsewhere in China have to keep a lower profile, so they often find each other through apps and social media, while knowing that the government heavily monitors these digital spaces. One such app was shut down because it helped mothers in Shanghai arrange same-sex "marriage" markets for their children—but while that particular app was deemed too dicey, others remain active. Even Grindr was owned for a few years by a Chinese gaming company,

Beijing Kunlun Tech, until the US government's Committee on Foreign Investment put an end to that.

Despite governmental sweeps in the twentieth century, gays managed to adapt, and cruising in Shanghai spread in cafes and parks known as "beats." More recent market reforms brought affluence and loosened regulations, and cafes and bars proliferated in this upscale city. The first bar I visited was in a former bomb shelter and had been a gay meeting spot for decades. My October visit happened to fall during the holiday commemorating the establishment of the People's Republic of China—originally called National Day, the celebration now stretches for seven days, so the bars and streets were packed each night for the whole of Golden Week. With bright lights in the birthplace of fireworks, I had a blast.

I had no inkling that Shanghai would have so many gay bars. There are lots! They have bars in the tourist section and others farther away, for the locals. There were butch queens, nelly queens, screaming queens, drama queens, and American tourists—just as I had seen all over the world. Indeed, everywhere you go these days, you'll find gay tourists being shown around by their one local contact. Fortunately, I had already looked up all the best spots to show my friends, and we sampled the culture. At the end of each night out, it was wonderful to take in the breezes from our hotel balcony, watching multitudes of people wander the Huangpu riverfront as buildings lit up both banks.

Charles and Ryan had found a guide for us, who would not only take us around Shanghai but also hand us off to a colleague in Beijing. For a single sum, our guide took care of all accommodations and transportation, and arrived at eight o'clock sharp the second morning after our arrival. What I did at night away from the guide and driver was my own business, and I used other references to get my bearings.

First on the agenda was shopping. For a city within a Communist country, Shanghai sure has some high-end retail, with Gucci stores and more, evoking a combination of Fifth Avenue and Rodeo Drive for the more discerning Chinese consumers. For dining, we sampled different foods on every part of the tour. During the week and a half we spent in Shanghai, we had the chance to see both fishing villages and palaces, traveling on wide, modern highways flanked with fields of manicured medians of red, yellow, and green flowers and plants of every shape and size. In the distance, in every direction, brand-new shopping centers and high-rises were sprouting up beyond remote suburbs.

After saying goodbye to our first guide, it was time to board the high-speed train to Beijing. These bullet trains were certainly state of the art, but packed, with each passenger on board carrying a little lunch to eat. And deep in this foreign country, what do you know? There were eight loud American queens insisting that the staff and those nearby speak to them in English. Why would they think that they wouldn't have to speak Chinese in China? We didn't speak the language, either, but we did secure a tour company where all the staff knew English. Plus, I think some of the workers on the train were only pretending not to understand the Loud Americans, as they each greeted me with perfect English diction.

The new tour guide and driver met us directly in front of the main train station in Beijing and went to work quickly. One took my bags right away, explaining that it was only proper, since I was "senior" to them.

"No, thank you!" I responded, "I'm still a young man."

When we started talking about current events, they proclaimed their love for Donald Trump! "We like him most because he'll help society make everyone even more money!"

I was not happy. I certainly wanted to discuss how gifted Trump was as a scammer and the pervasiveness of racism and discrimination in our economy, but we had just met. Just when I was ready for a bicker, triggered and red in the face, I took a walk to regain my composure and avoid overstepping my bounds.

The Beijing Wangfujing Park Plaza Hotel was a little over a mile from Tiananmen Square, in a neighborhood that was as bustling as Shanghai but more businesslike. When I arrived, not having known to pack myself

Charles Sydnor, Ryan Rydman, and Larry in Beijing, China [2018]
COURTESY OF THE AUTHOR

a lunch for the train, I was so starving that I went off in search of local cuisine, only to find a Kentucky Fried Chicken. I had two Number One meals because they misunderstood my selection of a single Number Two, but it was so good, I didn't care. With a full belly, I was grounded enough to realize that my temper with the guide was due to hunger, not real anger.

"I'm in a new city," I told myself, "where nobody knows me." I didn't want to be misunderstood if I looked grumpy. I wouldn't be able to use my body language to express myself if I was fuming hot. I needed to calm down. And by the end of our tour, the guide, the driver, Charles, Ryan, and I had all come to love each other.

Fundamentally, China is large and its cities crowded. With an unfathomable number of people, restraint is important, and getting along in China requires a bit of patience. The restraint is enforced from the top down—and unlike in Cuba or the United States, people generally understand that the opposite of restraint is chaos. Whether they like it or not, China's people accept order and rules to ensure that society can function. As foreign tourists on an organized tour, we didn't have to wait in line for anything, and our driver was always ready at the hotel for our next transfer. Maybe our penchant for convenience is a sign of our weakness.

As the capital city during both the imperial and the Communist eras, Beijing has been built on a scale to impress the masses. Ordinary avenues are the width of four New Orleans Canal Streets laid side by side. The Forbidden City takes up the area of eight Superdome complexes. China has high-speed trains, highways, waterworks, underground tunnels, and all manner of infrastructure that's brand new and clean. To a naive tourist, it all seemed like a vision of the future, making the United States seem almost stagnant in comparison. We've spent so little on building and infrastructure—and when we have invested in the future, it's often been at the expense of the less fortunate, with the highway cut through the heart of Tremé a case in point. Even New Orleans, with its largely liberal and affluent population, is skilled at shooting down construction projects for affordable housing or public services. Too many people prioritize their own freedom to live a cute way of life and keep it the way it's always been, no matter what pressing needs there are for the next generation.

The more I learned of China, however, the more I understood the bargain: trading freedom for affluence. The Chinese government has made the calculation that if people are well fed and happy, with perhaps a luxury purse by their side, they won't struggle against the entrenched leadership or ask for more freedom for the press or themselves. It's unfortunate that so many freedoms have been curtailed; as an American I've always counted freedom alongside equality as a core value. But lately, that's been a difficult stance. Chinese streets are spick-and-span thanks to their rules, whereas too many of my countrymen define "freedom" as the right to storm the Capitol. I see, but don't want to admit, that the world has passed America by.

My days in Beijing passed in a blur of impressions. Surrounded by bikes and tourists, flags and soldiers, I couldn't believe that a little boy from the Seventh Ward was standing in the middle of Tiananmen Square. It felt surreal, almost as if I were in a Broadway show.

As the sun went down in Beijing, our guides would take us to dinner—and then, rather than go to bed, we wanted to see the gay bars, which were massive! So much so that we didn't really like them. Beijing is a bit more conservative than Shanghai, toeing the line of the Communist government's "no approval, no disapproval, no promotion" policy toward alternative lifestyles. Gays in Beijing gather in clubs with floors upon floors of maze-like rooms filled with loud music. The three of us wondered aloud, "How do you meet anyone here?" as the bars are designed to foster anonymity rather than comity.

Friendly locals proceeded to explain to me that lesbians are known as *lalas* and are lumped with bisexuals and trans people as a somewhat invisible category of people, making it hard for them to find one another, too. But they manage to meet the (modern) traditional way—online. In a large, young population, queer women date, make art, and increasingly are spared from having to marry their gay best friends for appearance's sake. In China, like much of the rest of the world, there are the butch T's (for tomboy), the femme P's (for *po*, meaning wife), and those who fall in the middle.

Rather than get lost in the bars, Ryan, Charles and I would walk the long way around the Forbidden City and bicker about directions, in the familiar way that friends do when they get lost. The monuments were lit up, and the capital is beautiful at night.

Our itinerary left us with ample time to explore the countryside. We drove an hour or two north to see the Great Wall, and it sure was crowded. When climbing up the Great Wall, you can keep going higher and higher—as my friends did—and then, when you're ready to return, you can simply ride a toboggan slide back down to the ground.

Another day, we explored the gardens of the emperor. I love gardens, particularly those whose design transports you to a different place. Chinese-style gardens, in the cities I've visited around the world, have always carried my imagination to the East—and now, their inspiration was right there standing in front of me. Now that I had traveled to the home of these gardens, I floated somewhere even farther away, in my mind. Chinese gardens imbue both mind and body with serenity. The tactic works, for as I continue my meditation practice at home, I always picture myself back in those gardens.

My brother, Vernel, often visits Asia, eating his way through Vietnam, the Philippines, and Singapore with joy. Meanwhile, I don't have a taste for food, and I didn't understand the Asian philosophy and aesthetic around meals until I saw *Crazy Rich Asians*. For a silly movie about excess, it really did expose me to the quality and variety of life among certain well-to-do Asians, and the attention to detail that decorates their existence. While my upbringing might not seem to have much in common with that of stupendously wealthy Singaporeans, I recognized the familiar dynamic of family love and longing, jealousy and idle gossip, unity and commitment. It helped that so many of those boys in the movie were attractive, too.

My group didn't have time to visit Singapore, but we did squeeze in a side trip to Thailand. I didn't think too hard about the arrangements, trusting that Charles—having been there often—would take care of us in Bangkok. We all hoped to have a nice, trashy excursion, so we booked a hotel in a residential neighborhood just blocks away from the bar scene and right across the street from one of the city's very modern metro stations. While Charles and Ryan took a cooking class, I wandered the streets and explored.

Thailand is a majority-Buddhist country, and Buddhism teaches that all desire—including sexual desire—leads to dissatisfaction. It doesn't matter if it's between two men, two women, a man and a woman, or anything in between. Any desire causes suffering; even when we attain the object of our desire, it doesn't make us happy forever—eventually, the pleasure ceases to please. Perhaps this explains how a strange sort of tolerance has grown in Thailand for same-sex affairs, and many gays, lesbians, and trans people have grown to be rather successful—even while some workplaces still insist that women wear skirts. On the other hand, bias against LGBTQ+ people persists, and some Thais believe that the suffering life of a gay or a lesbian must be due to past sins, resulting in their reincarnation as a queer. That's almost the reverse of Western thinking, where doing gay things is a sin that results in punishment. If the Thai belief is true, I must've been terrible over and over again—and I must have enjoyed being punished so often, to end up where I am today!

Western mores and luxuries have seeped in, in Thailand, as they have in so many parts of the world. Yet unlike the other countries of Southeast Asia, Thailand has never been colonized, and it has had its own class of the crazy, rich, and blue-blooded. It once served as the crossroads for American soldiers on leave and international travelers. Now, sex tourism—both vanilla and kinky—has bloomed and is an important part of

Thailand's tourism economy. Thus, while Thailand's queer community is still beset by prohibitions on work, marriage, and adoption that range from the inconvenient to the dangerous, their tourism board is more than happy to draw in rich gay tourists by inviting us to "Go Thai! Be Free!"

We got off the Skytrain at the Sala Daeng stop and headed for the famous Silom district, with its Soi 2 and Soi 4 pedestrian alleys lined with bars and cafes of every shape and size. In the hot night, boys waited by the doorways. It was easy for them to spot tourists, lock eyes with them, and with no hint of shyness, try to drag their marks into their bars.

The alleys were tightly packed with drunk and happy Rice Queens from all over Europe and the Americas. You could see the synergy. The white tourists craved the taste of young Asian boys, and these young men from the countryside were more than happy to take their foreign currency. It's a routine everyone has learned really well, particularly the local tavern staff; it's their way to survive. A hint of something similar exists, of course, on Bourbon Street, but I like to pretend we're less transactional than that.

Whenever I travel, I not only want to fall in love with a person, but I want to fall in love with the experiences and culture that love brings into the equation. I want an equal exchange of thoughts, ideas, dalliances, and titillation. In Thailand, I wanted to see regular Thai gays having a quiet drink after work. Perhaps I had headed to the wrong spot, but all those hot boys in the doorway: they were all straight! I could tell in the way they looked at me, at each other, and at their patrons (who notice the deception, too, but are too aroused to care). This was all one big hustle.

Most visitors think of ladyboys when they think of Thailand's trans community. They're most visible to tourists when they're walking the streets, but they've been relatively lucky to reach a level of tolerance and respect across Thai society. Some of the best gender-affirming surgeons in the world come from Thailand, although very few are trans themselves. Transgender people are seen in many workplaces and are popular on television and in other forms of entertainment. This isn't to say that they haven't had to struggle for equality, legal recognition, and protection from discrimination, however.

The famous term in Thailand is *kathoey*, for ladyboy, but the trans women simply call themselves ladies. The k-word implies that they're simply very effeminate men, and the term can be bandied about like *faggot* is here. The visibility of trans women in Thai entertainment contrasts with the fact that many aren't yet accepted for being the women that they've always been—as if they're simply play-acting—and it's been a struggle correcting their documents to align with their true sexes and names. Yet the winners of beauty pageants for trans women are featured in the newspapers, and even rural locations host these raucous pageants. Recently, a successful Thai trans woman, a media mogul, purchased the Miss Universe pageant.

There's a whole assembly of queer tribes and terms in Thailand: for trans women who like other women, straight men who like butch women, and lipstick lesbians who are into all kinds of people. I'm reminded that Thai trans women—like many in the trans world, and indeed like many women—are vulnerable to exploitation and deserve protection as workers, as citizens, and as creative and striving individuals.

In the mornings, once I was up and moving, we would choose the day's destination from among dozens of temples. They were often dripping in gold and dazzling with intricate details. Instead of 250 years of history, Buddhism has closer to 2,500, and our culture holds no depth compared to the richness and breadth of theirs. The better to appreciate evolutions in philosophy and architectural style, and to aid my own meditative practice, I did my best to research the Hindu and Buddhist aspects of Thai history. It was a great experience tying everything together in real life as I witnessed elaborate rituals unfold before me.

One day, we happened upon a big celebration for a Hindu deity particularly venerated by the transgender community. We hadn't planned to be there; we got lucky to be in the right place at the right time! It's clear I like parades, and this one reminded me of Mardi Gras, with its painted altars, floats, and bands. I sat right on the curb in front of the hotel, just as we do in New Orleans, before deciding that I needed a drink to salute the celebration. I returned to my room, made me a vodka and cranberry, filled up a Coca-Cola bottle, and returned to my position. As the procession passed, I was able to admire the papier-mâché and brushstrokes that the transgender celebrants had put into their work. The look on their faces—a combination of thrill, anxious anticipation, and relief—reminded me of New Orleanians when we put on our big annual celebrations. This was my first Hindu celebration, and I thought they had done their gorgeous work to a T.

Afterward, it was time to go shopping for souvenirs and t-shirts and return to Beijing before heading back home to the States. While it had been relatively easy to pass inspection upon arrival to China, it proved tougher to leave. The lines were longer, and the authorities a bit tougher. Getting hot and aggravated, I heard a couple giggling loudly, which, considering that I'm half deaf, should tell you they were extremely loud. When I looked up, I saw an old Texas oilman in a ten-gallon hat with a young Asian woman hanging on his arm, cooing. I've never been one for cowboys; they give me flashbacks. I thought to myself, it must be money—and I scowled at the way that finances can warp the natural action of love and attraction, the special human fire of desire that keeps all of us young inside.

I wasn't the only one keeping my eye on the crowd. The airport had cameras everywhere, and the authorities were looking at everyone. They must've seen me pout and decided I was suspicious. I was stopped at the x-ray and made to dump out my suitcase—bursting with heaps of clothing and souvenirs for my many friends. I was scanned over and over, three times in all, to make sure that everyone was safe from me. I finally caught up to Ryan and Charles, sitting in the American Airlines lounge with free food and drinks. As much as I wanted to apologize, they were laughing too loud to hear. I meekly confessed that I was at fault for my own hassle, and Ryan kept laughing, teasing me about how proud he was that I could accept responsibility. They know full well I don't have a poker face. And when it came time to board, guess who was seated across the aisle from us? The same Texan and his barely legal bride.

There's so much that a humbler America could learn from other cultures around the world. I thought I was headed to China to see the future when, in reality, I encountered civilizations much, much older than ours. They don't seem to let the past keep them down, however, as everything was much newer and cleaner than I had expected. Over and over, I pondered why our country is no longer interested in restoring our bridges, tunnels, and other infrastructure. We've been ripping people off with our own imperial ambitions, yet somehow we also have the nerve to preach to them about the wonders of our democracy, our shining city on a hill, a vision which too many Americans are losing faith in. We need to take our freedom with responsibility.

Ultimately, I'm still happy I live in a multiracial, multicultural society, the one that reared me. China's population is very homogenous, overwhelmingly Han Chinese, and while Thailand is a bit more mixed, we have to master a way to coexist in the twenty-first century with different kinds of people living in our neighborhoods. The laws of entropy suggest that interactions with different cultures will only increase in the future—and any interventions in the name of homogeneity can only waste our society's resources.

It was a revelation to see different forms of government, different cultures, different everything on this trip—to learn about worship and belief in Thailand and to gain an appreciation for China without being scared of it. My Dad taught me full well not to believe everything they tell you in the schools and in the media, for he went abroad to fight in WWII and came back with a bigger, more global outlook on the world. He remembers fighting against his enemies only to find that we became friends not too long after. International trade and cultural exchanges are key; they uplift individuals as well as society as a whole.

We certainly have a strategic competition with China, but they're invested heavily in our economy, for now, and we can't worry that they're too much of a threat to our way of life. They need us as much as we need them.

CHAPTER TWENTY-ONE / *Finally*

Southern Decadence grand marshals Daryl Dunaway and Will Antill, with Larry and Tomy Acosta as lieutenants [2019]
COURTESY OF THE AUTHOR

21

LATELY, I'VE SETTLED INTO THE RHYTHM THAT MAKES NEW ORLEANS LIFE A JOY. I love living in a city that celebrates a diversity of cultures. And through our diversity, we discover unity, with offerings to delight all tastes. Young and old, people of all backgrounds can share a mutual love of food, music, architecture, and sports. I love watching the fireworks on the river on the Fourth of July and New Year's Eve. Mardi Gras is a great and ever-evolving tradition for me, and its spectacle continues to attract newcomers, who bring their own energy and life into this port city. New crowds arrive in the spring for French Quarter Fest and Jazz Fest, where I traipse about, trying new food and hearing old bands. Easter holds particular significance to the gay community, as our southern queens wait all year long to take out our seersucker clothing and spring hats to celebrate fertility.

At the same time, Texas is never far from my heart, and I book the same hotel rooms nearly every year for San Antonio's Fiesta in April and Houston Pride in June. If I'm not traveling, the summer begins on Memorial Day with the Quarter's Mascara 500 drag queen foot race, followed by the shouts of Labor Day's Southern Decadence amid the humid straitjacket of (hopefully quiet) hurricane season. My September birthday is always on the eve of Mexican Independence Day—and even during the COVID years I celebrated with friends and Superior Grill margaritas.

October is perfectly crisp in New Orleans, almost another spring, cool enough to grow fresh vegetables once again. Halloween marks the end of summer—and during the following months I join my family for large celebrations centered on gumbo, red beans, and oysters, whether for special occasions like Thanksgiving and Christmas or everyday miracles like Saints games. During my favorite season, Christmas, I never miss the romantic lights in City Park, and sometimes I even take a limo out to the bonfires of the River Parishes. Then, just as birds return from migration, society reassembles to ramp up for another Mardi Gras. A life lived celebrating each day is the greatest lesson my community can teach the rest of the world.

Each of the twelve months of our Louisiana calendar offers different and engaging ways to dress up and trade gossip with one's wide array of friends and family, whether the days are short or long. It's easy to forget that most cities, particularly in America, can't compete with this constant whirl of activity. I've seen big holidays around the world, and I travel nearly every month to reunite with my friends in Texas, but I've found no city that offers a warmer welcome than New Orleans—because we include everyone in our parties, friends and strangers alike.

Imagine growing up with a family that celebrated not only each holiday but each day as a blessing. As a child, I was surrounded by cousins, uncles, aunts, and grandparents in every direction. I've searched for that same intimate family feeling, and done my best to nurture it into reality, in every community the Lord has guided me toward.

I must emphasize, over and over again, how lucky gays and lesbians are to belong to a community of different ages, races, shapes, and sizes worldwide. Wherever we may be, anywhere in the world, we will always find a family, real as any other, with its dysfunctions, to be sure, but also its profound connections. I've found these deep bonds not only within my own Creole family, but also in the communities I've built in Houston and New York, in gay activism, in my travels, and even in corporate life—a phenomenon that nurtures my drive and lengthens the count of my blessings. I credit the fact that I grew up in a close and celebratory world for my ability to draw others into communion. Keeping a family intact is never as easy as it sounds. It's not blood or marriage that defines family, but the little pieces of ourselves that we share with others. That's what keeps us stuck with each other—no matter what comes, particularly when the going is tough.

Gay Mardi Gras is a storied scene, unique to New Orleans. The tableaus and royal rituals—the glitter, the multistory costumes—parody the ruling class and require the ultimate commitment from participants, for whom Carnival anchors the entire year. Only once in its nearly fifty-year history has *Saturday Night Live* ever broadcast from outside of New York—and that once came on a Sunday night in 1977, in New Orleans for Mardi Gras. NBC was expecting a parade, but no one reminded them that our parades were over by broadcast time. Instead, they took over Jackson Square, thronged with crowds, while John Belushi performed bits—riding in on a motorcycle dressed as a bumblebee, pretending to be Mussolini on the Cabildo balcony, and screaming for Stella, à la Stanley Kowalski. They even had actress Penny Marshall attend a gay Mardi Gras ball, the Mystick Krewe of Apollo, where my friend Bob Batson explained the system behind drag debutantes.

That this brotherhood and now sisterhood remains strong doesn't mean it's always been smooth. Like every family, it has its rivalries, and not all inherited coping strategies are healthy. Dysfunction lies in every family—and while members of the LGBTQ+ community draw strength from the global reach of our family, we need to be better at addressing our flaws. The gay community is already famous for its tribes and cattiness. Gay men are prone to the same misogyny that infects all too many straight men—and all of us must combat the impulse to practice race and class prejudice. After years of enduring brutality as others discriminated against us—and then discovering wells of tenderness as we cared for our brothers and sisters ill with AIDS—we emerged into a greater sense of our own humanity. But to this day, we must battle against our own dark instincts. An uncaring and superstitious society abandons too many of our youth to the streets; those same fears can make us turn a blind eye to the continuing violence against trans and Black queers.

In my time, I've seen several generations of gays coming out—predestined, or so it often seemed, to repeat the pattern of growing up, catching hell, and maybe catching a disease. I am proud, however, that today's youth appear to be much more inclusive, and their families more supportive. Many parents dote on their daughter's middle school girlfriend just as much as their son's. I'm often surprised by the boldness of modern drag and the everyday gender fluidity of our youth. Traditional masculinity is no longer a strict requirement for boys, or traditional femininity for girls, and today's young people operate without the oppressive memory of a more rigid society. The way we perform our gender and embody our love is deepening and expanding—and this holds true not only in New Orleans, unusual for its long history of straight men in drag, but also across the United States.

What a wonder, after all these years, to see how life is changing. It's natural for those in my generation to fear change. Imagine surviving the genocide of AIDS only to confront the deeper ignorance—and antagonism to science and other forms of expertise—that breeds both anti-mask hysteria and climate change denial. I wonder how today's kids must feel, growing up fully aware of the challenges our planet faces. When I ask them, they smile in return—knowing that each generation has its own trials and tribulations. They may face existential threats that I never knew, but today's gay youth have been able to date their high school girlfriends and boyfriends with ease.

Long the centers of our community—our temples, our refuges—many gay bars haven't kept up with the times and have closed. It's hard to say if this is a temporary tragedy or a permanent change. It's easy to blame Grindr and bachelorette parties—but remember, it has never been easier to live the "straight" life as a queer than it is today. Just like heterosexuals, queer youth can meet their life partners at church, or get set up by their parents, sidestepping the bars. Today, shy queer youth can skip the challenge of navigating the LGBTQ+ community. Social media serves the illusion of intimacy click after click, scroll after scroll, and the experience of meeting new people from new places has vanished. When chance encounters disappear, the LGBTQ+ community becomes less intergenerational, less culturally diverse, and less radical. Finally, legacy bar owners, beset with declining support, bury their heads in the sand and avoid appealing to more thoughtful, sober, and fabulous queer youth. Will my generation be the last that had no choice but to rebel against the straight life? The last that responded to such rejection with parties and self-expression, the last that forged a life without kids dedicated to celebration, travel, and the realization of new visions of the world?

With a shrug, I acknowledge that the modern gay bar needs bridal parties to survive. With dating apps, we cannot rely on the revenue of the scared and closeted. At least young female allies—and the straight boyfriends they drag around—know that we queers are always up to something interesting. It is a universal human impulse to birth something into life, nurture it, and pass it down into history; with luck, pieces of ourselves are written into the brittle memories of those we leave behind. That's why those who can and those who know work every day to cement our legacies through our celebrations and traditions. Since time immemorial, our love has been so strong, so loathed, and so feared that we were free to take the religious and ethnic celebrations of the straight world and make them our own. As a new world opens up, the straights find themselves welcome, inspired, and enraptured by the festivals and rituals we have revitalized. It's happening worldwide, but New Orleans remains unparalleled in its ability to throw a party.

Every time I shoot down Rampart Street, I remember how emotional I was on my last day at City Hall, which I had scheduled for the first Friday of Jazz Fest, 2018. I planned to walk back home taking the long route, and I made sure to bid farewell to my favorite ladies at the Catty Car Corner restaurant on Poydras. From there it's just a short hop to Rampart Street, which runs along one of the original borders of the colonial French settlement. Across Rampart's broad lanes lies Congo Square, where enslaved Africans could gather on Sundays to drum and dance, and the Tremé neighborhood, built and inhabited by free people of color in the early nineteenth century. Rampart was the main street of Storyville and later became home to several gay bars, including Wolfendale's, now Grand Pre's; the Ninth Circle, now the Black Penny; and the Voodoo Lounge, which is still there. Today, tall, antique, green streetlamps border a resurrected streetcar line and a vital, if dusty, bus route that passes the lit arch of a gated Armstrong Park. On certain Sundays, I follow Rampart Street to my favorite shrine, Our Lady of Guadalupe, to give thanks for the best job I ever had and to worship in celebration of all the gifts I've been given. It is also on this street that large, vinyl flags hang in formation like soldiers, one after another after another. They sport the colors of the rainbow, with the loving addition of pastel blue, pink, black, and brown. These flags signal to our LGBTQ+ community that this land is our home.

I've always loved flags. At the first March on Washington, I ordered fifty large Texas flags for our delegation, as a reminder that everything is bigger in Texas. For the next DC demonstration, I followed through with fifty rainbow flags.

Designed by Gilbert Baker, the rainbow flag debuted at the San Francisco Pride parade on June 25, 1978, with eight colors, including hot pink and turquoise. Soon after, the design was simplified to the familiar

Rainbow flag on Rampart Street, New Orleans [2024]
PHOTOGRAPH BY KEELY MERRITT, HNOC

six colors: starting from the top, stripes of red, orange, yellow, green, blue, and purple. By November 1978, the rainbow flag was flying at half-mast when Harvey Milk was assassinated, and from then on, it was ours.

Everyone bought into the flag right away. Some saw it as a symbol of the diversity of our multiracial community. Others had fond memories of Judy Garland, who by then was "Somewhere Over the Rainbow." The pink triangle—a mark of Nazi persecution, later appropriated by the gay community—remains a powerful symbol. But in the era of gay liberation, we had all decided we needed something with a bit of glitter and glitz to unite us. In the 1980s and '90s, the rainbow flag spread worldwide, flying mournfully for AIDS patients and jauntily at inaugurations. Pride celebrations began to spread across every continent, and the flag reached the darkest, most homophobic corners. Needless to say, marketers also slapped it onto all manner of liquors, lubes, and products every June.

Sadly, with progress comes backlash, and as the millennium turned, it became newly fashionable—and politically profitable—to whip up fear and hatred against gay people. I remember when, in 2002, during Ray Nagin's first administration, preacher Grant Storms of Metairie showed up on the scene to harass us at Southern Decadence. To call it a protest would be too gentle. Though he claimed to be a "man of God," Storms had no compunction about breaking police lines to sneer at us, spit on us, and threaten us. His vigilante mob—as many as three hundred strong—was convinced that their own shames and sins would be absolved if they put the faggots in their place. They were more than happy to start a fistfight to teach us a lesson, and we were more than happy to defend our manhood.

This bigoted political theater was unacceptable, and some sort of response was necessary. Emboldened by my position at City Hall, I knew our community, our businesses, bars, and restaurants needed to organize to make a statement. We had to mark our home and our land, and I was fortunate to have a mayor who supported us. Our community's bars raised $10,000 and partnered with the New Orleans Jazz and Heritage Foundation to procure hardware and print vinyl flags to hang all along

Rampart Street, welcoming our incendiary evangelical neighbors to Decadence.

When Storms demanded that Mayor Nagin "take down these flags of sin!" at his next rally, I knew I had gotten under his skin, right where I wanted to be.

The flags still fly along Rampart between Pride and Decadence, thanks to a nonprofit I founded with local lawyer Jack Sullivan and continued support from the Jazz and Heritage Foundation. Every five years, I raise another $10,000 to replace the faded flags—and I never fail to credit the bars that contribute in the gay press. I consider it important for people who arrive in New Orleans to know just whose hometown they're enjoying and just what kind of tolerance we expect of our visitors. Be nice or leave.

I like the trappings of home, but sometimes I get recognized too much. Cruising helps me feel young, and I don't always feel like being the face of the movement. On the road, I get to be a lone wolf and create my own fantasy. Lately, however, I have embraced a new role in my hometown. Mentorship made a difference in my life when I was shown the ropes and granted the right to swing by my favorite Xavier professor—and now I'm playing mentor every week to a spoiled young millennial.

I met Ryan, a suburban Washington, DC, transplant with a Filipino background, at the Mystik Krewe de la Rue Royale Revelers's famous Twelfth Night party in the Quarter, in 2016. I spotted something shiny across the torchlit French Quarter courtyard and approached him to ask about his metal mask. It was made of sheet brass, annealed, pounded, and polished into the shape of an Egyptian cat. Native New Orleanians like to complain about carpetbagging transplants and how crowded the French Quarter has become, and I'm no exception. It's a sport in Louisiana to see who knows how to pronounce which words correctly, where to find the best king cake, and what special spots just "ain't dere no more." At the same time, however, I'm proud that our community attracts so many creative people devoted to the culture. I'm almost jealous, as growing up, we were taught, for our own safety, to avoid crossing many different social and cultural lines. Ryan is an exemplar of this new trend toward openness and intersectionality. He vows every day to be a better New Orleanian and applies his curiosity, civic-mindedness, and spirit of revelry toward achieving that goal.

When we first met, however, I spotted trouble. He had recognized me instantly! Eager to stay anonymous, I blushed as Ryan spouted out facts about my career. "He knows too much!" I thought to myself. "I'd better keep him close."

We have opposite tastes in dates, yet we've become close friends. Ryan has a mind for facts and really loves New Orleans. As a millennial, he's lived through crises very different from the ones I grew up with, from September 11, the Great Recession, and COVID to the reality of a boiling planet. But he maintains a positive attitude. He always brings me the latest in trends and ideas, loves to bring up things he has read, and shares my tastes in TV and music.

I don't hang out with Ryan because I need a protégé, though. I hang out with him because he's funny, bright, and challenging. He's my sister! In exchange, I show him the ropes of the gay world, just as I was once shown. I like to think he does the same with his friends—because sometimes I forget how bewildering our community can be. So much of the illusion of gay happiness rests upon the shallowness of sex and image. We're all working through our own shame and trying to transcend our own backstories, but learning how to act right can go a long way. A young gay man should learn to tip generously, to serve as a good host, to harness his desire, and to wield his eyes and his personality in service of a life lived passionately. With an unyielding mind for facts and a dedication to making the world better, Ryan welcomes my lessons about mendacious politicians as well as the benefits of meditation. Young queers should stand proud and act honorably—the cheapest way to cover one's ass and sleep well at night. Our community's penchant for dressing up in tuxedos and having too much to drink at balls might be silly, but Ryan is really taking to it.

In exchange, he keeps pushing me. Every week he has a piece of art, gossip, career news, or silly boy story to share with me. I enjoy every bit—and even the fights help us both navigate our triggers and tempers. I'm so glad that my accumulated knowledge about leadership now has soil in which to germinate and bloom. In fact, I've only been able to put into words many of the lessons in this book because Ryan tricked me into sharing them.

The world today is wider than the one I grew up in. My generation's challenges were of a spiritual sort, where we debated the meaning of our inherent identities. We struggled for a world where we would not be shamed for choosing our true paths, whereas the young people of today are wrapped up in the secular concerns of fair pay, equitable healthcare, free speech—and teaching my generation how to use e-mail and open PDFs. I recommend everyone in our community either find a mentor or find the courage to serve as one. Frankly, so many people my age are happy to retire to their garden at home, but through mentorship I've discovered new ways to enjoy my city. This experience has reminded me that the challenges we share in the gay community are not new—and no matter how hard anyone tries to erase our learning and our memories, they will keep us young and help us live forever.

I've always enjoyed meeting new gay people whenever and wherever I am. My ability to laugh with people in a bar has been a superpower that has yielded many close friendships and fun times over the years. For instance, in the aftermath of September 11, I was at the Bourbon Pub joking with the bouncer who teasingly threatened to throw me out, as we often do. In the corner of my eye, I saw a young man who missed all the comedy and seemed genuinely alarmed by our exchange. So I turned to him to ask where he was from. He said, "New York City." In return, I then asked, "So, where are you from originally?"

It turned out he was Egyptian and his name was Tarek. In an effort to tease him like we gays love to do, I grinned as I screamed "there's a terrorist in the bar!" It took a minute to click, but in that moment he saw through my sarcasm how jovial and familiar we are as a community, particularly on Sundays. He started to laugh and in turn tried to land a few jokes on me.

He had only arrived recently from Egypt, where you can imagine it was very difficult to be homosexual. His job had recently transferred him down to New Orleans and I noticed he could use a few friends. Thus, from the time we met, I began to show him New Orleans gay life, rituals, and traditions. Soon after, he shared with me his favorite experiences in a New York I had never seen, and on and on we would trade happy memories for the next twenty-plus years of travelling together to Houston and beyond.

There are still places where it is difficult to be gay, and I can imagine that those places can be very lonely. On top of that, immigration to America is always difficult. Fortunately, Tarek has always had a kind and gentle heart and I'm thrilled to visit him and his husband Rodrigo, now both nationalized US citizens, in St. Petersburg, Florida, whenever I can.

The gift of being LGTBQ+ in a bar is that we already have something in common. Thus, I encourage anyone I can to put their phones down and meet the person next to you and make a friend for life.

One day during COVID, I received a phone call from someone who introduced himself as Harrison Guy of Houston. It was the first year of the pandemic, and I had no idea who this upbeat young man with lots of questions was.

"Were you president and vice president of GPC?"

"Did you really bring Tina Turner to the Houston Summit arena for Pride?"

"Were you the first African American director of the Pride parade?"

Turns out, Harrison Guy was doing research on the history of Houston's Gay Political Caucus—now the LGBTQ+ Political Caucus—after having his curiosity sparked, in 2019, while serving as the first African American grand marshal of the Pride parade. Harrison and I share the same build,

Larry with Tarek Barrawi [2013]
COURTESY OF THE AUTHOR

Larry and Harrison Guy, Houston LGBTQ+ Political Caucus Equality brunch [2021]
COURTESY OF THE AUTHOR

and he always has a pensive look on his face. He had only just learned that the entire parade was founded by an African American. Very quickly, from the time of that first phone call, I knew I had a new brother, and we soon formed a close bond. Harrison had participated in the Houston gay community; across several decades, many of the old challenges and triumphs remained the same (despite Houston's much larger population today). We shared the same sense of humor, sense of place, and sense of occasion. He informed me that the community was ready to honor me for all the work I had done over the years.

When the quarantine lifted, I went back to Houston as soon as I could to meet Harrison—and I fell in love with his attention to detail and dedication to the true story of our gay history. We then proceeded to tape an interview, which lasted over seventy-five nonstop minutes. We discussed Town Meeting One, the Gay Chicano Caucus, and the diverse family I had supported. Despite the parade being postponed for a year, the Pride committee staged an outdoor street festival in 2021 with masks and social distancing. I was introduced to the group's current leadership—positions that years ago had been filled by my friends.

On the eve of the 2022 Pride parade, Harrison put together a lavish dinner party and reception, the Bagneris Ball, on the thirty-fifth floor of Houston's Petroleum Club, at 1201 Louisiana Street. Harrison attended to every detail: the decorations, invitations, audio, dining, and trophies to regale a black-tie crowd celebrating the forty-fourth anniversary of Houston's Pride parade.

The next day, there I was, standing in the back of a Jeep on a 103-degree day, riding with two of my best friends. Ryan had brought ninety pounds of beads from New Orleans, and Randy had flown directly from New York to attend the ball and the festival. In the excitement of the lineup, we only found Harrison at the last minute. We handed him a sack of beads, he hopped on, and we told him to throw, throw, throw!

Everything I have ever done in my work has been designed to promote inclusion. As the crowd began to beg for beads, I held up a handmade sign decorated with a string of lights. Letters of construction paper, made lovingly by Ramon and David, exhorted all to "Vote Democrat!" It wasn't much, but I'm still devoting all I can to turn my beloved Texas as blue as it was when I left in 1986.

Playing in my head was Whitney Houston's "The Greatest Love of All," which I hope everyone has a chance to listen to. When I organized the fireworks in Spotts Park after my parades, I would always start with "The Star-Spangled Banner" and end with "We Are Family." The tearjerker was always "The Greatest Love of All"—George Benson's original version, back in the day.

"I believe the children are our future, teach them well and let them lead the way." The song teaches us to love ourselves, just as Harvey Milk told us to come out of the closet because our queerness is the special ingredient that ties us all together. *"Show them all the beauty they possess inside."* As I looked out upon the crowds on that hot Houston day in 2022, I hoped today's queers would never need to consider, as I had, the political ramifications of playing this song in public at a gay event. *"Give them a sense of pride, to make it easier."* In the old days I had my boyfriend Jimmy edit the word "children" out of the song when we used it in the fireworks mix because we didn't want to draw any controversy. May those days be forever over. *"Let the children's laughter remind us how we used to be."*

In the Jeep, rolling through the canyon of downtown Houston's fifty-story buildings, I looked across the multiracial crowd. My dream came true! Every bit of what I began to wish in New Orleans and put together in Houston had taken on a life of its own. Our protest is indeed a celebration, a celebration of our perfect gay lives.

ACKNOWLEDGMENTS

With this book, I honor all the people and places that led me to fall in love with life and filled me with pride as a gay, Creole man.

This book is only possible thanks to my partnership with the Historic New Orleans Collection. It was Daniel Hammer, president and chief executive officer, who introduced me to the HNOC's publishing arm, whom I warmly enjoyed working with. I wish to acknowledge Jessica Dorman, director of publications, for her patience and guidance; Cathe Mizell-Nelson for her expertise and counsel; and Siobhán McKiernan for her editorial assistance. I credit the process of designing the book and collecting the photos and mementos depicted throughout to the talented Alison Cody. Keely Merritt, HNOC's head of photography, also offered great support. It is thanks to them you are holding this fine book.

Above all, I thank my parents, who taught me sacrifice, hard work, and a celebration of life. From my father, Lawrence Bagneris Sr., I learned to appreciate travel as an education that reveals the richness of diverse lives and the potential we have to live as one. My mother taught me how to build a family as I collected friends throughout my journey. I would also like to remember my grandmother, Louise Imbert Bagneris, as I learned so much from the grand parties held at her house on the corner of St. Ann and Galvez, where a rainbow of people would gather to celebrate.

The comfort with which I live as a gay man would not be possible without my mentor and professor, James Schaffer, who taught me that there was nothing wrong with me. Furthermore, he went out of his way to introduce me to gay culture in the world beyond my hometown, taking me to New York City, California, and Mexico. I cannot imagine how different my life would have been without him.

My second home will always remain Houston, Texas, which allowed me to build an affluent life with larger opportunities than New Orleans could offer. I thank the large, new family I made in Texas, the first community I could build outside of my blood ties in Louisiana. I particularly dedicate this book to my deepest, longest friends, David Hernandez and Ramon Araiza. During my years in Houston, I was blessed to meet many inspirational activists whom I am honored to call friends, including Annise Parker, Troy Perry, and our eternal leader Harvey Milk.

I must also thank my family and friends in Chicago. The Windy City was the destination for my first trips to the North, and the city continued to inspire me as I returned again and again. I recognize how lucky I was to live in a time when diversity hiring was a mark of modernity and not controversy. Thus, I'm thankful to the coworkers I met at the Washington National Investment and Insurance Corporation. My job training agents not only provided me the opportunity to visit all fifty states, but during those travels, I also met leading gay activists in the largest cities as well as the smallest towns.

I also dedicate this book to the many peoples I have been fortunate to visit abroad. The gay communities I met worldwide were so similar to the ones I had met in the States, and we LGBTQ+ people should be proud we belong to a large family that transcends race and culture.

I am grateful to my friends at the Tulane School of Architecture, Mark Thomas and Gene Cizek, as well as Lloyd Sensat, who invited me to travel with them. Thanks to them, I was able to participate in deep explorations of Mexico City and witness many lands abroad: Brazil, Argentina, Croatia, Bosnia, Montenegro, Morocco, and more.

Additionally, this book has benefited immensely from the help of professional writers Frank Perez and Bobby Fieseler. Special thanks to Vanessa

Spinazola and Evelyn Pugh, whose earlier editing, encouragement, and friendship, together with that of Eva Hurst, will never be forgotten.

I want to finish with a particular nod of appreciation to my good friend and coauthor, Ryan Gomez. This book would not be possible without him. Ryan, as I have watched you grow in your youth, I have learned so much about the results of my efforts. As we grow together as friends I'm reminded over and over that the same spirit that saved me from the psychiatrist at the age of sixteen brought you into my life and to save other LGBTQ+ people who might doubt their existence. Let's hope that this book will guide them on their life's journey and give them hope for the future.

Bagneris collection of pins and buttons
COURTESY OF THE AUTHOR

NOTES ON IMAGES

Accent items on pages 9, 31, 67, 101, 125, 141, 165, 171, 179, 191, 205, 213, 221, 261, 271, 285, 299, and 317 are courtesy of the author, with photography by Keely Merritt, HNOC. The 1965 yearbook cover on page 47 is courtesy of Xavier University of Louisiana, *Xavierite*, Students on Campus, Print, Archives & Special Collections. The Harvey Milk memorial plaque on page 149 is courtesy of Creative Commons, with photography by Steven Damron (own work), 2008, Open Plaques 57032. The Razzoo bar sign on page 235 is courtesy of DigitalVues / Alamy Stock Photo. The can of drinking water on page 249 was distributed in the Gulf South by Anheuser-Busch Inc. after Hurricane Katrina and donated to HNOC by Mr. and Mrs. Daniel E. Sullivan (2010.0309.1).

We thank J. D. Doyle for his peerless documentation of Houston LGBTQ+ history at www.houstonlgbthistory.org and his generous assistance with image research. We are also grateful to Anna LeBlanc-Mulder at the Amistad Research Center, Tulane University; Vincent Barraza at Xavier University of Louisiana; Joyce Gabiola, LGBT History Research Collections Librarian at the University of Houston; and Lisa Svoronos at PARS International.

INDEX

Page numbers for illustrations appear in bold italics.

ABOUT THE AUTHORS

A native New Orleanian, **LARRY BAGNERIS** began his civil rights activism as a student at St. Augustine High School. He graduated from Xavier University of Louisiana and moved to Houston, Texas, where he was a two-term president of the city's Gay Political Caucus, chairperson of Gay Pride week, and, in 1979, founder of Houston's Gay Pride parade. Bagneris returned to New Orleans in the 1990s and became a lobbyist for the NO/AIDS Task Force. He served four mayoral administrations as executive director of New Orleans's Human Relations Commission before retiring in 2018.

RYAN GOMEZ was born to a Filipino family in Washington, DC, and graduated from Cornell University. At age twenty-five, he moved to New Orleans, where he participated in the redistricting cycle of 2020, helping create balanced city council and school board districts and a second Black congressional district in Louisiana. He works as a GIS specialist and demographer at the New Orleans District Attorney's office.